THE COMMONWEALTH AND INTERNATIONAL LIBRARY

Joint Chairmen of the Honorary Editorial Advisory Board

SIR ROBERT ROBINSON, O.M. F.R.S., LONDON

DEAN ATHELSTAN SPILHAUS, MINNESOTA

Publisher: ROBERT MAXWELL, M.C., M.P.

READINGS IN SOCIOLOGY

General Editor: A. H. RICHMOND

READINGS IN THE SOCIOLOGY OF MIGRATION

THE COMMONWEALTH AND INTERNATIONAL LIBRARY

READINGS IN SOCIOLOGY

Editorial Board

Forthcoming Volumes

READINGS IN THE SOCIOLOGY OF MIGRATION

CLIFFORD J. JANSEN, Ph.D.

Assistant Professor, York University,
Toronto, Canada

PERGAMON PRESS

Oxford · London · Edinburgh · New York
Toronto · Sydney · Paris · Braunschweig

Pergamon Press Ltd., Headington Hill Hall, Oxford
4 & 5 Fitzroy Square, London W.1

Pergamon Press (Scotland) Ltd., 2 & 3 Teviot Place, Edinburgh 1

Pergamon Press Inc., Maxwell House, Fairview Park, Elmsford,
New York 10523

Pergamon of Canada Ltd., 207 Queen's Quay West, Toronto 1

Pergamon Press (Aust.) Pty. Ltd., 19a Boundary Street,
Rushcutters Bay, N.S.W. 2011, Australia

Pergamon Press S.A.R.L., 24 rue des Écoles, Paris 5^e

Vieweg & Sohn GmbH, Burgplatz 1, Braunschweig

First edition 1970

Library of Congress Catalog Card No. 72–105954

Printed in Great Britain by A. Wheaton & Co., Exeter

0769,4857

08 006914 2 (flexicover)
08 006915 0 (hard cover)

Contents

Preface

THIS is one of a series of volumes published by the Pergamon Press. Each consists of a collection of articles on a specialized aspect of sociology, or social psychology, together with an introduction designed to relate the Selected Readings to the state of sociological knowledge and research in the field in question. Each volume of Readings has been prepared by a distinguished scholar who has specialized in the area. The individual editors have been supported by an editorial board of international repute.

A characteristic of the series is the inclusion in each volume of a number of articles translated into English from European and other sources. English-speaking scholars and students will have the opportunity of reading articles which would not otherwise be readily available to them. Many important contributions to sociology made by European and other writers will be given a wider circulation in this way. It is hoped that the series will contribute to an international cross-fertilization of sociological theory and research.

York University,   ANTHONY H. RICHMOND
Toronto   *General Editor*

Acknowledgements

ACKNOWLEDGEMENT is due to the publishers, editors, and authors whose material has been reprinted in this volume.

"Types of migration of the population according to the professional and social composition of migrants" by Pierre George was originally presented to the International Population Conference, 1959, and "The migrant population of a metropolitan area in a developing country" by L. J. Ducoff to the International Population Conference, 1961. La Nuova Italia Editrice gave permission for us to reproduce "Immigrants to Turin" from *Il Ponte* by Goffredo Fofi and *Quaderni di Scienze Sociali* permission to reproduce "Aspects of internal migration related to other types of Italian migration" by Francesco Alberoni. "Emigrants in the Upper Milanese area" by Cesare Mannucci is reproduced with permission from *Nord e Sud*. "A general typology of migration" by William Petersen, "Participation of migrants in urban structures" by Basil G. Zimmer, "Distance of migration and socio-economic status of migrants" by the late Arnold M. Rose, "Internal migration in Sweden and intervening opportunities" by E. C. Isbell, and "Family, migration, and industrialization in Japan" by Irene B. Taeuber all appeared originally in the *American Sociological Review* and are reprinted by permission of the American Sociological Association. "Kentucky Mountain migration and the stem-family: an American variation on a theme by Le Play" by J. S. Brown, H. K. Schwarzweller, and J. Mangalam is reprinted from *Rural Sociology* by permission of the Rural Sociological Society. *Norois* gave permission for us to reprint "Movements of the population in the Birmingham region" by Claude Moindrot. "The motivation and characteristics of internal migrants" by R. Illsley, A. Finlayson, and B. Thompson is reproduced from the *Milbank Memorial Fund Quarterly* by permission of the Milbank Memorial Fund. "The growing population of Paris" by the late G. Pourcher, "Geographical mobility and urban concentration in France" by A. Girard, H. Bastide, and the late G. Pourcher, and "Problems of adjustment in the case of internal migration: an example in Spain" by R. Duocastella, are reprinted from *Population* by permission of Institut National d'Études Demographiques.

INTRODUCTION

Migration: A Sociological Problem

C. J. Jansen

MIGRATION, especially in modern times, is a major symptom of basic social change. In most countries, industrialization is accompanied by vast movements of the population from farms to towns, between towns within the same country, and also between countries. These movements of the population attained great numerical importance at the turn of the last century in Europe and North America, while in the newly developing countries of Africa, Asia, and South America this process is still continuing on a large scale today.

The problem of international migrations has been treated more frequently than that of internal migrations. It is the object of these Readings to concentrate more on the latter, though frequent reference will be made to international migrations, especially when considering problems common to both groups and the more important factors which distinguish them.

Importance of Internal Migration

1. BRITAIN

It is quite common in Britain to hear of the "drift to the South". Between 1951 and 1961 South-east England (an area within the boundaries of a line running from about Bournemouth to Banbury and then across to The Wash) gained half a million persons by migration. Alongside this, the South-western region gained 78,000 persons, and the two regions bordering on these (Midlands and North Midlands) gained respectively 61,000 and

65,000. All other regions had net losses of population, main losing regions being the North, Scotland, and Wales. These net movements of population are generally the result of large gross movements both in and out of the regions.

Post-war movements of the British population, including gross movements, have been highlighted in a few studies. Two reports based on the National Register[83, 97] (set up in 1939 and continued after the war until 1952) cover movements of the population for the period 1948–50.

In the first of these, Newton and Jeffery found that during this period about 4 million moves were made per year. This was a period of little unemployment and an abnormal shortage of housing. Using the same source, Rowntree put the emphasis on the number of moves made by each migrant. He found that on average, each migrant made 1.6 moves in the three years 1948–50. While 61.4% of migrants had made only one move in this period, as much as one-fifth (23.1%) had made two moves, one-tenth (9.0%) had made three moves, and 6.5% had made four or more moves.

Using the 1951 census material on birthplace, Osborne[85] found that 12¾ millions (31%) of the 1951 population of England and Wales were then living outside their native county. The counties having largest net inward balances were: Middlesex (850,000), Surrey (505,000), Essex (455,000), Kent (240,000), Sussex (205,000) Hampshire (155,000), Hertfordshire (145,000), and Cheshire and Warwickshire (both 140,000). It will be noted that all of these counties except the last two (which surround Liverpool and Birmingham) are in South-east England around London. The highest net losses by migration were from the county of London (1,840,000), Durham (270,000), Lancashire (245,000), Glamorgan (140,000), Staffordshire (135,000), and East and West Ridings combined (95,000).

Using statistics of persons classified jointly by birthplace and by place of residence in subsequent censuses, Friedlander and Roshier[46] have contributed an important study on internal migration for the period 1851–1951.

However, it must be mentioned here that the use of birthplace statistics in a study of internal migration is subject to a number of limitations. First results of a survey of internal migrants to Bristol, being carried out by the present author, show that less than 50% of migrants have come directly to Bristol from their birthplaces, several making as many as five or six moves to other places between their birthplaces and Bristol. It is thus encouraging to note that recent censuses in Britain are including direct questions on migration.

In the 1961 sample census a question was asked about migration covering the year April 1960 to April 1961.[21a] First published results show that in England and Wales, while 2.34 million (5.1% of the population) had changed residence within local authority areas, a further 2.2 million (4.7%) had migrated between local authority areas. The number of persons who crossed regional boundaries in that year was 725,990, and from a study of regional migration the "drift to the South" is quite evident. Net losses of migration were sustained by the Northern region (10,540), the East and West Ridings (11,270), the North-western region (10,500), and Wales (5,270). London and the South-eastern region also showed a net loss of 58,250, but it is to be assumed that this is merely an indication of the expansion of the area as the two surrounding regions showed highest net gains, viz. Eastern region 44,560 and Southern region 28,370. Other net gains were shown by the South-western region (17,610) and the North Midlands region (6,410), while in the Midlands region gains and losses almost balanced out, the net loss to the Midlands being only 850. Again, it must be emphasized that net movements often represent only a small percentage of gross movements.

2. OTHER COUNTRIES

The "drift to the North" would be an appropriate way of describing population movements in Italy. Between 1951 and 1961 about 1.8 million southern Italians left their places of origin.

Some of these went abroad, but an appreciable number migrated to the north of the country.

Internal migration in Italy, which amounted to 1.28 million in 1955, had increased to 1.44 million (or 12.3%) by 1959. During this period the Italian population only increased by 4%. While movements between provinces and within provinces remained fairly stable in the 5 years (1955–9), interregional migration, especially between north and south, increased appreciably. For 100 migrants having moved between northern and southern Italy in 1955 there were close on 150 by 1959. In the 5 years, 610,908 southerners went to the northern provinces while the inverse movement was only 203,602 or a net loss of 407,306 for the south. For a loss of 100 migrants from the south in 1955 there was a loss of 121 in 1956, 131 in 1957, 142 in 1958, and 167 in 1959.

These southern migrants settle in the large towns of northern Italy thus aggravating an already acute situation of urbanization with problems of lodgings, work, transport, and the like. (See the three articles in these Readings on Italian migration.) A third of all in-migrants to Rome, Turin, Milan, and Genoa in 1959 had come from the south. In Turin between 1951 and 1960 an index of the numbers of migrants from the south rose from 100 to 818.

The problem of internal migration seems to present itself somewhat differently in France and Belgium. It is not so much a regional attraction as that of one big city: in both countries the capital cities seem to be attracting people at an alarming rate. It is estimated that in the 10-year period 1953–63, Paris has been gaining about 100,000 migrants per year from the provinces. The return movement to the provinces, on the other hand, is very slight, consisting mainly of retired persons. (See "The growing population of Paris" in these Readings.)

The population of Paris represents a larger and larger proportion of the French population as can be seen by comparing the population of the two departments surrounding Paris, namely Seine and Seine-et-Oise, at three censuses. In 1851 the two departments contained 5.3% of the population of France. In 1954 the proportion had risen to 15.8%. In 1962, out of a total population of 46.2 million, these two departments contained 7.9 million or 17.2%. Furthermore, the boundaries of these two departments do not adequately define the conurbation, for Paris overflows these limits into the departments of Seine-et-Marne, Oise, and Eure. The conurbation population could thus be considered as 9 million or 19.5% (nearly one-fifth) of the population of France.

It is estimated that between 1946 and 1954 in-migration accounted for 40% of the increase in population of the two departments around Paris and between 1954 and 1962 it accounted for 60% of this increase.

Brussels is in Brabant, one of the nine provinces of Belgium. In 1964 Brabant had net gains from all but one of the other eight provinces. These were as follows: from Hainaut 3414, Liège 802, East Flanders 444, West Flanders 370, Antwerp 320, Limbourg 168, and Luxembourg 59, while there was a net loss to Namur of 59. The total net gain to the Brabant province was thus 5518. This gain is typical of recent years. Within the province of Brabant itself, 130,435 persons changed residence from one commune to another in 1964. Comparing net gains of population between Brussels and a few large Belgian towns, one immediately sees how the capital stands out. The net differences from migration in 1962 (a boundary change renders 1964 figures incomparable) were as follows: Brussels 5841, Antwerp 860, Gand 143, Charleroi −1540, Liège −339, and Namur +411. It is evident that the capital has a great attracting influence and that some of the former large cities of Belgium are even on the decline.

In the United States of America, 3 out of 100 persons move from one State to another every year, many covering vast distances. In the 1950 census it was found that 25.1% of non-whites were living outside their State of birth. Among whites, every age group from 30 upwards had more than 30% living outside their State of birth with a peak of 38.1% for the over 70's. Among the non-whites, every age group over 20 had more than a third living outside their State of birth, but the peak of 45% was reached in the 40–49 year group, falling to 35.6% among the over 70's.

In the decade 1946 to 1955 there were over 100 million migrations. One of the main features of these migrations is the continued movement westward, principally from the south, midwest, and north-east. Between 1940 and 1945 California averaged a net gain of 385,000 persons per year by migration. This dropped after the war, but was still averaging 284,000 per year about 1955. On the other hand, Pennsylvania (near the east coast) and seven southern states have been losing 30,000 or more persons by migration annually since 1950. Favourable climate is a strong pulling force, especially in the older age groups, as is evident from the attraction of Florida where net gains by migration increased from 54,000 per annum between 1940 and 1945 to 130,000 per annum between 1950 and 1955.

In Latin American countries the problem of migration is closely linked with that of urbanization since the majority of moves made in these countries are from rural to urban areas. A sample survey carried out in six cities of Brazil,[66] namely Rio de Janeiro, São Paulo, Bel Horizonte, Americana, Volta Redonda, and Juiz de Fora, showed that only 25.8% of the adult population were born in the cities where they lived at the time of interview. Of the rest, 14.4% had been born in other large cities, 36.2% in small cities, 13.4% in Fazenda, Vile, etc., and the rest came from abroad. Making comparisons between cities it was seen that Rio de Janeiro as an attracting city was on the decline, since only 60% were not born in the city, compared to 98.8% in Volta Redonda.

In Mexico in 1950, those living in a State other than the one in which they were born represented 12.9% of the total native-born Mexican population. Of all life-time migrants, 80% were living in urban municipos. Between 1940 and 1950 there were increases in the number of persons not living in their State of birth: the increase was 69.7% for urban municipos but only 26.5% for rural municipos. About 42% of the metropolitan population of San Salvador in 1960 were migrants. Of the female population, 46% were migrants while this was 37% of the male population. (See the article "The migrant population of a metro-politan area in a developing country" in these Readings.)

One of the most important features of migration in Africa, south of the Sahara, is that political boundaries have never coin-cided with ethnic or cultural boundaries so that migration between countries could be considered more as internal rather than international migration. The labour force is the most important migrant group in Africa. This migration of labour differs con-siderably from migration in other countries as it is generally a temporary migration of the individual as opposed to the family. It is highly selective of young adult males who never settle at work places for periods of more than a year. A United Nations report in 1957 [126a] states that "... a large number, perhaps even a majority of people appearing in the census as town dwellers, cannot be con-sidered as permanently fixed in the cities". However, in a recent study by Gutkins[61] it was noted that since independence more and more Africans are staying longer in towns and fewer return to rural areas.

Some idea of inter-country migration is given by the number of "outsiders" in particular countries. In 1951 there were 650,000 "outsiders" in the Union of South Africa; in 1956 about 300,000 in Southern Rhodesia, 77,000 in the former Belgian Congo, 45,000 in Northern Rhodesia, and in 1957 about 55,000 in Uganda and 41,000 in Tanganyika.

The Asian countries show varying patterns of migration although urbanization accounts for a lot of the movement. In India between 1941 and 1951 about 9 million persons moved from rural to urban areas, representing 20% of the 1941 urban popu-lation. In Japan, between 1950 and 1955, 2.4 million persons moved from rural to urban areas, representing an in-migration rate of 5.4% to urban areas, but here, again, the capital city dominated, Tokyo prefecture accounting for 55% of all net gains.

From the foregoing it will be evident that migration is an important phenomenon in most countries of the world. What then are the sociological questions raised by these shifts in population?

Theories of Migration

1. SIZE AND DIRECTION OF MOVEMENT

As we have seen, industrialization, especially at the turn of the century, was accompanied by vast shifts of the population. These movements have been an important subject of sociological inquiry.

As early as the 1880's, Ravenstein [93] presented papers entitled "The laws of migration". At the end of a long statistical study, Ravenstein put forward the following laws or trends:

1. We have already proved that the great body of our migrants only proceed a short distance and that there takes place consequently a universal
shifting or displacement of the population, which produces "currents
of migration" setting in the direction of the great centres of commerce
and industry which absorb the migrants. . . .
2. It is the natural outcome of this movement of migration, limited in range,
but universal throughout the country, that the processes of absorption
go on in the following manner:
   The inhabitants of a country immediately surrounding a town of
rapid growth, flock into it; the gaps thus left by the rural population are
filled up by migrants from more remote districts, until the attractive
force of one of our rapidly growing cities makes its influence felt, step
by step, to the most remote corner of the Kingdom. Migrants enumerated
in a certain centre of absorption will consequently grow less with the
distance proportionately to the native population which furnishes
them. . . .
3. The process of dispersion is the inverse of that of absorption and exhibits
similar features.
4. Each main current of migration produces a compensating counter-
current.
5. Migrants proceeding long distances generally go by preference to one of
the great centres of commerce and industry.
6. The natives of towns are less migratory than those of rural parts of the
country.
7. Females are more migratory than males.

These broad generalizations of Ravenstein's have been shown to be correct in several studies though his thesis on migration by stages has never been adequately verified. [63, 76, 115, 120, 121]

Hill, concentrating on the rural districts of Essex, showed that the direction of migration from these districts was mostly short distance into the neighbouring counties. In his study of the Glamorganshire coalfield, Brinley Thomas also showed the importance of short-distance movement. Taeuber and Taeuber, in their study of movements between cities and suburbs, supported the law that each current of migration was accompanied by a significant counter-current in the opposite direction. This law is also supported by Ministry of Labour data for regions of Britain. For example, between 1954 and 1963 the number of employees leaving the South-western region for all other regions was 431,000, while the number coming to the South-west was 438,000—a small net gain of only 7400 or 0.85% of the gross movement.

But though many authors agree that most people go a short distance while few people go a long distance, recent theories have looked at movements not in mere terms of distance but also in terms of opportunities. In 1940 Stouffer[109] presented his theory of intervening opportunities. The theory proposes that ". . . the number of persons going a given distance is directly proportional to the number of opportunities at that distance and inversely proportional to the number of intervening opportunities". The biggest problem in testing this theory is that of defining opportunities. In his original study Stouffer used census tract data of Cleveland Metropolitan District to study the number of persons moving house. "Opportunities" were defined as the number of vacant houses (in a given rental group) in a given tract X. Similar vacancies between tract Y and X were called "intervening opportunities". He found that agreement between expected and observed values were high.

Other authors[15, 66a] have applied Stouffer's theory to internal migration with encouraging results. The article by E. C. Isbell, where "opportunities" are defined as the number of males settling in a county, including those migrating from one community to another within the county as well as in-migrants from all other counties, is included in these Readings.

In a paper presented in 1960 Stouffer[110] introduced a further variable: "competing migrants". Thus his original model became an attempt to express, for a specific time interval, the number of migrants from city A to city B as a direct function of the number of opportunities in city B and an inverse function of the number of opportunities intervening between city A and city B, as well as the number of other migrants competing for opportunities in city B. A recent study applied this new model to an interpretation of United States 1960 census data. The authors[47] found, however, that the 1935–40 census data (used by Stouffer) fitted more closely than the 1950-60 data, though differences were small.

Concentrating on "distance and opportunities" in migration, Rose tested the following hypothesis in Minneapolis: "higher status persons, seek better jobs or 'opportunities' must move a greater distance to find them, on average, than do persons whose skills and aspirations direct them to look for less desirable opportunities". This article is also included in these Readings. He concluded that lower-class people find many more intervening opportunities in a given distance than do upper-class people. This hypothesis was re-tested in Duluth by Stub. [111] This study confirmed that of Rose, for professionals and managers were found to migrate longer distances than lower-status migrants.

In a study of migration of labour from farming, Burford, [17] referring to the distance factor of migration, considered what he called "psychological distance": "More important than actual geographic distance as a determinant of migration from farms, is how far farmers 'feel' that they are from non-farming opportunities." He thus constructed a "remoteness index" taking into account the distance between a county seat and the nearest town of 25,000 population; number of secondary cities (10,000–25,000) within a radius of 30 miles; sum of percentage levels of unemployment in cities involved.

The "push–pull theory" has long been one of the most important in migration. These "push" and "pull" attributes of communities of origin and destination are considered by Bogue[11] as independent migration variables which account for the selectivity of certain groups (other independent variables are the characteristics of migrants).

In a paper presented at the 1961 Population Conference, Bogue put forward the following hypothesis:

Migration that has a very strong "push" stimulus tends to be much less selective, with respect to the community of origin than migration which has a very strong "pull" stimulus. Where there is a condition of very strong "push" but no strong "pull" (extreme cases are disasters such as famine, drought, floods, exhaustion of a resource), origin selectivity is at a minimum. In other words, selectivity of out-migrants from any community tends to vary directly with the strength of attractive "pulls" from other communities and inversely with expulsive "pushes" from the community itself.[12]

In a paper presented at the 1959 International Population Conference, George considers geographical movements of the population in two forms: (1) moves caused by *necessity* or *obligation*; (2) moves caused by *needs* (termed "economic"), in certain countries. (The article is included in these Readings.) Characteristics of the first type are that they generally have political or religious causes, that they "push" certain classes or racial, religious, or national groups who are mostly not suited to conditions in their place of destination. In the second type, pressure from place of origin (push), is accompanied by a need (pull) in the place of destination. Examples from several countries are given.

Rossi divided reasons for moves into those which pertain to the decision to move out of the former home (pushes) and those pertaining to the choice among places to move to (pulls). He found that about 1 out of 4 residential shifts could be classified as either involuntary or the logical consequence of other decisions made by the household. "Pushes" were caused by evictions or destructions of dwellings and decisions which led to moves included marriage, divorce or separation, and job changes. "Pulls", where people had a clear choice of going or staying, were prompted by the desire for more dwelling space, better neighbourhoods, and cheaper rents.

The "push–pull" theory was seen from another angle by Mac-Donald[74] in a paper presented at the 1961 International Population Conference. He found that while all the "push" factors were operational in some rural areas of Italy, still a large proportion of the population did not migrate, though free to do so. He thus examined migration differentials in relation to frequency of other forms of action directed to economic betterment and found that labour militancy played an important part in keeping the population at home as an alternative to migration.

The foregoing are some of the most important "theories" concerning size and direction of migratory movements. Sociologists are interested in certain other problems, such as selectivity, motivations, and the social integration of migrants.

2. DIFFERENTIAL MIGRATION

Differential migration is the selectivity of certain persons or the tendancy of certain groups (age, sex, class, etc.) to be more migratory than others. Demographers have repeatedly tried to establish "universal" migration differentials which would apply in all countries and at all times. But to date the only differential which seems to have stood the test, in research undertaken in various countries and at various times, is that persons in young adult ages 20–34 are more prone to migrate than other age groups.

This finding has been supported in several studies. In a survey of migrants conducted in Paris (see "The growing population of Paris" in these Readings) it was found that 44% of migrants were aged 20–34 years. Studying inter-state migration in the United States, Thomas,[122] covering the period 1870–1950, found that net gains in inter-State migrants were highly concentrated in the age range 20–34 years for both sexes during the whole period. Studying labour migration from Wales to Oxford between 1928 and 1937, Daniel[30] found that at the time of migration 64% of the migrants were in the age group 20–34 years.

In his paper presented to the 1961 International Population Conference, Bogue (ref. 12, pp. 1, 4–6) suggests that apart from age ". . . further universal differentials do not exist and should not be expected to exist". He proposes instead to test hypotheses which express *principles* of selectivity under specified combinations of environmental and population conditions at places of origin and destination. He submits the following hypotheses which tend to characterize data in the United States and which may be consistent with migration elsewhere. His hypotheses are summarized as follows:

1. There is a series of stages in the development of any major migration stream. From initial invasion it develops into a phase of settlement which at its peak becomes routine, institutionalized. In initial stages, men outnumber women, but with the settlement phase sex selectivity tends to disappear or even favour women. During initial stages, migration is highly selective of young but mature adults, persons who are single, divorced, or widowed.

2. Migration stimulated by economic growth, technological improvement, etc., attracts the better educated. Conversely, areas tending to stagnation lose their better educated and skilled persons first.

3. If between two population points streams of equal size tend to flow, neither making net gains, then the composition of migration streams in each direction tends to be of minimum selectivity. If the stream flowing in one direction is greater than that flowing in the other direction, there is greater selectivity in both streams. But the place showing a net gain would have a greater proportion of males, young adults, single, divorced, and widowed, while the place having a net loss would have high proportions of "migration failures" (returnees), employees of new establishments, local migrants "passing through" on their way to bigger centres and retired migrants returning to place of origin. (It should be noted, however, that not all returnees are failures, a large majority simply fulfilling original intentions to return. This is well illustrated in a study of immigrants to Canada by Richmond,[94] where only 16% of returnees to Britain expressed dissatisfaction with their experience in Canada.)

4. Where the "push" factor is very strong (famine, drought, etc.), origin selectivity is at a minimum. Where "pull" stimulus is greater, there will be an appreciable selectivity.

5. In modern technological societies, major streams which flow between metropolitan centres tend to have very little selectivity of migrants.

Other migration differentials have been shown to be important in particular places and times. Even the universal finding on age selectivity has some exceptions. One of the most obvious of these is the migration of persons to areas of better climate, which is usually selective of older and retired persons.

For instance, in the United States between 1940 and 1950 net gains of those 65 years and over were 13,000 in California, 66,000 in Florida, and 8900 in Arizona. In England the 1951 census revealed a growing population in the 60 mile stretch along the southern coast. Over 65-year-olds represented 24% of the population of Worthing, 21.1% in Hove, 19.7% in Hastings, and 19% in Eastbourne. These populations are also characterized by a strong desequilibrium in sex ratios (Worthing 1480 females per 1000 males), high mortality rates (18–21 per 1,000) a small proportion of young people (under 15's in Hove 15.8%), and a large number of widows and widowers.

Another exception to the age finding is that of migration of families from central cities to suburbs where migrants tend to be more in the 30–40 year age groups.

The following are differentials other than that of age which affect the selectivity of migrants in different places and at different times.

Sex Selectivity

In a paper presented to the 1961 International Population Conference, Lee,[71] studying birthplace statistics for 1950 in the United States, shows very little sex selectivity of those living outside State of birth. For all age groups the proportion of the population living outside State of birth for white and non-white males exceeded that of females by only 0.2% (whites: M 25.2%,

F 25.0%; Non-whites: M 29.3%, F 29.1%). The highest proportion of males exceeding females in both groups were found in age categories 50–59 and 60–69 where white males exceeded females by 1.5% and 1.6%, respectively, and non-white males exceeded females by 3.9% and 2.7% respectively.

Arias,[4] in a paper on Guatemala, found that in general, males were more migratory than females except in a few cases, including the capital of the country, where the male net gain was 26,000 compared to a 39,000 female net gain in the 1950 census.

In a study of urban Brazil, Hutchinson[66] shows that a slightly higher proportion of males tended to come from other large cities (M 15.1%; F 13.8%), but in the move from smaller cities and rural areas, proportions of females were higher (M 47.7%; F 51.4%).

In a paper by Dandekar[29] of the Demographic Training and Research Centre, Bombay, taking the total and urban populations of India in 1941 as bases, it was found that in the 10–year period 1940–1951, 16.5 per 1000 females and 14.7 per 1000 males migrated between states while the net rural–urban migration among persons aged 10 years and over was 163 per 1000 females and 152 per 1000 males.

For Japan, between 1950 and 1955, the overall sex ratio of net migrants in thirty-five cities of over 200,000 population was 110 males per 100 females. But the predominance of males among net migrants declined with the decrease in the size of towns.

In Ceylon, between 1946 and 1953, males were found to be more migratory than females in all age-groups. On the other hand, in the Philippines there were 98 males per 100 females in eight net in-migrant provinces between 1939 and 1948.

In England and Wales during the year April 1960 to April 1961 more women than men crossed regional boundaries (M 357,000; F 369,000), but migrants represented 1.6% of the male population as opposed to 1.55% of the female population.

This diversity in "sex selectivity" in time and place seems to give very little support to a law of differential sex migration.

Urban–Rural Selectivity

As we have seen, industrialization has been accompanied by vast shifts from rural to urban areas. Another important characteristic of migrants, then, is their rural or urban origin. In the study "The growing population of Paris" (in these Readings) it will be seen that for an index of 100 given to the rate of out-migrants (proportion of out-migrants to population of origin) in rural communes of France, the index was 106 for urban agglomerations of under 5000 inhabitants, 91 for agglomerations of 5000–20,000; 89 for those 20,000–50,000; 79 for those 50,000–200,000; and only 44 (less than half the rural index) for cities of over 200,000. It seems, then, that the more an area tends to be rural the more likely the rate of out-migration tends to be high.

Using the electoral register as a source for studying internal migration in France, Croze[27] shows some interesting facts of rural–urban selectivity by age group. France is divided into five categories: (1) Paris region; (2) large cities: 50,000+; (3) medium cities: 10,000–49,999; (4) Small cities: 10,000; (5) rural areas. Figures relate to 1953.

In the 21–29-year-old group, rural areas showed a net loss of 9991, while urban areas showed the following net gains: small cities 1217, medium 1008, large 2252, Paris 5514. A similar pattern of losses and gains was found in the age group 30–44 years: rural areas − 3340; small cities + 1662, medium + 146, large + 67; Paris + 1465. But in the next age group the pattern starts reversing: rural + 9272, small cities + 1307, medium − 1404, large − 3289, Paris − 5886. In the 60 + -year-old group rural areas gained 2779, small cities 1767, and medium 722, while losses from large cities and Paris were, respectively, 1527 and 3761. It would seem that the rural–urban characteristics of migrants are further influenced by age.

In the United States a larger proportion of non-farm population tends to change residence in general (except between counties within states) than farm population. Between April 1948 and April 1949, for instance, for the population 18 years and over,

10.8 % of the farm population and 13.5 % of the non-farm population changed residence within the same county; 3.9 % of farm and 2.4 % of non-farm population migrated between counties within states, while these percentages between states were farm 2.4 % and non-farm 3.2 %.

Hutchinson,[66] in his study of urban Brazil, concluded that migrants from small cities were more likely to be women than men, while the migrant stream from rural areas was even more heavily female in its composition (100 F per 77 M).

From the foregoing we may conclude that the urban–rural differential as such is not directly selective but depends on other factors like age and sex.

Status Selectivity

Social status and to a large extent occupation selectivity are also important especially in contemporary migrations. In these Readings, the article by Rose shows that professional people have to move longer distances than lower status persons to find job opportunities.

On the other hand, the article on "The growing population of Paris", shows that migrants to Paris are representative of several occupations with as many as 28 % being manual workers and 26 % (19 % farmers and 7 % farm workers) coming from farms.

In his study of urban Brazil, Hutchinson[66] found that the city-born and migrants from other large cities were of significantly higher social status than the average, while those from small cities and rural areas were of lower-class origin. He concluded that these differences reflected one of the main original motives for rural–urban migration—the hope of social and economic advancement.

Studying the inter-county movements of the civilian labour force in the United States between April 1949 and April 1950, Tarver[118] found that of twelve major occupations the professional, technical, and kindred workers were by far the most mobile. On the other hand, municipal and county officials were rather immobile, while various craftsmen were tied to their jobs by seniority and pension plans.

In a study of Norristown, Pennsylvania, Goldstein[52] noted that while high rates of in- and out-migration had not affected the total size of the Norristown population between 1910 and 1950, the fact that the opposing streams of movement were selective of persons in different occupational groups meant that migration served to alter the occupational composition of the male labour force. At the beginning of the period, three groups, namely professional, proprietors, and unskilled labourers, had net gains of over 300 per 1000 persons. By 1930–40, however, all groups except professionals and semi-skilled workers experienced net losses through migration.

Thus the selectivity of migrants of particular social status and occupation tends also to vary in time and place.

Other than the foregoing migration differentials, studies have also covered migration selectivity of ethnic or racial groups (US: whites and non-whites; Latin America: Indian and non-Indian, etc.), educational level—which is generally well correlated with social or job status—and religion. But, as we have seen, none but the age differential seems to stand the test in time and space. It would be truer to say that migration is selective of persons having certain combinations of traits rather than attributing selectivity to one particular differential.

3. MOTIVATION FOR MIGRATION

The motivation of migrants is another question which sociologists have studied. Unless one undertakes a social survey, very little is known from the migrants themselves about their reasons for moving. Even in the censuses it is rare to see a question about motive for moving. Though this may often be inferred by studying the characteristics of migrant streams it reveals nothing about the "personal decision" to move and all that it involves. Rossi[96] in his work *Why Families Move* pays particular attention to the decision to move and choice of destination. In these Readings, the article entitled "The growing population of Paris" also touches on motivation for migration. However, the book with the same title [90] devotes a whole chapter to this important problem.

Here, motives for moving to Paris are divided into seven main divisions, each of these being divided into about five or six subdivisions. Among recent migrants the main reasons for coming to Paris were: (1) motives concerning the labour market in Paris ("pulls"), 35.3%; (2) motives concerning the labour market in the provinces ("pushes"), 20.5%; (3) family, housing, health motives, 15.1%; (4) marriage and motives independent of the mover (children accompanying parents, etc.), 11.7%; (5) love of change, etc., 8.3%; (6) studies, 6.4%; (7) wars, political events, military service, 2.7%.

The importance of the "work" motive is immediately evident. But the word "work" can take on many shades in the context of migration. A person who is completely jobless might migrate to another area in the hope of finding any kind of work. This tends to be the case of many migrants from rural to urban areas in Africa, Asia, and South America. On the other hand, a person might have a good job in one place but he might migrate in search of a better job—a job with more pay, a job in healthier surroundings, a job which is more suited to his particular abilities. In the first case one might say that the person is "pushed" out of his original place because of complete lack of work, while in the second he is "pulled" by the attractions of a better job without his job at the point of departure being threatened. Then, again, many persons are appointed by their firms to work in another place—in a branch of the firm found in another part of the country or the firm itself might decide to move from one area to another. Most students migrate on completing their studies in search of their first job in a place other than the one where their university or school is found. Other jobs require routine changes of residence. These include migratory farm work, construction, and the like. Many moves are motivated by seasonal changes. Those with the many service jobs associated with the summer holidays migrate to the seaside and other resorts for the whole of the holiday period to cater for the thousands of holiday makers and tourists. In the Flemish part of Belgium it is a well-known fact that families of farmers spend part of the year on their farm and the other part in all types of jobs required along the sea coast during the holiday season. Although quite rare today, there are persons who only work for part of the year, then return to their homes until the next working season. This is the case of Africans employed in the mines of South Africa, who work for a 9-month period at the mines. They then migrate back to their homes which might be in Lesotho, Botswana, Rhodesia, Mozambique, or Angola for the rest of the time. A similar phenomenon is known among Sicilians working in the northern part of Italy or in other European countries.

As we have seen, work is not the only motive for migrating. Accounting for at least a quarter of all moves are those linked in some way with family motives. Many people migrate at the time of marriage. Some people migrate because of a lack of an offer of marriage in their place of origin.

Kin and family relationships are strong motivating forces in the decision to move. A larger proportion of persons move in order to rejoin families or relatives. At moments of death, divorce, or separation it is not uncommon for one of the partners to rejoin members of his or her original family. Families are known to move in order to improve opportunities in schooling, training, and jobs for their children. We have already seen the importance of the migratory move on retirement from work. There are also an appreciable number of people who simply like moving from place to place gaining the experience each place has to offer or simply because they cannot settle down in one place.

To these general motives for moving could be added those of particular circumstances. A student might migrate to several parts of a country in search of a better education because he wants to follow a particular course which is well taught in one particular place, etc. This type of move is generally of limited duration—the time it takes to complete the course—although once completed the student may not necessarily return to his former place but seek employment elsewhere.[39, 104] Young men doing National Service are in similar circumstances: they may be moved all over the country during this time and a number may not return to their original areas once discharged.

Finally, among motives for migration there are occasional "mass migratory moves" caused by disasters like droughts, floods, and war.

While the above motives might "decide" one to move, they do not in all cases determine where one will go. There are several factors which influence choice of destination, assuming that there is freedom to make this choice. Many people, if given the choice between two places, would prefer going to one where they already had relatives or friends or even acquaintances of their own friends. Very few like taking a "plunge in the dark". Others have some knowledge—through previous visits, holidays, travel, or reading—of the place they decide to go to. The cost of moving might be an important factor in deciding one's destination. Climate and general surroundings play an important part in determining choice too. All these factors could be considered as the "pulling" factors as opposed to the "push" factors which force one to make a move, no matter where one decides to move to.

There is much scope for further study of "motivation" and "choice of destination" as the two articles on France in these Readings illustrate.

4. MIGRATION AND INTEGRATION

Another aspect of migration which would be studied by sociology is that of the integration of the migrant. Firstly, would the migrant family be integrated or is migration the cause of disintegration of the family? Do migrants integrate well with new neighbours? Do migrants participate fairly soon in local formal and informal organizations?

One may ask "Do family and kin relations encourage migration?" The reply to this question has to be seen both from place of origin and place of destination. If one has many kin and family ties in a particular place, one is less likely to go elsewhere. On the other hand, the fact that one has relatives in another part of the country may be considerably important in the decision to migrate as well as in determining choice of destination. (*The International Journal of Comparative Sociology*, **6** (1), March 1965, is devoted to "Kinship and geographical mobility".)

In these Readings an article on "Kentucky Mountain migration" shows that migrants from the area studied all tended to go to the same places, while in-migrants all tended to come from the same places. It was discovered that there were close kin connections in both in- and out-migrant groups.

In another article in these Readings, "Family, migration, and industrialization in Japan", Taeuber shows the important role of the family in structuring migration. The codified household law prohibited a change of residence without the consent of the head of household. While inter-provincial migration for boys and girls under 10 years of age were proportionately similar, with adolescence, proportionately more boys than girls were "permitted" to migrate, but by the early thirties the relationship between migrant status of men and women was fairly close. The author also describes the effects of migration in transforming the family.

As is to be expected, non-migrants are likely to have more contact with relatives living close by, while contacts of relatives by migrants will be limited by the distance factor. Margaret Stacey,[108] in her study of Banbury, England, compares migrants (who came to Banbury after age 7) with Banburians. Residents, on average, maintained more contact with their relatives, for while nearly 90 % of them had at least one relative living near Banbury, less than one-third of migrants had relatives near Banbury.

In many cases the father of the family migrates first and once he is settled the rest of the family joins him, thus creating a difficult period for the family. Once the family joins the head, a place large enough to house them must be available, schools must be sought for the children, and, while the husband's first contacts would probably be among his workmates, it is generally more difficult for the wife to make friends. She will become entirely dependent on her husband to keep "in touch" with the new community. In many cases these circumstances "force" the husband to spend more of his free time about the home; more household duties are shared between husband and wife; the wife will know more about her husband's job since much of the daily discussion will centre around this. In general, the pattern of conjugal roles will tend to be quite different among migrant couples. The wife in these circumstances usually looks back on her life in the previous residence with some nostalgia and regret at the loss of assistance given her by relatives and friends in the former place.[14, 131] Many are the wives who look forward to the day when, liberated from the constant care demanded by young children, they will be able to go out and work themselves.

How well does the migrant integrate with new neighbours and friends? Migrants have been heard to complain "We heard that people are friendlier here, but that is not so", or "People here are not as friendly as where we lived before". Are the migrants themselves to blame or are they really resented by local residents? In these Readings the article on "Emigrants to Milan" shows that one of the complaints of residents was that migrants did not "acculturate" themselves in their new surroundings: they "imported" their culture and beliefs from their place of origin.

Integration of the migrant could be facilitated in cases where he knew friends at the place of destination before migrating. A good example of this is the international migration of Italians to a particular country: they have often all come from the same village in their own country.[75]

Studies have shown that in many cases the migrant's closest friends are other migrants—people in similar circumstances who have faced similar problems to his own. Then the working migrant is likely to make friends among workmates before meeting neighbours, while migrants wives will make friends with neighbours sooner, especially if both she and her neighbours have children of similar ages. Then, little by little, the circle of friends will grow by meeting people at the local pubs, the shopping centres, the school gate or launderette, and, if the migrant participates in local associations (clubs, churches, etc.), he will enlarge his circle of friends even further.

The problem of participation in organizations is covered in these Readings by Zimmer in his article "Participation of migrants in urban structures". He not only compares membership of migrants and residents in formal organizations but also the holding of office of members. In a recent article, Jitodai[67] studied the relationship between migrant status and church attendance. He states that one could expect rural migrants to show higher rates of church attendance than urban migrants because the church seemed to be the most obvious channel for rural migrants to enter the network of groups, while urban migrants would be more familiar with other urban organizations. In fact rates of attendance were higher for urban migrants. Jitodai felt that the main reason for this was the difference in organization of urban and rural churches. The urban church was characterized by its large size, professionalized staff, and a general structure of secondary and impersonal relationships, and had become a meeting place for many kinds, both secondary and primary groupings—sport, social, professional, and intellectual as well as religious. The rural church was organized around more communal and primary relationships.

Large groups of migrants could also have a profound effect on local government policy. Four articles in these Readings touch on this problem. These include "Movements of the population in the Birmingham region", two articles on Italy, and one on Spain. It would seem that the most important problem created by large migrant groups is that of housing or re-housing if they have initially tended to cluster in poorer type areas. In Birmingham, since 1950, skyscraper flats are being built while the population is encouraged to move to the outskirts of the city and to commute back and forth, thus creating the added problem of adequate travelling facilities. In Cinisello, north Italy, over 2000 dwellings, of which 95% went to migrant families, were built in 10 years, but about 200 families were still living in shanties and stables. Then migrants tend to get housed with other migrants, so that while they have an added sense of protection, on the one hand, their integration and contact with local residents is limited, as can be seen in the article on "Immigrants to Turin". Similar problems were met by migrants in Mataro, Spain, but the author states that though reputed to be lazy, the migrants, in fact, adapted themselves quickly to local conditions in spite of great personal difficulties.

Another important problem created for local authorities is that of schools for the migrant children. These become rapidly insufficient as the migrant stream grows, but even when there are enough schools there might be a serious discrepancy in the standard of education by migrant children compared to local children and special courses for the former may be necessary.

In an article on the effect of migration on children at school in Britain, where "Every local authority has the duty to organize its schools on the needs and conditions of its own area" Taylor[119] argues that since Britons are becoming nearly as mobile as Americans, the extent of migratory habits of children should be assessed before local systems of education are finalized. In international migration there is the added problem of language spoken by children. This is not only a handicap for children at school but also for adults at work. This problem does arise in internal migration as well in countries like Belgium (where in some parts of the country only Flemmish is spoken while in others only French is spoken) or South Africa (English–Afrikaans). In these Readings the article on Spain, where Catalonians speak a language which differs considerably from Spanish, refers to this question.

The foregoing are but a few of the problems covered by sociological inquiry in the study of migration. Most of these problems are covered by one or several of the articles in these Readings. It is clear that there is considerable scope for further study of the social implications of a phenomenon which is becoming more and more the rule rather than the exception in modern society.

References and Bibliography

1. ALBERONI, F., Caratteristiche e tendenze delle migrazioni interne in Italia (Characteristics and trends of internal migrations in Italy), *Studi di Sociologia*, 1 (1) (Jan.–March 1963), 23–50.

2. ANDRÉ, R., Mouvements migratoires intérieures en Belgique pendant la période 1954–1958 (Internal migratory movements in Belgium, 1954–1958), *Bulletin de la Société Royale Belge de Géographie*, 84 (1960), 99–105.

3. ANSELMOTTI, G., I movimenti migratori a Torino negli anni di rapido sviluppo economico (Migratory movements to Turin in the years of rapid economic development), *Realtá de Mezzogiorno*, 3 (2) (Feb. 1963), 265–79.

4. ARIAS, J. B., Internal migration in Guatemala, *International Population Conference 1961*, paper 120.

5. BARBANCHO, A. G., Los movimientos migratorios en Espana (Migratory movements in Spain), *Revista de Estudios agro-sociales*, 12 (43) (April–June 1963), 47–88.

6. BARBERIS, C., Due sondaggi sull'esodo (Two surveys on exodus), *Quaderni di Sociologia rurale*, 2 (1) (1962), 12–35.

7. BARGHINI, A., Aspetti dei movimenti di popolazione nell'Africa Occidentale (Aspects of population movements in West Africa), *Quaderni di Sociologia rurale*, 3 (2–3) (1963), 76–89.

8. BEIJER, G., *Rural Migrants in Urban Setting; An Analysis of the Literature on the Problem Consequent on the Internal Migration from Rural to Urban Areas in 12 European Countries, 1945–1961*, The Hague, M. Nijhoff, 1963, xiv + 327 pp.

9. BELTRAMONE, A., Sur la mesure des migrations intérieures au moyen des données fournies par les recensements (Measuring internal migration from census data), *Population*, 17 (4) (Oct.–Dec. 1962), 703–24.

10. BOEKESTIJN, C., *Binding aan een streek. Een empirisch onderzoek naar de migratie uit de provincie Zeeland onder jongere arbeiders in Walcheren en Zuid-Beveland* (Attachment to a region. An empirical research on migration of young workers from the Province of Zeeland to Wallachia and South-Beveland), Leiden, Verhandeling van het Nederlands Instituut voor Praeventieve Geneeskunde, 1961, 259 pp.

11. BOGUE, D. J., Internal migration, in P. M. Hauser and O. D. Duncan, *The Study of Population*, University of Chicago Press, pp. 486–509.

12. BOGUE, D. J., Techniques and hypotheses for the study of differential migration, *International Population Conference 1961*, paper 114.

13. BOSCO, G., Migrazione, congéuntura e programmazione economica (Migrations, economic situation and economic development), *Rassegna del Lavoro*, 10 (5) (May 1964), 657–67.

14. BOTT, E., *Family and Social Network*, London, Tavistock Publications, 1957.

15. BRIGHT, M. L. and THOMAS D. S., Interstate migration and intervening opportunities, *American Sociological Review*, 6 (1941), 773–83.

16. BURCHINAL, L. G. and JACOBSON, P. E., Migration and adjustment of farm and non-farm families and adolescents in Cedar Rapids, Iowa, *Rural Sociology*, **28** (4) (Dec. 1963), 364–78.

17. BURFORD, R. L., An index of distance as related to internal migration, *Southern Economic Journal*, **29** (2) (Oct. 1962), 77–81.

18. BURNIGHT, R. G., Estimates of net migration, Mexico, 1930–1950, *International Population Conference 1961*, paper 42.

19. CASCINO, N., Le migrazioni interne (Internal Migrations), *Quaderni di Azione Sociale*, **13** (3) (May–June 1962), 469–82.

20. CAVALLI, L., *Gli immigrati meridionali e la società ligure* (Southern Italian immigration and society in Liguria), Milano, Angeli, 1964, 228 pp.

21. CECCHELLA, A., Le migrazioni della manodopera nei paesi dell'Africa centrale: Aspetti economici e sociali (Migration of the labour force in the countries of Central Africa: economic and social aspects), *Africa (Roma)*, **17** (4), (July-Aug. 1962), 173–7.

21a. *Census 1961, England and Wales*, Migration: National Summary Tables, Part II, tables 4 and 5.

22. CÉPÈDE, M. *et al.*, Mobilité des travailleurs en agriculture et influence du Marché Commun (Mobility of agricultural workers and influence of the Common Market), *Economie rurale*, **58** (Oct.–Dec. 1963), 17–28.

23. CHARRIER, J. B., Problèmes de l'exode rurale: l'attraction démographique de Nevers, Dijon, Paris sur les communes rurales de la Nièvre et de la Côte d'Or (Problems of rural exodus: the demographic attraction of Nevers, Dijon, Paris on rural communes of Nièvre and Côte d'Or), *Revue géographique de l'Est*, **4** (2) (April–June 1964), 145–62.

24. CHATELAIN, A., Les Migrations de la population (Population migrations), *Revue économique*, **14** (1) (1963), 1–17.

25. CHATELAIN, A., Les Migrations quotidiennes du travail dans les régions françaises hors de l'agglomération française (Daily migrations of workers in regions other than the French agglomeration), *Revue économique*, **14** (5) (1963), 659–94.

26. COMPAGNA, F., Dopo i primi anni di esodo rurale (After the first years of rural exodus), *Nord e Sud*, **8** (22) (Oct. 1961), 6–16.

27. CROZE, M., Un instrument d'étude des migrations intérieures: les migrations d'électeurs (An instrument for studying internal migrations: movements of voters), *Population*, **2** (1956), 235–60.

28. DAMAS, H., Population de la Belgique: les migrations intérieures (Belgian population: internal migrations), *Population et Famille*, **4**, 31–62.

29. DANDEKAR, D. P., Internal migration in some countries of the East, *International Population Conference, 1961*, paper 111.

30. DANIEL, G. H., Labour migration and age composition, *Sociological Review*, **31** (3) (1939), 281–308.

31. DANIEL, G. H., Labour migration and fertility, *Sociological Review*, **31** (4) (1939), 370–400.

32. DAS GUPTA, A. Types and measures of internal migration, *International Population Conference, Vienna 1959*, presented by L. Henry and W. Winkler, pp. 619–23.

33. DAVIS, S. G., The rural–urban migration in Hong Kong and its new territories, *Geographical Journal*, **128** (3) (Sept. 1962), 328–33.

34. DELOGU, I., L'Immigrazione sarda a Torino (Sardinian immigration in Turin), *Cronache meridionali*, **11** (4) (April 1964), 21–50.

35. DOBYNS, H. F. and VASQUEZ, M. C. (eds.), Migracion e integracion en el Peru (Migration and integration in Peru), Lima, *Editorial Estudios Andinos*, 1963, 196 pp.

36. DOMINION BUREAU OF CENSUS, LABOUR DIVISION, *Movements within the Canadian Insured Population*, 1952–1956, Feb. 1960, 21 pp.

37. DONNISON, D. V., The movement of households in England, *Journal of the Royal Statistical Society*, **124** (1) (1961), 60–80.

38. FAKIOLAS, R., Problems of labour mobility in the USSR, *Soviet Studies*, **14** (1) (July 1962), 16–40.

39. FERRISS, A. L., Predicting graduate student migration, *Social Forces*, **43** (3) (March 1965), 310–19.

40. FISCHLOWITZ, E., Las Migraciones internas en Brazil (Internal migration in Brazil), *Revista mexicana de Sociologia*, **24** (3) (Sept.–Dec. 1962), 705–33.

41. FISK, E. K., The mobility of rural labour and the settlement of new land in underdeveloped countries, *Journal of Farm Economics*, **43** (4) (Nov. 1961), 761–78.

42. FLAUS, L., Aperçu sommaire sur l'accroisement de la population des départements de la Seine et de la Seine-et-Oise et sur l'importance de l'immigration dans ces 2 départements entre 1872 et 1962 (A short review of population increase in the departments Seine and Seine-et-Oise and of the importance of immigration to these 2 departments between 1872 and 1962), *Journal de la Société de Statistique de Paris*, Nos. 10–12 (1963), 249–53.

43. FOFI, G., L'Immigrazione meridionale a Torino (Southern immigration to Turin), Milano, Feltrinelli, 1964, 359 pp.

44. FONTANI, A., L'Immigrazione nel triangolo industriale (Immigration in the industrial triangle), *Cronache meriodionali*, **9** (6) (June 1962), 27–47.

45. FORTE, F., Le Migrazioni interne come problema di economia del benessere (Internal migrations as a problem of welfare economics), *Studi economici*, **17** (2–3) (March –June 1962), 97–124.

46. FRIEDLANDER D. and ROSHIER R. J., A study of internal migration in England and Wales, *Population Studies*, Part I, **19** (3) (March 1966), 239–79; Part II, **20** (1) (July 1966), 45–59.

47. GALLE, O. R. and TAEUBER K. E., Metropolitan migration and intervening opportunities, *American Sociological Review*, **31** (1) (Feb. 1966), 5–13.

48. GERMAIN, C., Mouvements migratoires et croissance démographique de Montréal (Migratory movements and demographic growth of Montreal), *Actualité économique*, **38** (3) (Oct.–Dec. 1962), 345–67.

49. GIRARD, A., Les Changements de profession au cours de la vie active; les mouvements migratoires des retraités (Changes of profession during active life; migratory movements of the retired), *Population*, **2** (1947), 368–70.

50. GIRARD, A., Mobilité de la population et développement économique (Mobility of the population and economic development), *Revue du Conseil économique wallon*, Nos. 27–29 (1957–8), 1–20; 1–15; 16–25.

← 51. GITTUS, E., Migration in Lancashire and Cheshire, *Town Planning Review*, **32** (2) (July 1961); 141–156.

← 52. GOLDSTEIN, S., Migration and occupational mobility in Norristown, Pennsylvania, *American Sociological Review*, **20** (1955), 402–8.

· 53. GOLDSTEIN, S. and MAYER, K., The relation of migration and intra-urban mobility to population decline in an American city, 1950–1960, *International Population Conference 1961*, paper 11.

· 54. GOLDSTEIN S. and MAYER K., *Residential Mobility, Migration and Commuting in Rhode Island Providence*, Planning Division, Rhode Island Development Council, State Planning Section, 1963, vi + 65 pp.

· 55. GOLDSTEIN S. and MAYER K., Migration and the journey to work, *Social Forces*, **42** (2) (May 1964), 472–81.

56. GOTTMANN, J., Expansion urbaine et mouvements de population (Urban expansion and movements of the population), *REMP Bulletin*, **5** (2) (April–June 1957), 53–61.

57. GRAUMAN, J. V., Development of a model of rural-urban population change, with relevance to Latin America, *International Population Conference 1961*, paper 58.

58. GROAT, H. T., Internal migration patterns of a population subgroup: college students, 1887–1958, *American Journal of Sociology*, **69** (4) (Jan. 1964), 383–94.

59. GUILBERT, M., Les mouvements du personnel dans quelques industries de la région parisienne (Movements of employees of some industries in the Paris region), *Sociologie du Travail*, **4** (1) (Jan.–Mar. 1962), 45–59.

60. GUNZERT, R., Innerstädtische Wanderungen (Intra-urban movements), *International Population Conference, Vienna 1959*, presented by L. Henry and W. Winkler.

61. GUTKINS, P., African urbanism, mobility and social network, *International Journal of Comparative Sociology*, **6** (1) (March 1965).

62. HAMILTON C. H., Some problems of method in internal migration research, *Population Index*, **27** (4) (Oct. 1961) 297–306.

63. HILL, A. B., *Internal Migration and its Effects upon Death Rates with Special Reference to the County of Essex*, Medical Research Council.

64. HILL, P., *Migrant Cocoa Farmers of Southern Ghana*, London, Cambridge University Press, 1963, xv+265 pp.

65. HITT, H. L., The role of migration in population change among the aged, *American Sociological Review*, **19** (2) (1954), 194–200.

65a. HUBERT, J., Kinship and geographical mobility in a sample from a London middle-class area, *International Journal of Comparative Sociology*, **6** (1) (March 1965), 61–80.

66. HUTCHINSON, B., The migrant population of urban Brazil, *América latina*, **6** (2) (June 1963), 41–71.

66a. ISBELL, E. C., Internal migration in Sweden and intervening opportunities, *American Sociological Review*, **9** (1944), 627–39.

67. JITODAI, T. T., Migrant status and church attendance, *Social Forces*, **43** (2) (Dec. 1964), 241–8.

68. JORDAO NETTO, A., São Paulo e o problema das migracoes internas (São Paulo and the problem of internal migrations), *Sociologia (São Paulo)*, **25** (3), (Sept. 1963), 209–12.

69. KEYFITZ, N., L'Exode rurale dans la province de Québec, 1951–1961 (Rural exodus in the province of Québec), *Recherches Sociographiques*, **3** (3) (Sept.–Dec. 1962), 303–16.

70. LA CALLE CONTRERAS, L. De, La Emigracion campesina en la gran cuidad (Rural exodus in the great city), *Seminarios*, **17** (1963), 336–54.

71. LEE, E. S., Migration differentials by state of birth in the United States, *International Population Conference 1961*, paper 61.

72. LEGENDRE, P., Les Migrations rurales (Rural migrations), *Droit social*, **26** (11) (Nov. 1963), 513–28.

73. LEO, M. Di., L'Emigrazione meridionale nelle regioni del Centronord dal 1955 al 1959 (Southern emigration to Centre-north regions from 1955–1959), *Réalta del Mezzogiorno*, **3** (4) (April 1963), 424–37.

73a. LESLIE, G. R. and RICHARDSON, A. H., Life-cycle, career pattern, and the decision to move, *American Sociological Review*, **26** (6) (Dec. 1961), 894–902.

74. MACDONALD, J., Migration versus non-migration: regional migration differentials in rural Italy, *International Population Conference 1961*, paper 107.

75. MACDONALD, J. and MACDONALD, L., Chain migration, ethnic neighbourhood formation and social networks, *Social Research*, **29** (4) (Winter 1962), 433–48.

76. MAKOWER, H., MARSCHAK, J. and ROBINSON, H., *Studies in the Mobility of Labour*, Oxford Economic Papers, **1**, Oct. 1938; **2**, May 1939; and **4**, Sept. 1940.

77. MANGIN, W. and COHEN, J., Kulturelle und psychologische Charakteristika nach Lima einwandernder Gebirgsbewohner (Cultural and psychological characteristics of mountain migrants to Lima), *Sociologus*, **14** (1) (1964), 81–87.

78. MASI, D. De, Migrazioni e congiuntura a Milano (Migrations and economic situation in Milan), *Nord e Sud*, **11** (58), (Oct. 1964), 62–66.

79. METGE, A., *A New Maori Migration: Rural and Urban Relations in Northern New Zealand*, London, University of London, Athlone Press, 1964, x + 299 pp.

80. A decade of internal migration, *Metropolitan Life Insurance Co. Statistical Bulletin*, **31** (5) (May 1950), 5–7.

81. Population still moving westward, *Metropolitan Life Insurance Co. Statistical Bulletin*, **36** (6) (June 1955).

82. MOINDROT, C., Les Villes de retraités de la côte de Sussex (Retirement towns on the Sussex Coast), *Population*, April–June 1963, 364–6.

83. NEWTON, M. and JEFFERY, J., *Internal Migration*, General Register Office, Studies on Medical and Population Subjects, No. 5; London, HMSO, 1951, 41 pp.

84. OLIVER, F., Inter-regional migration and unemployment 1951–1961, *Journal of the Royal Statistical Society*, **127** (1) (1964), 42–75.

85. OSBORNE, R., Internal migration in England and Wales 1951, *Advancement of Science*, **12** (1955–6), 424–34.

86. PACI, M., Immigrazione di manodopera e mobilità del lavoro nell' industria edilizia milanese (Labour migrations and labour mobility in the Milan building industry), *Quaderni di Sociologia*, **12** (4) (Oct.–Dec. 1963), 435–52.

87. PACI, M., L'Intergrazione dei meridionali nelle grandi città del nord (Integration of southern immigrants in large northern towns), *Quaderni di Sociologia*, **13** (3) (July–Sept. 1964), 341–9.

88. PEARSON, J. E., The significance of urban housing in rural–urban migration, *Land Economics*, **39** (3) (Aug. 1963), 231–40.

89. POBLETE TRONCOSO, M., El exodo rural, sus origines, sus repercusiones (Rural exodus, its origins, its repercussions), *America latina*, **5** (1–2) (Jan.–June 1962), 41–49.

90. POURCHER, G., *Le Peuplement de Paris* (The peopling of Paris), Paris, Presses Universitaires de France, 1964, 310 pp.

91. RAIMON, R., Interstate migration and wage theory, *Review of Economics and Statistics*, **44** (1962), 428–38.

92. RAVAULT, F., Kanel: l'exode rurale dans un village de la vallée du Sénégal (Kanel: rural exodus in a village of the Senegal valley), *Cahiers d'Outre-mer*, **17** (65) (Jan.–March 1964), 58–80.

93. RAVENSTEIN, E., The laws of migration, *Journal of the Royal Statistical Society*, **48** (June 1885), 167–235; **52** (June 1889), 241–305.

94. RICHMOND, A., The standard of living of post-war immigrants in Canada, *Canadian Review of Sociology and Anthropology*, **2** (1), 41–51.

95. RITA, L. and IACONO, G., Aspetti psicologici dei meridionali in rapporto ai problemi dell'immigrazione (Psychological aspects of southern Italians in relation to the problems of immigration), *Studi di Sociologia*, **2** (2) (April-June 1964), 170–7.

96. ROSSI, P., *Why Families Move: A Study in the Social Psychology of Urban Residential Mobility*, Free Glencoe Press, 1955.

97. ROWNTREE, J., *Internal Migration*, General Register Office, Studies on Medical and Population Subjects, No. 11, London, HMSO, July 1957, 11 pp.

98. SANTOS, M., As migraçoes para Salvador através da analise do ficario eleitoral (Migrations to Salvador through analysis of the electoral register), *Revista brasileira de Estudos politicos*, **15** (Jan.–July 1963), 127–50.

98a. SAVILLE, J., *Rural Depopulation in England and Wales, 1851–1951*, London, Routledge and Kegan Paul, 1957, xvi + 253 pp.

99. SAXENA, D., Emigration and rural social change, *Indian Sociological Bulletin*, **1** (4) (July 1964), 20–23.

100.   SCHWARZ, H., Chinese migration to north-west China and inner Mongolia, 1949–1959, *China Quarterly*, **16** (Oct.–Dec. 1963), 62–74.

101.   SCHWARZ, K., Migration in the Federal Republic of Germany by Town and Country, *International Population Conference, 1961*, paper 97.

102.   SHANNON, L. and KRASS, E., The economic absorption of in-migrant laborers in a northern industrial community, *American Journal of Economics and Sociology*, **23** (1) (Jan. 1964), 65–84.

103.   SHRYOCK, H., The efficiency of internal migration in the United States, *International Population Conference, Vienna 1959*, presented by L. Henry and W. Winkler.

104.   SHRYOCK, H. and NAM, C., Educational selectivity of inter-regional migration, *Social Forces*, **43** (3) (1965), 299–310.

105.   SMITH, T., Gente que se mueve (People on the move), *Revista mexicana de Sociologia*, **25** (3) (Sept.–Dec. 1963), 981–94.

106.   SOPHER, D., Population dislocation in the Chittagong Hills, *Geographical Review*, **53** (3) (July 1963), 337–62 (Pakistan).

107.   SOVANI, N., Potential out-migrants and removable surplus population in three districts of Orissa (India), *International Population Conference, Vienna 1959*, presented by L. Henry and W. Winkler.

108.   STACEY, M., *Tradition and Change: A Study of Banbury*, London, Oxford University Press, 1960, xiv + 231 pp.

109.   STOUFFER, S., Intervening opportunities: a theory relating mobility and distance, *American Sociological Review*, **5** (Dec. 1940), 845–67.

110.   STOUFFER, S., Intervening opportunities and competing migrants, *Journal of Regional Science*, **2** (Spring 1960), 1–26.

111.   STUB, H., The occupational characteristics of migrants to Duluth: a retest of Rose's migration hypothesis, *American Sociological Review*, **27** (1) (Feb. 1962), 87–90.

112.   TABAH, L. and CATALDI, A., Effets d'une immigration dans quelques populations modèles (Effects of immigration on some population models), *Population*, **4** (1963), 683–96.

113.   TACHI, M., Regional income disparity and internal migration of population in Japan, *Economic Development and Cultural Change*, **12** (2) (Jan. 1964), 186–204.

114.   TAEUBER, I., Hong Kong: migrants and metropolis, *Population Index*, **29** (1) (Jan. 1963), 448–51.

115.   TAEUBER, K. and TAEUBER, A. White migration and socio-economic differences between cities and suburbs, *American Sociological Review*, **29** (5) (Oct. 1964), 718–29.

116.   TAGLIACARNE, G., Population employment and migration between the 1961 census and today, *Review of Economic Conditions in Italy*, **18** (4) (July 1963), 247–64.

117.   TARVER, J., Interstate migration differentials, *American Sociological Review*, **28** (3) (June 1963), 448–451.

118.   TARVER, J., Occupational migration differentials, *Social Forces*, **43** (2) (Dec. 1964), 231–41.

119.   TAYLOR, G., Children on the move, *The Guardian*, 10 Feb. 1965.

120. Thomas, B., The migration of labour into the Glamorganshire coalfields, *Economica*, **10** (1930),

121. Thomas, B., The influx of labour in London and the South-east, 1920–1936, *Economica*, **4** (1937), 323–36.

122. Thomas, D. S., Age and economic differentials in interstate migration, *Population Index*, Oct. 1958, 313–25.

123. Thomas, D. S., Internal migration in Sweden: a recent study, *Population Index*, **29** (2) (April 1963), 125–30.

124. Thomas, D. S. and Zachariah, K., Some temporal variations in internal migration and in economic activity, United States, 1880–1950, *International Population Conference 1961*, paper 60.

125. Thomas, L., Brève typologie des déplacements de populations au Sénégal (Short typology of population movements in Senegal), *Cahiers de Sociologie économique*, **10** (May 1964), 247–84.

126. Udo, R., The migrant tenant farmer of Eastern Nigeria, *Africa* (*London*), **34** (4) (Oct. 1964), 326–39.

126a. United Nations, *Report on the World Social Situation*, New York, 1957, p. 147.

127. Vergottini, M. de, Migrazioni interne e sviluppo demogràphico (Internal migrations and demographic development), *Rivista italiana di Economia, Demografia e Statistica*, **18** (3–4) (July-Dec. 1964), 9–23.

128. Villani, A., Migrazioni interne e insediamento urbano (Internal migrations and urban settlement), *Aggiornamento sociali*, **15** (7–8) (July-Aug. 1964), 529–48.

129. Villani, A., Migrazioni interne e sviluppo economico nella recente esperienze italiana (Internal migrations and economic development in the recent Italian experience), *Aggiornamento sociali*, **15** (12) (Dec. 1964), 779–96.

130. Whetten, N. and Burnight, R., Internal migrations in Mexico, *Rural Sociology*, **21** (2) (1956), 140–51.

131. Willmott, P. and Young, M., *Family and Class in a London Suburb*, London, Routledge and Kegan Paul, 1960, xiii + 187 pp.

132. Zanini, E., Esodo rurale e problemi che ne derivano (Rural exodus and resulting problems), *Rivista internazionale de Scienze sociali*, **69** (6) (Nov.–Dec. 1961), 569–77.

PART I

TYPOLOGIES

Types of Migration of the Population According to the Professional and Social Composition of Migrants

P. George

GEOGRAPHICAL movements of population today fall into two broad categories. In the one, population movement occurs in which the need or obligation for exodus is so strong as to put economic considerations into the background. In the other, population movement is the outcome of certain economic factors, in particular the need for specific types of labour in another country.

The first of these is dictated by political or religious considerations which determine the extent of the migrating group whose members may be from one social class or from a particular racial, religious, or national group. Depending on the nature of the pressures at work, either certain age groups only will elect to emigrate—older people, for example, tend to resign themselves to conditions facing them in their country of origin—or else a complete group will leave the country. Thus the occupational composition and age structure of the migrating population is quite varied. It may be a former ruling class departing after a revolution, or the more active elements of a persecuted group migrating in a steady flow, or the sudden mass exodus of a complete group. The group's standing in the social hierarchy and occupational structure of the country of origin may lend a certain tonality to the migration. In all else, however, it is no more than the movement of a population of different ages and occupations. It will be appreciated that such a transfer *en masse* to a different geographical environment is

39

always very difficult. The structure of the group is based on a stage of development in a given country. By definition it cannot therefore correspond exactly to that of a likely receiving nation, and when transposed to a new environment it does not necessarily fit the development needs of that environment.

In the course of such a transfer, therefore, the group must disintegrate in order to supply individual elements which will help in the reconstruction of a new society or which will fit into corresponding blanks of such a society. A process of disassociation like this calls for occupational changes and for intensive methods of vocational training; and despite hard work, frequent setbacks in social standing, compared to pre-departure positions are to be expected.

Economic migration takes places when demographic pressures in one country are met by a corresponding readiness to receive population in another. The numerical proportions are rigidly determined by the development requirements of the new country whose human resources are generally inadequate for the achievements of its objectives. However, the existence of a frontier produces two types of migration. Where economic circumstances render the condition of people in one region of a country quite intolerable, a large scale exodus gets under way. If there is no outlet in another country for this offer of population, the national frontier presents an insurmountable barrier. The exodus comes to a halt at the gates of the large towns in the country concerned. For most of the migrants it becomes a migration with a departure and no arrival. In countries under strong demographic pressures and not well developed, this situation has led to a proliferation of shanty towns. Before international migration can be effected there must be a balance between arrival and departure.

Two sides of the question have to be taken into account—the economic and social condition of the exporting country and the employment needs of the receiving country. The migratory phenomenon is in fact adjusted between these two situations. The offer of migrants stems from a saturation of the labour market in which the level of skills varies with the standard of development of the country in question. Underdeveloped countries have at their disposal surpluses of rural workers only, whose aptitudes and former experiences may perhaps suit them for work as carpenters, labourers, and construction workers. By contrast a more advanced country may at some stage find it has a surplus of one particular type of skilled labour which cannot be employed because of the state of its market. But at all events it does have a system of cultural and vocational training, and even at the lowest social level its population has a better standard of education than that of the underdeveloped countries.

Of greater importance, however, is the nature of the receiving country's requirements. There is little need to repeat that economic migration does not take place without an appeal for manpower and the subsequent signing of labour agreements and issuing of entry permits. Manpower requirements are strictly determined by the state of development and the state of the labour market of the receiving nation. The great transoceanic migrations of the nineteenth century were prompted by the need for vast numbers of able-bodied workers to clear and cultivate virgin land, open up mines, construct roads and bridges, lay railways, build new towns, etc. Once these requirements were met and a certain saturation of the labour market, which was a more or less permanent feature for almost half a century, was relieved, then a new type of movement was substituted. This movement meets the specific requirements of particular sectors where there is no saturation and where the economy needs supplementary manpower at a lower cost than either the national labour force or the systematic mechanization of the particular activity (were it technically possible).

A study of samples of migrants either at departure from their own country or on arrival in the receiving country, compared with identical geographical samples taken over different periods, is of value. It reveals a preponderance of type I (exodus) movements over type II (economic migration), or vice versa as the case may be, the nature of the manpower available for dispersal in different economic and social contexts, the variation in demand in relation to the receiving country's internal development, and so on.

1. Mass Migration

The best example of this is immigration into Isreal. During the 4 years 1951–4, when there was an intake of nearly 400,000, the sex ratio was 96 [ratios to base 100 female] and the proportion of inactive persons, that is children, old people, and untrained women, was as high as 66%. Classification according to occupations is as follows:

		% of the active population
Category I	Agriculture	4.7
Category II	Unskilled labourers	8
	Industrial workers	22
	Building workers	2
Category III	Public services and transport	3
	Teaching and the professions	5.8
	Commerce & administration	29
	Miscellaneous services	6
Unclassified		19.5

In greater detail it appears that the largest group among industrial workers is in the garment trade (nearly 5000 in 1951), followed by leatherworkers (2200) and jewellers and watchmakers (1400) out of a total of 14,000 skilled workers. This corresponds closely to the social structure of Jewish groups in the exporting countries, particularly in central Europe, since agricultural workers tend to come from the Mediterranean countries. There is no need to stress the necessity for occupational changes if the economic requirements of Israel are to be met.

German emigration in recent years may to a certain extent be considered as planned exodus in the sense that it is the continuation, after a period of stabilization, of refugee movements. Numerical characteristics place it midway between the Jewish emigrations and true economic migrations: sex ratio 102, inactive 41%, active migrants with category I occupations 9%, category II 42%, category III 49%. The main problem seems to be to find employment in the receiving country for migrants in category III. Naturally in such a comprehensive group distinctions of professional competence have to be recognized.

2. Economic Migration from an Underdeveloped Country

The major part of European emigration at the beginning of the twentieth century and up to the First World War (from Mediterranean and central and east European countries) falls under this heading. It is represented today by emigration from Portugal. Figures show a sex ratio of 154, which is evidence of the survival of a tradition for men to migrate alone. The number of inactive emigrants is only 20%. Migrants of working age are of both sexes: 32.7% being women classified as domestics, 29.5% agricultural workers, and 14.5% construction workers. Only 10% fall clearly into category III (unclassified 13.3%).

Despite variation in methods of recording occupations, similar type migrations are found in Irish emigration during the inter-war years. In 1926 there were 10% inactive, while 78% of all active migrants were agricultural workers and 85% of the women were registered as domestic workers.

Italian emigration in the twenties followed a similar course— sex ratio 220, inactive 30%, agricultural and construction workers 56%. However, unemployment in the important industrial region of northern Italy does drive industrial workers to emigrate (18% of the total number of emigrants). It is likely that the 20% or so who did not indicate their occupation when registering could be classed with the non-skilled agricultural workers and labourers. This brings to more than 75% the number of manual workers with no skill beyond their experience in building and on the land. (Sample of intercontinental emigration taken in 1920.[1])

One last example of an historical nature is the 1929 Polish

---

[1] Composition of emigration to other European countries—especially to France—for the same period, is slightly different: there were fewer agricultural workers (21% against 38%), more construction workers (nearly 40%), and more industrial workers (nearly 25%).

emigrations: inactive persons numbered 12.6%, agricultural workers 64% of the active, unclassed 30%, miners 4%, tradesmen and others 2%.

3. Economic Emigration from an Industrial Country

The Netherlands, the most populous country in Western Europe, produces between 60,000 and 80,000 overseas emigrants a year. Sex ratio is 114, the number of inactive 47%; the largest group of Dutch emigrants (44%) are tradesmen and 35% are employed in the professions in management. Barely 10% of the active emigrants are farmers. Separation of the agricultural occupations takes place before emigration which, generally speaking, follows upon the acquisition of a vocational training (1954).

In 1954, 136,000 English emigrated overseas from the British Isles. The sex ratio, at 82, was quite exceptional. The number of inactive of all ages was 56% and, as in the previous example, it was for the most part family emigration. Half the inactive emigrants were women and half were children under 18. The bulk of the total active emigrants fell into three occupational groups—business, banking, and insurance 26.5%; skilled workers (including construction workers) 30%; and the professions 25%. Only 3.3% were in agriculture, 9.5% in transport and unskilled labouring, 2.8% in domestic work. This represents less than 5% in category I, 35% in category II including transport, and 60% in category III.

By contrast, during the 1925 coal crisis 25% of emigrants were miners and unskilled labourers. At this time agriculture still accounted for 15%, and nearly 25,000 young women left the United Kingdom to take up domestic work in overseas countries, i.e. 14% of the total number of emigrants. These three groups together amounted to 47%. Male emigrants still predominated (sex ratio about 150) and there was a large proportion of single emigrants (only 35% inactive and 20% under 18). Classification by category then was roughly 40%, 30%, and 30% (half of category III being female domestic workers).

Emigration from Italy today is considered to be from an industrial economy, even though it is still largely supplemented by emigration from the agricultural regions of southern Italy and the islands. Its composition lies midway between emigrations immediately after the First World War and present-day emigration from countries like the United Kingdom and the Netherlands—inactive 55%, agricultural workers still 37%, construction workers 17%. The proportion of industrial workers has risen to 33% and category III workers to 10%, with 3% unclassified.

4. Immigration into an Industrial Nation

By definition only industrial nations with an expanding economy or with a shortage of manpower in certain sectors of their economy, are receiving nations. Compared with the nineteenth century their requirements have changed radically.

In 1954 the United States accepted 237,800 immigrants of whom 50% were inactive. Unskilled labourers and agricultural workers, who between 1920 and 1925 represented 40% of total immigration, now account for only 22%. The next largest quotas are: skilled workers 20.5%, office personnel 15%, members of the professions 8.5%, domestic workers 10%, etc. Considered in terms of the occupational divisions this is: one-fifth in category I, one fifth in category II, and three-fifths in category III.

Canadian immigration, with a sex ratio of 120 and 55% inactive (1952), accepts only 28% agricultural workers and unskilled labourers (between 1918 and 1930 the proportion was over half). By contrast it is open to skilled workers (more than 25%), clerical staff, and members of the professions (15%). Proportions by category are comparable to those recorded above for the United States: about one-quarter in each of categories I and II and one half in category III.

Australia has a different pattern. In immigration of 104,000 (1954), the sex ratio was 114 and the number of inactive 55%. But, while agricultural workers amount to 15% of the active immigrant population and unskilled labourers to 11%, the number of skilled workers and managerial class immigrants is 46% of the total. This leaves less than 30% in category III of whom 12% are in business, 9% in the professions, and 7% in domestic services.

France, the largest receiving nation in Europe, has a specific immigration pattern relating to certain occupations which the native population is deserting. In addition to single workers from North Africa and workers who leave their families behind, there is a tendancy to receive single male immigrants in France rather than complete families. Between 1946 and 1955 the proportion of inactive immigrants varied between 20% and 30%. More than two-thirds of the immigrants fall into the categories of manual labourers, agricultural workers, miners, and construction workers.

Conclusion

Now that we have made this comparison of the basic facts in the above cases, it is apparent that the occupational and social composition of migrations today differs widely from the migrations at the start of the century. The extent of these changes cannot be fully appreciated, however, without more precise information on the vocational training and level of education of the migrants.

Nevertheless, it is possible to make certain observations. Migration as it evolved during the nineteenth century and up to the First World War, i.e. the movement of unskilled labour, recruited in the poorest and most overpopulated rural regions of Europe and containing a high proportion of unmarried males, is now almost entirely at a standstill. The Portuguese emigrations described above are now the only movements of this type in Europe. Comparable situations are to be found in the current intra-African migrations which are part of the massive urbanization phenomenon in inter-tropical Africa, and perhaps in certain internal population movements in Latin America.

Emigration and immigration in their present forms are, in the first place, movements either of complete groups of population from advanced European countries or of former ruling or privileged classes. This means either they are representative of the whole social and occupational scale of the advanced countries, or they belong to a somewhat narrow occupational group which is characterized by a preponderance of skilled workers and management and other category III occupations. In the second instance the present-day movements meet the requirements of the so-called "new countries" which today need managerial and specialist skills rather than mere physical strength. Facts show that, with a certain amount of adaptation to the economic needs of the receiving nation, persons with a good general education and a knowledge of the language of the country to which they are emigrating, may be admitted in large numbers under category III. Unskilled workers, however, are only accepted in very small numbers. The effect of mechanization in agriculture and in public works, of improved mechanical handling techniques, and of the widespread introduction of automatic machinery in industry, has been far-reaching. The door of emigration is now closed to the masses from underdeveloped countries who are condemned to misery and geographic inertia because of the fundamental opposition between the offer of "muscle power" from backward and over populated economies and the demand for "brain power" in the increasingly complex technical economies.

Most of the figures quoted were taken from *Migrations internationales selon les caracteristiques*, United Nations, Demographic Studies, No. 12, 1958.

A General Typology of Migration[*]

W. PETERSEN

MOST studies of international migration are focused on the movement from or to one particular country, and virtually all of the other, somewhat broader works are concerned with a single historical era. Moreover, the emphasis is usually on description rather than analysis, so that the theoretical framework into which these limited data are fitted is ordinarily rather primitive. In this paper, an attempt is made to bring together into one typology some of the more significant analyses of both internal and international migration, as a step toward a general theory of migration.

The best known model for the analysis of migration is the typology constructed some years ago by Fairchild.[1] He classifies

[*] An earlier version of this paper was presented at the annual meeting of the American Sociological Society, Washington, DC, Aug. 1957. It was written as a chapter of a volume on population to be published in 1959.

[1] Henry Pratt Fairchild, *Immigration: A World Movement and Its American Significance*, rev. ed., New York, Macmillan, 1925, pp. 13 ff. In spite of the fact that it has all the faults of a pioneer effort, this classification has been adopted uncritically in several other works on the subject. See, for example, Maurice R. Davie, *World Immigration with Special Reference to the United States*, New York, Macmillan, 1949, pp. 2–3; Julius Isaac, *Economics of Migration*, London, Kegan Paul, Trench, Trubner, 1947, p. 1. The most recent and in many respects the best text in the field takes over Fairchild's four types and adds a fifth, *compulsory migration;* see Donald R. Taft and Richard Robbins, *International Migrations: The Immigrant in the Modern World*, New York; Ronald Press, 1955, pp. 19–20.

Several other discussions are decidedly better than Fairchild's, though not nearly so well known. I found two particularly stimulating—Rudolf Heberle, "Theorie der Wanderungen: Sociologische Betrachtungen," *Schmollers Jahrbuch*, LXXV:1 (1955); and Ragnar Numelin, *The Wandering Spirit: A Study of Human Migration*, London, Macmillan, 1937. See also Howard Becker, Forms of population movement: prolegonema to a study of mental mobility, *Social Forces*, 9 (Dec. 1930), 147–60; and 9 (March 1931), pp. 351–61.

migration into *invasion*, of which the Visigoth sack of Rome is given as the best example; *conquest*, in which "the people of higher culture take the aggressive;" *colonization*, when "a well established, progressive, and physically vigorous state" settles "newly discovered or thinly settled countries;" and *immigration*, or the individually motivated, peaceful movement between well established countries "on approximately the same stage of civilization." That is to say, Fairchild uses, more or less clearly, two main criteria as his axes—the difference in level of culture and whether or not the movement was predominantly peaceful. His four types, thus, can be represented schematically as follows:

Migration from	Migration to	Peaceful Movement	Warlike Movement
Low culture	High culture		Invasion
High culture	Low culture	Colonization	Conquest
Cultures on a level		Immigration	

Reducing the implicit underlying structure to this schematic form has the immediate advantage of indicating its incompleteness. Two types are lacking from the classification,[2] although they are well represented in history.

Such a paradigm, moreover, suggests even more strongly than the dozen pages of text it summarizes that the two axes are not the best that could have been chosen. An attempt to distinguish between "high" and "low" cultures is an invitation to ethnocentrism, which Fairchild does not always avoid. The contrast between "progressive" England and "newly discovered" India, for example, can hardly be termed a scientific analysis of *colonization*.

[2] It is patent that this omission was not intentional; this is not an example of what Lazarsfeld terms "reduction"—that is, the collapsing of a formally complete typology in order to adjust it to reality. See Paul F. Lazarsfeld, "Some remarks on the typological procedures in social science," mimeographed translation of an article that appeared originally in *Zeitschrift für Sozialforschung*, **6**, 1937.

Similarly, Rome's *conquest* of her empire was not merely the migration of a people of higher culture: much of Rome's culture was adapted from that of conquered Greece. Nor is the distinction between "peaceful" and "warlike" always an unambiguous one. Colonization is ordinarily neither one nor the other;[3] and the Visigoths' *invasion* of Rome, Fairchild's main example of this type, was predominantly a peaceful interpenetration of the two cultures, accomplished (as Fairchild points out) over more than two centuries.[4]

This criticism of Fairchild's classification illustrates two general points: that it is useful to make explicit the logical structure of a typology, and that the criteria by which types are to be distinguished must be selected with care.

[3] According to Fairchild, "while the resistance of the natives may be so weak as to make the enterprise hardly a military one, yet colonization is carried on without the consent, and against the will, of the original possessors of the land, and is, consequently, to be regarded rightly as a hostile movement. . . . [Moreover,] not infrequently the rivalry of two colonizing powers for some desirable locality may involve them in war with each other" (*op. cit.*, p. 19). In spite of this hedge, classifying *colonization* as "peaceful" is in accord with his main argument, for this is how he distinguishes it from *conquest*.

[4] On the one side, Germans were taken into the Roman army, granted land in the border regions and civil rights in the city; on the other side, after Wulfilas's translation of the Bible into Gothic, Roman culture made deep inroads among the Germans through their conversion to Christianity. The relation between the two cultures, therefore, was expressed not merely in a sharp confrontation on the field of battle, but also in the divided loyalties of marginal types. Alaric, leader of the Visigoths, was a romanized German, a former officer in the Roman army, a Christian; and Stilicho, the *de facto* emperor after Theodosius's death, was a German-Roman, a German by descent who had reached his high post through a successful army career. Alaric's purpose was not to overthrow Rome but, within the framework of the Empire, to get land and increased pensions (!) for his followers; Stilicho's purpose, similarly, was not to oust the Visigoths, whom he sought as allies against Constantinople, but to keep them under control. The interpenetration of the two cultures, that is to say, was a complex and subtle process, not too different from the present-day acculturation of immigrant groups. That Alaric put pressure on the Senate by marching his army into Italy was not the characteristic of "a rude people, on a low stage of culture," but the time-honored mode of lobbying used by Roman generals. Historical studies substantiate this account of the facts; I have used principally J. B. Bury, *The Invasion of Europe by the Barbarians*, London, Macmillan, 1928.

M.—C

Psychological Universals

Together with most other analysts of migration, Fairchild implies that man is everywhere sedentary, remaining fixed until he is impelled to move by some force. Like most psychological universals, this one can be matched by its opposite: man migrates because of wanderlust. And like all such universals, these cannot explain differential behavior: if all men are sedentary (or migratory) "by nature," why do some migrate and some not? If a simplistic metaphor is used, it should be at least as complex as its mechanical analogue, which includes not only the concept of forces but also that of inertia.

Thus one might better say that a social group at rest, or a social group in motion (e.g., nomads), tends to remain so unless impelled to change; for with any viable pattern of life a value system is developed to support that pattern. To analyze the migration of Gypsies, for example, in terms of push and pull is entirely inadequate—no better, in fact, than to explain modern Western migration, as Herbert Spencer did in terms of "the restlessness inherited from ancestral nomads".[5] If this principle of inertia is accepted as valid, then the difference between gathering and nomadic peoples, on the one hand, and agricultural and industrial peoples, on the other hand, is fundamental with respect to migration. For once a people has a permanent place of residence, the relevance of push and pull factors is presumably much greater.

Sometimes the basic problem is not why people migrate but rather why they do not. The vast majority of American Negroes, for example, remained in the South until the First World War, in spite of the Jim Crow pattern and lynch law that developed there from the 1870's on and, as a powerful pull, the many opportunities available in the West and the burgeoning northern cities.[6]

[5] Herbert Spencer, *The Principles of Sociology*, 3rd ed, New York, Appleton, 1892, Vol. I, p. 566.

[6] See Gunnar Myrdal, *An American Dilemma: The Negro Problem and Modern Democracy*, New York, Harper, 1944, ch. 8, for an extended discussion of this point. For an international example, see William Petersen,

If wanderlust and what might be termed sitzlust are not useful as psychological universals, they do suggest a criterion for a significant distinction. Some persons migrate as a means of achieving the new. Let us term such migration *innovating*. Others migrate in response to a change in conditions, in order to retain what they have had; they move geographically in order to remain where they are in all other respects. Let us term such migration *conservative.* When the migrants themselves play a passive role, as in the case of African slaves being transported to the New World, the migration is termed innovating or conservative depending on how it is defined by the activating agent, in this case the slave-traders.

The fact that the familiar push–pull polarity implies a universal sedentary quality, however, is only one of its faults. The push factors alleged to "cause" emigration ordinarily comprise a heterogeneous array, ranging from an agricultural crisis to the spirit of adventure, from the development of shipping to over-population. Few attempts are made to distinguish among underlying causes, facilitative environment, precipitants, and motives.[7] In particular, if we fail to distinguish between emigrants' motives and the social causes of emigration—that is, if we do not take the emigrants' level of aspiration into account—our analysis lacks logical clarity. Economic hardship, for example, can appropriately be termed a "cause" of emigration only if there is a positive correlation between hardship, however defined, and the propensity to migrate.[8] Often the relation has been an inverse one; for example, the mass emigration from Europe in modern times developed

Planned Migration, Berkeley, University of California Press, 1955, chapter 3, which discusses the several factors in prewar Holland that seemingly should have induced a large emigration, but did not.

[7] Cf. R. M. MacIver, *Social Causation*, Boston, Ginn, 1942.

[8] Similarly, no principled difference is usually made between what is sometimes termed "absolute overpopulation," which results in hunger and starvation, and milder degrees of "overpopulation," which reflect not physiological but cultural standards. In the first case the aspiration of emigrants can be ignored, for it is a bare physiological minimum that can be taken as universal; but in the second case it is the level of aspiration itself that defines the "overpopulation" and sets an impetus to emigrate.

together with a marked *rise* in the European standard of living. As has been shown by several studies, the correlation was rather with the business cycle in the receiving country,[9] and even this relation explains fluctuations in the emigration rate more than its absolute level. Nor can the class differential in the rate of emigration be ascribed simply to economic differences. The middle class lived in more comfortable circumstances, but for many a move to America would have meant also a definite material improvement. During the period of mass emigration, however, this was stereotyped as lower-class behavior, as more than a bit unpatriotic for the well-to-do. For a middle-class person to emigrate meant a break with the established social pattern; therefore in the middle class, especially marginal types like idealists or black sheep left the country, and these for relevant *personal* reasons. Once a migration has reached the stage of social movement, however, such personal motivations are generally of little interest.

This kind of confusion is not limited to economic factors. Religious oppression or the infringement of political liberty was often a *motive* for emigration from Europe, but before the rise of modern totalitarianism emigrants were predominantely from the European countries least marked by such stigmata. An increasing propensity to emigrate spread east and south from Northwest Europe, together with democratic institutions and religious tolerance. Again, we are faced with the anomaly that those who emigrated "because" of persecution tended to come from countries where there was less than elsewhere.

When the push–pull polarity has been refined in these two senses, by distinguishing innovating from conservative migration and by including in the analysis the migrants' level of aspiration, it can form the basis of an improved typology of migration. Five broad classes of migration, designated as primitive, forced, impelled, free, and mass, are discussed below.

[9] Harry Jerome, *Migration and Business Cycles*, New York, National Bureau of Economic Research, 1926; Dorothy Swaine Thomas, *Social and Economic Aspects of Swedish Population Movements, 1750–1933*, New York, Macmillan, 1941, ch. 9.

Primitive Migration

The first class of migration to be defined is that resulting from an ecological push, and we shall term this *primitive* migration. Here, then, primitive migration does not denote the wandering of primitive peoples as such, but rather a movement related to man's inability to cope with natural forces. Since the reaction to a deterioration in the physical environment can be either remedial action or emigration, depending on the technology available to the people concerned, there is, however, a tendency for primitive migration in this narrower sense to be associated with primitive peoples.

Many of the treks of preindustrial folk seem, moreover, to have been conservative in the sense defined above. "There is often a tendency for [such] a migrating group to hold conservatively to the same type of environment; pastoral people, for example, attempt to remain on grasslands, where their accustomed life may be continued."[10] Such conservative migrations are set not by push and pull, but by the interplay of push and control. The route is shaped by both natural and man-made barriers: mountains, rivers, or rainfall or the lack of it; and the Great Wall of China or other, less monumental, evidence of hostility toward aliens. If they are indifferent about where they are going, men migrate as liquids flow, along the lines of least resistance. Conservative migrants seek only a place where they can resume their old way of life, and when this is possible they are content. Sometimes it is not possible, and any migration, therefore, may be associated with a fundamental change in culture.

The frequent designation for migrations of prehistoric primitives used to be "wandering of peoples," a translation from the German that, however inelegant, is nevertheless appropriate, for it denotes two of the characteristics that define it. For usually peoples as a whole migrate, not merely certain families or groups, and they leave without a definite destination, as "wander" implies

[10] Roland B. Dixon, Migrations, primitive, *Encyclopedia of the Social Sciences*, New York, Macmillan, 1934, **10**, 420–5.

in English. Let us, then, term migrations induced by ecological pressure as the *wandering of peoples*. Unintended movements over the ocean—an analogous type of primitive migration, which can be termed *marine wanderings*—have occurred more frequently than was once supposed.

> There are countless examples . . . [of] more or less accidental wanderings from island to island over oceanic expanses of water, brought about by winds and currents. The space of time and extent of these voyages seem to play a subordinate part. Journeys covering 3000 miles are not unusual. They may last six weeks or several months. Even without provisions the natives can get along, as they fish for their food and collect rainwater to drink.[11]

Contemporary primitives also often move about in a way directly related to the low level of their material culture. A food-gathering or hunting people cannot ordinarily subsist from what is available in one vicinity; it must range over a wider area, moving either haphazardly or back and forth over its traditional territory. Such movements can be called *gathering*. The analogous type of migratory movements of cattle-owning peoples is called *nomadism*, from the Greek word meaning to graze. Gatherers and nomads together are termed *rangers*.

The way of life of rangers is to be on the move, and their culture is adapted to this state. Their home is temporary or portable; some Australian peoples have no word for "home" in their language. Their value system adjudges the specific hardships of their life to be good; the contempt that the desert Arab feels for the more comfortable city Arab is traditional. Although their ordinary movement is usually over a restricted area, bounded by either physical barriers or peoples able to defend their territories, rangers are presumably more likely to migrate over longer distances (apart from differences in the means of transportation) simply because they are already in motion. Whether any particular nomad people settles down and becomes agricultural does not depend merely on geography. Geography determines only whether such a shift in their way of life is possible—it is barely feasible on

[11] Numelin, *op. cit.*, pp. 180–1.

the steppe, for example; but even when physical circumstances permit a change, the social pattern of ranging may be too strong to be broken down. The Soviet program of settling the Kirghiz and other nomad peoples on collective farms, for example, succeeded because it was implemented by sufficient terror to overcome their opposition.[12] That is to say, ranging, like wandering, is typically conservative.

A primitive migration of an agrarian population takes place when there is a sharp disparity between the produce of the land and the number of people subsisting from it. This can come about either suddenly, as by drought or an attack of locusts, or by the steady Malthusian pressure of a growing population on land or limited area and fertility. Persons induced to migrate by such population pressure can seek another agricultural site, but in the modern era the more usual destination has been a town: the migration has ordinarily been innovating rather than conservative. The Irish immigrants to the United States in the decades following the Great Famine, for example, resolutely ignored the Homestead Act and other inducements to settle on the land; in overwhelming proportion, they moved to the cities and stayed there. Let us term such an innovating movement *flight from the land* (again, an inelegant but useful translation from the German).

To recapitulate, primitive migration may be divided as follows:

Primitive	Wandering	Wandering of peoples
		Marine wandering
	Ranging	Gathering
		Nomadism
	Flight from the land	

[12] For a documentation from two sources of divergent political views, see Rudolf Schlesinger, *The Nationalities Problem and Soviet Administration*, London, Routledge & Kegan Paul, 1956; Walter Kolarz, *The Peoples of the Soviet Far East*, New York, Praeger, 1954.

These are the types of migration set by ecological push and controls, usually geographical but sometimes social.

Forced and Impelled Migrations

If in primitive migrations the activating agent is ecological pressure, in forced migrations it is the state or some functionally equivalent social institution. It is useful to divide this class into *impelled* migration, when the migrants retain some power to decide whether or not to leave, and *forced* migration, when they do not have this power. Often the boundary between the two, the point at which the choice becomes nominal, may be difficult to set. Analytically, however, the distinction is clearcut, and historically it is often so. The difference is real, for example, between the Nazis' policy (roughly 1933–8) of encouraging Jewish emigration by various anti-Sematic acts and laws, and the later policy (roughly 1938–45) of herding Jews into cattle-trains and transporting them to camps.

A second criterion by which we can delineate types of forced or impelled migration is its function, defined not by the migrant but by the activating agent. Persons may be induced to move simply to rid their homeland of them; such a migration, since it does not ordinarily bring about a change in the migrant's way of life, is analogous to conservative migration and can be subsumed under it. Others are induced to move in order that their labor power can be used elsewhere; and such a migration, which constitutes a shift in behavior patterns as well as in locale, is designated as innovating.

Four types are thus defined, as follows:

	Impelled	Forced
To be rid of migrants (conservative)	Flight	Displacement
To use migrants' labor (innovating)	Coolie trade	Slave trade

In all of human history, *flight* has been an important form of migration. Whenever a stronger people moves into a new territory, it may drive before it the weaker former occupants. The invasion of Europe during the early centuries of the Christian era thus was induced not only by the power vacuum resulting from the disintegration of the Roman Empire, but also by a series of successive pushes, originating from either the desiccation of the Central Asian steppes (Huntington) or the expansion of the Chinese empire still farther east (Teggart).[13]

Many more recent migrations have also been primarily a flight before invading armies.[14] In modern times, however, those induced to flee have often been specific groups among the population, rather than everyone occupying a particular territory. Political dissidents, of course, always were ousted when they became a danger to state security; but with the growth of nationalism ethnic as well as political homogeneity has been sought. The right of national self-determination proclaimed by the Treaty of Versailles included no provision for the minorities scattered through central Europe; and in the interwar period the League of Nations negotiated a series of population transfers designed to eliminate national minorities from adjacent countries or, more usually, to legitimate expulsions already effected.[15] The separation of Pakistan from India, another example, was accompanied by one of the largest migrations in human history, in part induced by terrorist groups on both sides and in part arranged under official auspices.

It is useful to distinguish between two classes of those who have

[13] Ellsworth Huntington, *Civilization and Climate*, New Haven, Yale University Press, 1951; Frederick Teggart, *Rome and China: A Study of Correlations in Historical Events*, Berkeley, University of California Press, 1939.

[14] See, for example, Eugene M. Kulischer, *Europe on the Move*, New York, Columbia University Press, 1948.

[15] Cf. Stephen P. Ladas, *The Exchange of Minorities: Bulgaria, Greece and Turkey*, New York, Macmillan, 1932, p. 721: "Both conventions [of Neuilly and Lausanne], and especially that of Lausanne, proved to be agreements confirming accomplished facts," and the Greek-Turkish exchange, while "voluntary in theory, became in fact to a great extent compulsory."

fled their homeland—*émigrés*, who regard their exile as temporary and live abroad for the day when they may return, and *refugees*, who intend to settle permanently in the new country. Under otherwise similar circumstances, the occulturation of the latter would presumably be much more rapid than that of persons still living spiritually in another country.

Frequently, even the pretense that the movement is voluntary has been lacking. As part of its European population policy, Nazi Germany exported Jews to camps and imported forced laborers from all occupied countries. The latter movement was a modern variant of the earlier slave-trade, but the largely successful attempt to kill off some millions of persons because of their supposed racial inferiority was something new in history. In the jargon of official bureaus, those that survived such forced migration have been termed "displaced persons," a designation that clearly implies their passive role. The forced movement itself is here called *displacement*.

The forced migrations under Soviet auspices have typically served two purposes, to remove a dissident or potentially dissident group from its home[16] and to furnish an unskilled labor force in an inhospitable area. During the first two five-year plans, several million "kulaks" were removed *en masse* to the sites of cities-to-be, and the inhabitants of the five national units of the USSR

[16] For example, after Poland was divided between Nazi Germany and Communist Russia in 1939, the more than a million Poles deported to Asiatic Russia were chosen not merely on the basis of actual or alleged opposition to their country's invasion but more often as members of a large variety of occupational groups, which were defined as potentially oppositionist. "Regarded as 'anti-Soviet elements,' and so treated, were administrative officials, police, judges, lawyers, members of Parliament, prominent members of political parties, non-communist non-political societies, clubs, and the Red Cross; civil servants not included above, retired military officers, officers in the reserve, priests, tradesmen, landowners, hotel and restaurant owners, clerks of the local Chambers of Commerce, and any class of persons engaged in trade or correspondence with foreign countries—the latter definition extending even to stamp collectors and Esperantists—were also deported. Many artisans, peasants, and laborers (both agricultural and industrial), were banished too, so that, in effect, no Polish element was spared." Edward J. Rozek, *Allied Wartime Diplomacy: A Pattern in Poland*, New York, Wiley, 1958, p. 39.

abolished during the war were deported wholesale to forced-labor camps.[17] Such movements combine displacement with *slave trade*, or the forcible migration of laborers. While the overseas shipment of Africans during the mercantile age differed in some respects from the use of forced labor in an industrial economy, the two criteria that define the type are the same—the use of force and the supply of labor power.

The analogous form of impelled migration is termed *coolie trade*. This includes not only the movement of Asians to plantations, the most typical form, but also, for example, the migration of white indentured servants to the British colonies in the eighteenth century. Such migrants, while formally bound only for the period of a definite contract, very often are forced into indebtedness and thus to extend their period of service indefinitely.[18] But as in other cases of impelled and forced migration, even when the difference between historical instances becomes blurred, the analytical distinction is clear. Another important difference between slave and coolie migration is that many coolies eventually return to their homeland. The total emigration from India from 1834 to 1937, for example, has been estimated at slightly more than 30 million, but of these almost 24 million returned, leaving a net emigration over the century of only 6 million.[19]

[17] The Volga-German ASSR, the Kalmyk ASSR, the Chechen-Ingush ASSR, the Crimean ASSR, and the Karachayev Region were designated as "disloyal nationalities", and the major portion of the 2.8 million inhabitants were removed from their immemorial homeland. The million or so Tatars brought into Crimea to replace the deportees also proved to be unreliable, and in 1945 most of these were also deported to forced labor. See David J. Dallin and Boris I. Nicolaevsky, *Forced Labor in Soviet Russia*, New Haven, Yale University Press, 1947, pp. 274–7. According to a decree dated Jan. 9, 1957, the survivors among five of the uprooted peoples are to be shipped back to their homes over the next several years. Even under this new policy, however, the Volga Germans and the Tatars are presumably to be left in their Siberian exile (*New York Times*, Feb. 12, 1957).

[18] See, for example, Victor Purcell, *The Chinese in Southeast Asia*, London, Oxford University Press, 1951, p. 345.

[19] Kingsley Davis, *The Population of India and Pakistan*, Princeton, Princeton University Press, 1951, p. 99.

Free Migration

In the types of migration discussed so far, the will of the migrants has been a relatively unimportant factor. A primitive migration results from the lack of means to satisfy basic physiological needs, and in forced (or impelled) migration the migrants are largely passive. We now consider the types in which the will of the migrants is the decisive element, that is, *free* migrations.

Overseas movements from Europe during the 19th century afford important illustrations of this class of migration. Because of the excellence of its formal analysis, Lindberg's monograph on emigration from Sweden[20] has been chosen as an example. Lindberg distinguishes three periods, each with a characteristic type of emigrant. During the first stage, beginning around 1840, emigrants came principally from the two university towns of Upsala and Lund; they were "men with a good cultural and social background, mostly young and of a romantic disposition" (p. 3). Since the risks in emigration were great and difficult to calculate, those who left tended to be adventurers or intellectuals motivated by their ideals, especially by their alienation from European society during a period of political reaction. The significance of this *pioneer* movement was not in its size, which was never large, but in the example it set: "It was this emigration that helped to break the ice and clear the way for the later emigration, which included quite different classes" (p. 7). These pioneers wrote letters home; their adventures in the new world were recounted in Swedish newspapers. Once settled in the new country, they helped finance the passage of their families or friends.

Imperceptibly, this first stage developed into the second, the period of *group migration*—the emigration, for example, of Pietist communities under the leadership of their pastor or another person of recognized authority. Even when not associated through their adherence to a dissident sect, emigrants banded together for

<hr/>

[20] John S. Lindberg, *The Background of Swedish Emigration to the United States: An Economic and Sociological Study in the Dynamics of Migration*, Minneapolis, University of Minnesota Press, 1930.

mutual protection during the hazardous journey and against the wilderness and the often hostile Indians at its end. Again, the significance of this group migration lay not in its size but in the further impulse it gave. During the decade beginning 1841, an average of only 400 persons left Sweden annually, and during the following decade, this average was still only 1500.

Mass Migration

Free migration is always rather small,[21] for individuals strongly motivated to seek novelty or improvement are not commonplace. The most significant attribute of pioneers, as in other areas of life, is that they blaze trails that others follow, and sometimes the number who do so grows into a broad stream. Migration becomes a style, an established pattern, an example of collective behavior. Once it is well begun, the growth of such a movement is semi-automatic: so long as there are people to emigrate, the principal cause of emigration is prior emigration. Other circumstances operate as deterrents or incentives, but within this kind of attitudinal framework; all factors except population growth are important principally in terms of the established behavior. As we have already noted, when emigration has been set as a *social* pattern, it is no longer relevant to inquire concerning the *individual* motivations. For the individual is, in Lindberg's phrase, in an "unstable state of equilibrium," in which only a small impulse in either direction decides his course; hence the motives he ascribes to his emigration are either trivial or, more likely, the generalities that he thinks are expected.[22]

---

[21] As in general throughout this essay, the words used to designate the classes or types of migration are terms in common usage rather than neologisms. Since they are here more precisely defined than in most contexts, however, they denote a narrower range of meaning; thus free migration is not all unforced migration, for it is one of five rather than two classes.

[22] Hansen has pointed out that the migrant's motivation was likely to be pruned to suit the person asking for it. The official in the home country was told of material difficulties, but to cite these in America would confirm the natives' belief that the foreigner was a dangerous economic competitor. The village clergyman, should he attempt to dissuade a prospective migrant, was

The development of migration as collective behavior is aptly illustrated by the Swedish case. During the decade 1861–70, when the average number of emigrants jumped to 9300 per year, the transition to the third stage of *mass* emigration began. Transportation facilities improved: railroads connected the interior with the port cities, and the sailing ship began to be replaced by the much faster and safer steamer. While its relation to mass migration was important, this improvement in transportation facilites was not a cause; rather, it is "possible and even probable that emigration and the development of transportation were largely caused by the same forces" (p. 15, n. 17). Not only was the geographical distance cut down but also what Lindberg terms the social distance: as communities in the new country grew in size and importance, the shift from Sweden to America required less and less of a personal adjustment. Before the migrant left his homeland, he began his acculturation in an American-Swedish milieu, made up of New World letters, photographs, mementoes, knick-knacks. There developed what the peasants called "America fever": in some districts, there was not a farm without some relatives in America, and from many all the children had emigrated. According to a government report that Lindberg quotes, children were "educated to emigrate," and he continues—

---

told that his sons were growing up without a future and becoming lazy and shiftless; but in America these moral motives would give point to the argument that immigrants were depraved. Hence, "the newcomer said, 'I came to the United States to enjoy the blessings of your marvelous government and laws,' [and] the native warmed to him and was likely to inquire whether there was not something he could do to assist him. Immigrants soon learned the magic charm of this confession of faith. They seized every opportunity to contrast the liberty of the New World with the despotism of the Old." Marcus Lee Hansen, *The Immigrant in American History*, Cambridge, Harvard University Press, 1940, pp. 77–78.

This is a good example of why public opinion polling can be deficient as a method of social—rather than social psychological—analysis. Each respondent queried replies in terms of his own norms, and for the whole sample these may differ considerably, depending on how heterogeneous the respondents are with respect to the subject of the poll. To sum up the yes's and no's without taking into account the criteria that determined these replies is appropriate only when we are interested solely in the sum, as in an election.

When they finally arrived at a decision, they merely followed a tradition which made emigration the natural thing in a certain situation. In fact, after the imagination and fantasy had, so to speak, become "charged with America," a positive decision *not* to emigrate may have been necessary if difficulties arose (pp. 56–57).

The Swedes who migrated to Minnesota became farmers or small-town craftsmen or merchants. In a more general analysis, it is useful to distinguish the types of mass movement according to the nature of the destination—*settlement*, such as Lindberg described, and *urbanization*, or mass migration to a larger town or city. No distinction in principle is made here between internal and international migration, for the fundamentals of the rural–urban shift so characteristic of the modern era are generally the same whether or not the new city-dwellers cross a national border.

Relation	Migratory force	Class of migration	Type of migration	
			Conservative	Innovating
Nature and man	Ecological push	Primitive	Wandering	Flight from the land
			Ranging	
State (or equivalent) and man	Migration policy	Forced	Displacement	Slave trade
		Impelled	Flight	Coolie trade
Man and his norms	Higher aspirations	Free	Group	Pioneer
Collective behaviour	Social momentum	Mass	Settlement	Urbanization

Conclusions

The typology developed in this paper is summarized in the attached table. Such a typology is a tool, and it is worth constructing only if it is useful. What is its utility?

This question may be answered against a perspective of the present undeveloped status of migration theory. Classifications of modern migrations tend to derive from the statistics that are collected, whether or not these have any relevance to theoretical questions. It is as if those interested in the *causes* of divorce studied this matter exclusively with data classified according to the *grounds* on which divorces are granted. Even the principal statistical differentiation, that between internal and international migration, is not necessarily of theoretical significance.[23] Similarly when the species *migrant* is set off from the genus *traveler* by arbitrarily defining removal for a year or more as "permanent" migration, such a distinction clearly has little or no theoretical basis, and it is not even certain that it is the most convenient one that could be made.[24] The preferable procedure in any discipline is to establish our concepts and the logical relation among them, and to collect our statistics in terms of this conceptual framework. The principal purpose of the typology, then, is to offer, by such an ordering of conceptual types, a basis for the possible development of theory. "Since sound sociological interpretation inevitably *implies* some theoretic paradigm, it seems the better part of wisdom to bring it out into the open," first of all because such a paradigm "provides a compact parsimonious arrangement of the central concepts and their interrelations as these are utilized for description and analysis."[25]

[23] The movement westward across the United States, for example, included a swing northward to the western provinces of Canada at the turn of the century, and today American cities attract both American and Canadians. In both cases, one may interpret English-speaking North America as a single labor market, with the international border acting primarily as an added friction to free mobility. See Brinley Thomas, *Migration and Economic Growth: A Study of Great Britain and the Atlantic Economy* (National Institute of Economic and Social Research), London, Cambridge University Press, 1954, pp. 134–8.

[24] Thus in his recent study of British migration, Isaac found it useful to distinguish between those who intend to settle elsewhere permanently and what he termed "quasi-permanent" migrants or those who leave for a year or more but intend to return. See Julius Isaac, *British Post-War Migration* (National Institute of Economic and Social Research), Occasional Paper XVII, Cambridge University Press, 1954, p. 2.

[25] Robert K. Merton, *Social Theory and Social Structure*, Glencoe, Ill., Free Press, 1949, p. 14. For an interesting article exemplifying the usefulness of such a typology, see Merton, "Intermarriage and the Social Structure: Fact and Theory," *Psychiatry*, 4 (Aug. 1941), 361–74.

Migration differs from fertility and mortality in that it cannot be analyzed, even at the outset, in terms of non-cultural, physiological factors, but must be differentiated with respect to relevant social conditions. This means that the most general statement that one makes concerning migration should be in the form of a typology, rather than a law.[26] While few today would follow Ravenstein's example by denoting their statements "laws,"[27] most treatments of migratory selection still imply a comparable degree of generality. Even the best discussions[28] typically neglect to point out that selection ranges along a continuum, from total migration to total non-migration, or that the predominance of females in rural-urban migration that Ravenstein noted must be contrasted with male predominance in, for example, India's urbanization. As we have seen, the familiar push-pull polarity implies a universal sedentary tendency, which has little empirical basis in either history or psychology. Analogously, the distinction between conservative and innovating migration challenges the usual notion that persons universally migrate in order to change their way of life.

Sometimes an analytical problem can be clarified by defining more precisely the two more or less synonymous terms that denote a confusion in concepts. For example, the question of whether the secular decline in the Western birth rate was due to a physiological deterioration or to new cultural standards was often not put clearly until *fecundity* was precisely distinguished from *fertility*. Several such pairs of terms are differentiated here. Whether a movement from the countryside to towns is *urbanization* or *flight from the land* can be a very important distinction; the discussion of Canada's immigration policy, for example, has largely centered on this point.[29] While the distinction between *urbanization* and

[26] This point is very effectively argued by Heberle, *op. cit.*

[27] E. G. Ravenstein, The laws of migration, *Journal of the Royal Statistical Society*, **48** (June 1885), 167–235; **52** (June 1889), 241–305.

[28] See, for example, Dorothy Swaine Thomas (ed.), *Research Memorandum of Migration Differentials*, New York, Social Science Research Council, Bulletin 43, 1938; E. W. Hofstee, *Some Remarks on Selective Migration*, The Hague, Nijhoff, 1952.

[29] See Petersen, *op. cit.*, pp. 202 ff.

settlement would seem to be so obvious that it can hardly be missed, one can say that the national-quota system of American immigration law is based in part at least on neglect of the implications of this differentiation. [30] The most useful distinction in the typology, perhaps, is that between *mass* migration and all other types, for it emphasizes the fact that the movement of Europeans to the New World during the nineteenth century, the migration with which we are most familiar, does not constitute the whole of the phenomenon. When this type of migration declined after the First World War, largely because of new political limitations imposed by both emigration and immigration countries, this was very often interpreted, not as a change to a different type, but as the end of significant human migration altogether.[31] A world in which hardly anyone dies in the place where he was born, however, can hardly be termed sedentary.

[30] The main source of immigration to the United States shifted from northwest Europe to southern and eastern Europe at about the same time that the American economy underwent a fundamental transformation from an agrarian to an industrial base; consequently *some* of the observed differences between the "old" and the "new" immigration were due not to variations among European cultures, as is assumed in the law, but to the different rate of acculturation of peasants undergoing settlement or urbanization.

[31] The two best known statements of this point of view are W. D. Forsyth, *The Myth of Open Spaces*, Melbourne, Melbourne University Press, 1942, and Isaiah Bowman (ed.), *Limits of Land Settlement*, New York, Council on Foreign Relations, 1937.

PART II

THE PROBLEM IN VARIOUS COUNTRIES

The United States

Participation of Migrants in Urban Structures*

B. G. ZIMMER

HISTORICALLY cities have been dependent upon migration for growth or even maintenance of size. Important as migration is to the city very little is known concerning the behavior of migrants in these centers. It has long been known that cities are made up of migrants, but just what this means to the city is as yet relatively unexplored. Most of the work in the area of migration to date has been concerned with the volume and direction of movement, reasons for movement, and the demographic characteristics of the persons engaged in the movement. From these kinds of data the significance of migration to the receiving communities has been inferred.

There is a great deal of conjectural literature concerning the social implications of migration, but the empirical studies attempting to measure some of the implications, as far as specific types of behavior are concerned, are limited. Generally, those available have been concerned with very select groups.[1]

* This article is based on the writer's unpublished doctoral dissertation, University of Michigan, 1954. Particular indebtedness is due to Ronald Freedman, chairman of the writer's doctoral committee and to Amos Hawley, Werner Landecker, and Robert Blood for their criticisms and many helpful suggestions. For funds with which to complete the larger study, the writer is indebted to the Human Resources Research Institute and the Chicago Community Inventory.

[1] Louis Killian, Southern white laborers in Chicago's West Side (unpublished Ph.D. dissertation, University of Chicago, 1949). Grace G. Leybourne, Urban adjustment of migrants from the southern Appalachian plateaus, *Social Forces*, **16** (Dec. 1937), 238–46.

The only type of behavior which has received systematic analysis in relation to migration status is occupational role both before and after migration. Perhaps the reason for this is that migration studies have been, for the most part, limited to census materials.

Significant as these studies have been, it appears to the writer that a fruitful area for research, in order better to understand both the city and the consequences of migration, is to measure selected types of behavior in the urban community of destination in relation to migrant status. This is the problem of the present study. Specifically, we will test whether migrants to an urban center, considered as a group, ever become participants in the activities of the community to the same extent as the non-migrant natives, and if so, how long a period of time is required. Further, we will test whether specific types of migrants enter the formal activities of the community more rapidly than other types of migrants. It is expected that migrants coming from an environment culturally similar to the present community will participate more rapidly than persons coming from dissimilar environments.[2]

We will test the following hypotheses:

Hypothesis I. Migrants differ from the natives in level of participation but they become more similar to the natives in their behavior the longer they live in the community.[3]

Hypothesis II. Urban migrants tend to enter the activities of the community more rapidly than farm migrants.[4]

The data on which this investigation is based were gathered by the personal interview survey method during the spring and early summer of 1951. The interviews were obtained from the occupants of a random sample of dwelling units in a mid-western community

[2] This is based on the notion that even though migration itself may limit behavior, previous training to live in an urban setting will facilitate participation in the urban community, whereas, the lack of such training or experience will retard participation.

[3] Natives include those who have lived in the community since birth, and those who entered the community before attaining 10 years of age and have lived in the community continuously since that time.

[4] Migrants are classified according to type of community of birth.

with a population of nearly 20,000. The data presented here are limited to married males. Thus, marital status and sex are automatically controlled.

Three different types of activity in the community are studied: membership in formal organizations,[5] officership in organizations, and registration to vote. The analysis of participation[6] in each type of behavior is a separate test of the general hypotheses. If the hypotheses are valid they should be supported for each type of behaviour studied.

Prior researchers have investigated these types of behavior but most studies have emphasized that participation varies by demographic characteristics such as age, sex, education, and occupation.[7] The importance of these variables is already known; the present study will employ these as controls. Thus, the significance of migrant status itself can be demonstrated.

Membership in Formal Organizations

Membership in formal organizations tends to increase directly with length of time in the community within age, occupational and educational categories, as is shown in Table 1. Migrants, as a group, within each control category, have a lower participation rate than the natives, but the rate among the migrants becomes more similar to the natives the longer the former reside in the community.

[5] Formal organizations refer generally to those groups which are ordinarily thought of as clubs and societies by the people in the community. However, church organizations, such as missionary societies, usher clubs, choir, and the like, have not been included. Although not reported here these latter have been analyzed separately.

[6] Participation means only that persons belong to any organization, holds or has held an officership position, or is registered to vote. It does not measure intensity of activity.

[7] Mirra Komarovsky, The voluntary associations of the urban dwellers, *American Sociological Review*, 2 (Dec. 1946), 468–98. Herbert Goldhamer, Some factors affecting participation in voluntary associations (unpublished Ph.D. dissertation, University of Chicago, 1943). William C. Mather, Income and social participation, *American Sociological Review*, 6 (June, 1941), 380–4.

TABLE 1. PER CENT BELONGING TO FORMAL ORGANIZATIONS WITHIN AGE, OCCUPATIONAL, AND EDUCATIONAL CATEGORIES, BY LENGTH OF TIME IN COMMUNITY

Length of time in community (years)	Age		Occupation		Education		
	Under 40 yrs.	40 yrs. plus	WC	MW	GS	HS	Col
Less than 2	25[a]	22	33	16	5	10	47
2–5	37	36	53	22	15	37	54
6–10	45	31	46	35	18	42	58
11–19	50	40	67	30	29	49	60
20 and over	...[b]	51	73	37	35	47	92
Natives	56	54	63	48	33[c]	50	74
Total	41	42	56	32	24	41	61

[a] The complement of this percentage would be the percentage of those who do *not* belong.
[b] Less than 10 cases.
[c] Less than 20 cases.

Within each sub-group the lowest participation rate is found among migrants in the community less than 2 years, whereas, migrants who have been in the community 20 years or more have the highest participation. Among the white-collar workers and the college trained, migrants who have been in the community over 20 years have a participation rate higher than the natives. In all other sub-groups, the natives have the highest membership rate.

Within age groups we note that, among the younger persons, migrants approximate the level of participation of the natives after 10 years of residence, whereas in the older age group this does not occur until migrants have been in the community for 20 years or more. Apparently younger persons are less affected by migration than older persons.[8]

[8] From these data differences by age are not evident. However, a more detailed breakdown by age shows the middle age groups to have the highest participation, whereas the rate is lower for the younger and older migrants. A similar pattern was observed in a preliminary report issued by the Detroit Area Study.

Among white-collar workers the difference between migrants and natives in memberships also tends to disappear after 10 years of residence. At this point white-collar migrants seem to participate at about the same rate as the natives, or even at higher rates. However, among the manual workers, migrants never do attain the level of participation of the natives at the same occupational level. It may be that there is a standardized urban culture shared by white-collar workers which soon transcends the limiting influence of migration. This is to say that, in preparing for or in the pursuit of white collar work, persons learn at the same time an urban way of life, which is carried with them in their migration. This urban culture makes for a more rapid adjustment in the new community. Such a culture is not found among manual workers. Thus it takes the manual worker longer to become similar to the native in participation. In each length of time in the community category white-collar workers have a much higher membership rate than manual workers. The importance of occupational status is strikingly evident when we note that white collar workers in the community from 2 to 5 years, have a higher membership rate than native manual workers.

Within each educational group participation increases consistently with length of time in the community; however, marked differences by education are found. The lowest membership rate, only 5 per cent, is found among grade school persons with less than two years of residence in the community. At the college level nearly half are members. The importance of education is also strikingly evident by the fact that college migrants who have lived in the community less than 2 years have a membership rate which is much higher than the natives in the grade school group and is nearly equal to the natives at the high school level.

At each educational level it takes at least 10 years or more before migrants approximate the natives of equal education in level of participation. Generally, after 10 years of residence migrants become quite similar to the natives; however it seems that, at the lower levels of education, migrants become similar to the natives of equal education sooner than at the college level. It may be that college persons join more exclusive groups which are more difficult to enter. Such groups are likely to offer more restrictions to migrants than other type formal organizations.

At any rate hypothesis I is supported by the data. The length of time required to become active in the community varies according to the personal characteristics possessed by the migrants. High status facilitates participation. However, regardless of status, it takes migrants 10 years or more to become integrated in this aspect of the organized structure of the community.

The rate of entering formal organizations varies by migrant type as demonstrated in Table 2. However, for each migrant type, membership increases with length of time in the community. Farm migrants have the slowest entrance rate, but contrary to expectations urban migrants do not enter more rapidly than rural non-farm migrants. Nevertheless, they do exceed them in memberships after the first two years. Persons from rural non-farm areas tend to enter the organizations sooner than those from urban areas, but after a time in the present community the urban born have a higher membership rate than is found among the rural non-farm migrants. Thus, eventually urban migrants attain the highest participation rate.

The high participation on the part of rural non-farm migrants as a group was not expected according to our cultural similarity hypothesis. It may be that the rural non-farm category does not properly "fit" on a rural-urban continuum since it is a recognizable ambiguous category. For this reason the emphasis of our discussion is centered on the differences between urban and farm migrants. These two categories do clearly represent distinctly different types of communities.

A second possible explanation for this finding is that, insofar as rural non-farm areas are small villages, it may be that formal organizations play a more important role in such communities than in larger urban areas. These organizations may be quite accessible to all members of the community in that sharp status differences on which to select members may be lacking or at least quite limited. Thus, living in rural non-farm areas may expose persons to formal organizations even more so than living in the city. It is suggested that the diversity of such groups may be rather limited in small villages as compared to urban centers, but the actual level of participation may be more frequent in the former.

TABLE 2. PER CENT BELONGING TO FORMAL ORGANIZATIONS, BY LENGTH OF TIME IN COMMUNITY, BY MIGRANT TYPE

| Length of time in community (years) | Type of migrant | | | | | |
| | Farm | | Rural non-farm | | Urban | |
	Per cent	Number	Per cent	Number	Per cent	Number
Less than 2	14	(29)	41	(17)	26	(39)
2–5	29	(56)	38	(29)	43	(60)
6–10	29	(56)	39	(23)	47	(62)
11–19	39	(49)	53	(17)	41	(44)
20 and over	48	(54)	52	(25)	57	(35)
Total	33	(244)	44	(111)	43	(240)

Thus, rural non-farm migrants may have learned to participate in such groups more so than other types of migrant. It may be that their participation rate decreases proportionately because of migration, but they continue to have a higher level of participation than other types of migrant. Perhaps an analysis of membership before and after their migration would show that their high participation rate in the present community is due to the fact that they have transferred their memberships to local chapters of national organizations to which they had previously belonged. One of the important functions of national organizations may be to cushion the limiting effects of migration.

Although membership increases steadily for the farm migrants by length of time in the community, these never do reach the level of participation of the natives. Also we note that no matter how long farm migrants have been in the community they have a lower participation rate than do other types of migrant who have lived in the community the same length of time.

For memberships in formal organizations, hypothesis II is also supported by these data. Farm migrants enter this activity less rapidly than rural non-farm or urban migrants. Here also, as within sub-groups, we find that, regardless of type, it takes at least ten years or more for migrants to become similar to the natives in level of participation. Farm migrants, however, never do attain the level of participation of the natives.[9] We will now turn to a different type of behavior in order to test further the same hypotheses.

Officership

The extent to which migrants may obtain officership positions is dependent upon their rate of membership in the organizations of the community. For this reason our discussion on officership is limited only to those persons who belong to an organization in the community and are thus exposed to officership positions.[10] Officership refers to any specially recognized position in the group.

The participation rate in the officership class increases directly by length of time in the community within each control category. These data are presented in Table 3. As in formal organizations, those who have been in the community less than 2 years have the lowest proportion in the officership group, whereas those who have lived in the community 20 years and over have the highest percentage. Even though there tends to be a steady increase in the proportion who are in the officership group by length of time in the community, within age groupings, the main difference among the younger persons is found between those who have lived in the community 5 years or less and those who have lived in the community for more than 5 years. However, among the older people the migrants never do reach the natives in the proportion who are in the officership class. Thus, for this category,

[9] When migrants are classified according to last place of residence, the participation rate of farm migrants is lower than is found according to the place of birth criterion.

[10] All persons without an affiliation have been dropped from the sample for this discussion. Included here are members of formal organizations, church organizations, and of the union. Therefore, the differences reported are not due to differential membership by length of time in the community.

the effects of migration are never overcome. Differences in the officership rate are also found by age. Older persons, as a group, have a higher proportion in the officership class than do younger persons.

When we control for occupation it is only during the first 5 years that migrants are distinct by their low participation. Migrant white-collar workers, after living in the community more than 5 years, have a higher percentage in the officership class than the natives of equal status. However, among the manual workers, as among the older people, migrants never do reach the natives in level of participation, but the differences are not marked after the the first 5 years. Thus, among manual workers, it seems that during the second five years in the community the officership rate is more than double the rate for the first 5 years. Thereafter, even though the proportion in the officership class increases, the differences are slight. Marked differences by occupation are found. High status migrants enter officership positions more rapidly than low status workers. For example, white-collar migrants, in the community less than 2 years, have an officership rate equal to the natives in the manual worker group. White-collar workers, as a group, have an officership rate double that of the manual workers.

TABLE 3. PER CENT IN OFFICERSHIP CLASS WITHIN AGE, OCCUPATIONAL, AND EDUCATIONAL CATEGORIES, BY LENGTH OF TIME IN COMMUNITY

Length of time in community (years)	Age		Occupation		Education		
	Under 40 yrs.	40 yrs. plus	WC	MW	GS	HS	Col
Less than 2	23	8[b]	33	10	8[b]	. .[c]	45
2–5	23	26	37	13	9	29	31
6–10	37	31	53	27	16	36	58
11–19	37	35	47	30	31	33	50
20 and over	. .[a]	37	58	24	19	36	64
Natives	31	56	49	33	17[b]	42	48
Total	30	34	46	24	18	32	48

[a] Less than 10 cases. [b] Less than 20 cases.   [c] None in the officership group.

Similarly, within each educational level, migrants approximate the natives in the proportion who are in the officership class after five years of residence. Again we find that after long residence migrants are likely to have a higher participation rate than the natives. In other words, the limiting influences of migration are lost. Marked differences are found by education. The college trained migrants enter officership positions much more rapidly than migrants at the lower levels of education. Again we observe that the possession of high status characteristics facilitates adjustment. For this type of behavior also hypothesis I is supported by the data.

Within each migrant type (Table 4) the proportion in the officership class also tends to increase with length of time in the community. Farm migrants, however, take longer to enter the officership roles than do the other types of migrant. Farm migrants have a particularly low participation rate during the early years in the community. Among the farm migrants we note a steady increase in the proportion in the officership group by length of time in the community, whereas the proportion of the other migrants in the officership class increases only during the first 5 years in the community, then begins to level off and remains relatively constant.

TABLE 4. PER CENT IN OFFICERSHIP CLASS BY LENGTH OF TIME IN COMMUNITY, BY MIGRANT TYPE

Length of time in community (years)	Type of Migrant					
	Farm		Rural non-farm		Urban	
	Per cent	Number	Per cent	Number	Per cent	Number
Less than 2	12	(17)	28	(14)	20	(20)
2–5	18	(40)	30	(20)	32	(41)
6–10	20	(41)	29	(17)	44	(52)
11–19	25	(40)	31	(13)	43	(35)
20 and over	42	(38)	32	(22)	35	(29)
Total	24	(176)	30	(86)	37	(177)

Apparently rural non-farm and urban migrants attain their normal participation rate in about 5 years, whereas, farm migrants are continually adjusting.

Thus, hypothesis II is again found to be supported by the data in that urban migrants tend to make a more rapid adjustment than other migrants. The effects of migration appear to be temporary, for migrants soon approximate the native population in level of participation and in many instances the migrants are even more active than the non-migrant natives. A third test of the hypotheses is presented below in terms of registration to vote.

Registration to Vote

In so far as registration to vote is a measure of the level of participation in the political affairs in the community, the data presented here do not indicate that migration cuts a person off from participation. On the contrary, after living in the community for a certain length of time, migrants become as active, and in some cases even more active, than the native population in terms of the proportion who are registered. It is evident from the data in Table 5, that only those who have been in the community less than 5 years have a lower proportion registered to vote than do the natives.[11] Thus, migration has the effect of decreasing participation in the political life of the community, but this is only temporary. Registration to vote varies also by age. Older persons are more likely to be registered than younger persons.

Within each occupational and educational category a similar pattern is found. After 5 or more years in the community the migrants become very similar to the natives of equal status and even exceed the natives in the proportion who are registered voters. No consistent difference in the proportion registered is found by occupational or educational status.

Thus, in terms of this type of behavior also, hypothesis I is

[11] The same pattern of difference is found when those who have not yet established legal residence are dropped from the sample.

TABLE 5. PER CENT REGISTERED TO VOTE WITHIN AGE, OCCUPATIONAL, AND EDUCATIONAL CATEGORIES BY LENGTH OF TIME IN COMMUNITY

Length of time in community (years)	Age		Occupation		Education		
	Under 40 yrs.	40 yrs. plus	WC	MW	GS	HS	Col
Less than 2	18	44	24	25	20	28	25
2–5	63	77	74	63	51	77	70
6–10	82	97	87	89	89	88	94
11–19	92	93	. .[b]	89	90	91	. .[b]
20 and over	. .[a]	94	98	91	93	95	96
Natives	84	89	89	83	86[c]	84	93
Total	66	88	79	77	75	81	76

[a] Less than 10 cases.   [b] All registered.   [c] Less than 20 cases.

supported by the data. After a period of adjustment, migrants, as a group, tend to become quite similar to the natives.

The rate of entering the formal political activities of the community varies by type of migrant. Our data[12] show that it takes the farm and the rural non-farm migrants 10 years or more in the community before they equal or exceed the natives in proportion registered, whereas, the urban migrants exceed the natives after they have lived in the community for only 5 years or more. After ten years in the community the migrant types can no longer be clearly distinguished from each other in the proportion registered, and in most cases migrants have a higher proportion registered than do the natives. Here again, hypothesis II is supported by our data.

Summary

These data have shown that: (1) migrants differ from the natives in level of participation, but they become more similar to the natives in their behaviour the longer they live in the community,

[12] Due to space limitations these data are not presented here, but are available upon request to the writer.

and (2) urban migrants tend to enter the activities of the community more rapidly than farm migrants.

On the basis of a case study of a single community, it seems that migration does limit participation in community activities, but the initial limiting influences of migration are only temporary for these types of behavior, at least in that, with time, migrants either equal or exceed the natives in level of participation. When migrants first enter the new community they are much less active in the formal structure than are the natives, but with time their participation rate increases. The adjustment takes at least 5 years, however, and in some types of behavior migrants possessing low status characteristics never do attain the same level of participation as the natives. The possession of high status personal characteristics facilitates the adjustment.

Farm migrants have the slowest rate of entering. They seem to be particularly limited during the first 5 years or so in the community. However, the longer they live in the community, the higher their rate of participation. All migrant types eventually become similar to the natives in their behavior.

Distance of Migration and Socio-Economic Status of Migrants*

A. M. ROSE

Hypothesis

Since Stouffer's study in 1940, there have been a number of investigations corroborating his findings that there is a relationship between the number of migrants and some measure of the distance migrated.[1] Despite the careful procedure and high quality of the research, it has not moved significantly beyond the framework given it by Stouffer, at least not in the direction of relating his variables to other sociological variables. This paper

* The author wishes to express his appreciation to the Graduate School of the University of Minnesota for a grant-in-aid to conduct the research on which this article is based. The author is also grateful to Joseph Shechtman for his careful and intelligent assistance in carrying out the laborious work in connection with this research.

[1] Samuel A. Stouffer, Intervening opportunities: a theory relating mobility and distance, *American Sociological Review*, **5** (Dec. 1940), 845–67; Margaret L. Bright and Dorothy S. Thomas, Interstate migration and intervening opportunities, *ibid.*, **6** (Dec. 1941), 773–83; Eleanor C. Isbell, Internal migration in Sweden and intervening opportunities, *ibid.*, **9** (Dec. 1944), 627–39; Donald J. Bogue and Warren S. Thompson, Migration and distance, *ibid.*, **14** (April 1949), 236–44. Strodtbeck has also corroborated Stouffer's conclusion while providing an addition to his theory: Fred Strodtbeck, Equal opportunity intervals: a contribution to the method of intervening opportunity analysis, *ibid.*, **14** (Aug. 1949), 490–7. Zipf has also provided a corroboration, although he used a less adequate theory—as shown by Anderson: George Kingsley Zipf, The $P_1 P_2/D$ hypothesis: on the intercity movement of persons, *ibid.*, **11** (Dec. 1946), 677–86; Theodore R. Anderson, Intermetropolitan migration: a comparison of the hypotheses of Zipf and Stouffer, *ibid.*, **20** (June 1955), 287–91. With a still different theoretical framework, Dodd has also corroborated the finding: Stuart C. Dodd, The interactance hypothesis: a gravity model fitting physical masses and human groups, *ibid.*, **15** (April *1950*), 245–56.

reports an attempt to relate distance of migration to the sociological variable of socio-economic status, thereby tying migration theory into social stratification research. Our hypothesis is that higher status persons, seeking the better jobs or "opportunities", must move a greater distance to find them, on the average, than do persons whose skills or aspirations direct them to look for less desirable opportunities. Perhaps this means, in part, that large corporations, which control many of the "opportunities" for which people move, are more likely to move their top people than their lower level personnel. Our hypothesis is limited to movement into urban American areas, and our data are limited to migrants into the Minneapolis area.

Procedure

The most complete list of in-migrants to the Minneapolis area would seem to be a compilation of the names of new customers of the local electric company, whose service almost everyone in a metropolitan area uses. The Northern States Power Company kindly supplied data for the period March 15–July 1, 1955, listing each of its new residential accounts whose last previous address was outside the company's service area (Minneapolis, its suburbs, and some of the outlying parts of Hennepin County to the south and west of Minneapolis). Both the new local address and the place moved from were listed. Not all in-migrants to Minneapolis are immediately included in the sample: while practically everybody in and near a city uses electricity, people who rent hotel rooms, other furnished rooms and occasionally apartments may not become customers of the electric company, as some landlords assume the costs of electricity themselves (a customary practice when single rooms are rented). If these persons later move into their own homes or apartments, however, they become new customers of the electric company, and so get into our sample.

We used an "ecological" technique to obtain an index of the socio-economic status of our migrants. Each census tract and suburb of Minneapolis was ranked on four characteristics, as indicated by the Census:[2] (1) median rent, (2) median school years completed, (3) percentage of professional workers among all employed workers, and (4) percentage of native whites in the population.[3] These rankings were divided into quintiles, and the mean of the four quintile ratings was calculated for each tract. The means were designated the "socio-economic status index". These means were then grouped into quintiles, which were arbitrarily designated the "class" for each tract or suburb. The "address moved to" of each person on the list was then located by census tract or suburb and characterized by this class number. The class of the in-migrant is thus ecologically determined on the basis of the characteristics of the community into which he moved.

The "place moved from" was classified as falling within one of nine concentric rings drawn to cover the entire United States, with the center at Minneapolis. The rings are as follows:

Zone 1—0–25 miles from Minneapolis Zone 6—401–625 miles
Zone 2—26–80 miles   Zone 7—626–920 miles
Zone 3—81–160 miles   Zone 8—921–1200 miles
Zone 4—161–240 miles   Zone 9—1200 + miles
Zone 5—241–400 miles

In addition, each "place moved from" was classified as being either east or west of the Mississippi River (on which Minneapolis is located), and the Southern states (as defined by the Census) were kept in a separate category. Previous residences outside the continental United States were also separately counted.

The total number of newcomers to the Minneapolis area that became customers of the electric company during the period March 15–July 1, 1955,[4] was 1454. Of this number, 203 were drop-

[2] US Bureau of the Census, *Census of Population: 1950*, Vol. III, Census Tract Statistics, chap. 33 (Washington, DC: US Government Printing Office, 1952). The technique was developed by Albert Mayer for the Chicago Community Inventory of 1949, and was transmitted to us by Leo Reeder.

[3] *Ibid*. Selected from Tables 1, 2, and 3.

[4] While our complete sample is only for this $3\frac{1}{2}$ month period, we spot-checked the migrants during the rest of the year to make sure that there was no significant difference in distribution by socio-economic class between the migrants during the sample period and those who migrated in other seasons of the year.

ped because they moved into rural areas of Hennepin County for which there are no data to characterize socio-economic status, and another 30 were dropped because of errors or ambiguities in the listing—leaving a total of 1221 cases. The distribution of these cases, according to class of neighborhood moved into as well as distance and direction of previous residence, is shown in Table 1. (A highly disproportionate percentage—44 per cent—of the cases moved into class I neighborhoods. This indicates the vigorous growth of the new, more desirable residential suburbs as well as the "upper class" character of so many in-migrants.)

Findings

It will be noted from the table that the distance moved steadily declines with the class of neighborhood moved into, from class I to class IV, thus supporting our general hypothesis. Class V presents the exception. The median distance migrated is 237.6 miles for those moving into class I neighborhoods down to 124.6 miles for those moving into Class IV neighborhoods. On the other hand, those moving into class V neighborhoods come from about the same distance as those moving into class II neighborhoods—177 miles and 180 miles, respectively.

Our first thought upon discovering this exception was that non-whites (predominantly Negroes) provided the exception, since they usually had to migrate considerable distances in order to go to Minneapolis and yet their general social circumstances put them into the lowest class neighborhoods. By dividing class V neighborhoods into those that were also in the highest quintile of percentage non-whites (called "non-white neighborhoods") and those that were in the four other quintiles (called "white neighborhoods"), this guess is shown to have considerable merit (see the last two columns of the table). The migrants into the non-white class of neighborhoods moved 194 miles on the average, whereas the migrants into the white neighborhoods moved only 150 miles. This suggests that our general hypothesis covering the relation between class of migrant and distance migrated is limited to whites and does not apply to disadvantaged minority groups: poor Negroes (predominantly from the South) migrate a considerable distance, and one might say that their motivation to migrate is greater than that of whites. Partly for this reason, our hypothesis may be termed "culture-bound".

But even those who migrate into "white" class V neighborhoods have migrated a greater distance than they should have, according to our general hypothesis. We have no satisfactory explanation of this finding, unless it be that our technique of separating whites from non-whites is inadequate. The data on which neighborhoods are classified are as of 1950 whereas the migration data are as of 1955; there had been very heavy migration of Negroes during the intervening period.[5] It should also be noted that a significant proportion of Minneapolis Negroes do not live in Negro neighborhoods.[6]

Another interesting finding is that, while migrants into class I neighborhoods are more likely to come from the east than from the west, the reverse is increasingly the case for migrants moving into neighborhoods II to IV. What seems to be indicated here is that many upper class migrants are coming from the large urban centers to the east, while the middle class migrants come primarily from the rural and small town areas to the west (Minneapolis is the nearest metropolis for people living in the Dakotas and Montana as well as those in rural Minnesota). A check on the specific places of origin of the migrants shows this to be the fact. Again, class V migrants provide something of an exception: while a majority of them come from the west, the proportion coming

[5] The census of 1950 records 6,807 Negroes in Minneapolis. On Aug. 9, 1957, the director of the Minneapolis Urban League estimated that there were 10,000 Negroes in the city (Shelton B. Granger, Statement for the Legislative Interim Commission, State of Minnesota, unpublished, Aug. 9, 1957). Except for the in-migration of Negroes—who still constitute less than 2 per cent of the total population—Minneapolis neighborhoods have changed relatively little since 1950, so that the use of data from the two dates would have no other implications for the findings of this paper.

[6] Even by 1950, Negroes were reported living in 82 per cent of the city's census tracts.

from the west is not as great as might be expected from observing the trend as we move down the class level of neighborhood.

Conclusion

These data indicate that the "upper class" neighborhoods are being disproportionately filled with persons who have migrated a long distance, while the opposite is true for the "poorer class" neighborhoods. The exception is for the poorest class of neighborhoods, but most of these contain disproportionate numbers of Negro residents who are being augmented significantly by migrants coming all the way from the South.

In Stouffer's terms it might be said that, generally speaking, lower-class people find many more intervening opportunities in a given distance than upper-class people do. Relatively specialized persons and others who seek the better-paying jobs must move a greater distance to find them, while those who are less specialized —whose remuneration is lower on the average—can find their "opportunities" close by. Similarly, when employers seek employees to fill specialized (including managerial) positions, they must look farther afield and move them a greater distance, than when they seek workers to fill relatively unspecialized positions.

The fact that the non-whites move a considerable distance and hence are an exception to our general conclusion, serves to indicate that the main finding is culture-bound. Migrant Negroes are of the lowest socio-economic status, and generally must accept the poorest jobs and residences in this Northern city— jobs and residences which, if racial discrimination was absent, they could find much closer to their original homes. Their reason for migrating the unusually long distance seems to be to vacate the Southern culture area. (The relatively small number of Negroes migrating to Minneapolis probably often select this particular community because friends or relatives have already established a community there.)

Another finding indicating that our general conclusion is culture-bound is that upper class migrants come predominantly from the east (from urban centers), whereas, the middle and lower class migrants come predominantly from the west (from rural areas and small towns). In other words, the geographic position of a city can have different significance as an "opportunity" for migration for different segments of the population.

The migrants who move into the lowest class areas provide something of an exception to these general findings, but they also constitute the smallest number among the classes of migrants (only 9.7 per cent). On the whole, "intervening opportunities" during migration mean different things to upper, middle, and lower class people, to Negroes and whites, and to eastern urbanites and western rural people.

Kentucky Mountain Migration and the Stem-family: An American Variation on a Theme by Le Play[1]

J. S. BROWN, H. K. SCHWARZWELLER, and J. J. MANGALAM[2]

Abstract

In studying Kentucky Mountain migration, the authors found Frédéric Le Play's *famille-souche* or "stem-family" concept useful in understanding the functions of the kinship structure in (a) the processes of migration and (b) the adjustment of individuals within a migration system.

Case study of three Eastern Kentucky neighborhoods (Beech Creek) over a period of 20 years shows that (a) members of the same extended family in 1942 tend to migrate to the same places, (b) migrants from these neighborhoods now living in a given town are almost all related by close kinship ties, and (c) migration destination appears to be social class-oriented (closely related to kinship structure).

We conclude that the consistency of the directional pattern of Eastern Kentucky's out- and in-migration may well be due to kinship relationships.

Finally, many Beech Creek families, like Le Play's stem-family, facilitate and encourage migration and provide in crises "havens of safety". Furthermore, "branch-families" in the new communities provide a socio-psychological "cushion" for the migrant during the transitional phase.

Introduction

In this paper we are concerned with functions performed by kinship groups in the migration of persons from the rural areas of

[1] Paper prepared for the annual meeting of the American Sociological Association, St. Louis, Missouri, Sept. 1, 1961. This is the first of a series of working papers from the Beech Creek Study which is sponsored by the National Institute of Mental Health in cooperation with the Kentucky Agricultural Experiment Station.

[2] James S. Brown is an associate professor of rural sociology, and Harry K. Schwarzweller and J. J. Mangalam are assistant professors of rural sociology at the University of Kentucky.

Eastern Kentucky to the more urbanized, industrial areas of Ohio, Indiana, and elsewhere.[3]

Though this exploratory attempt to indicate functional connections between kinship structure and migration process in the case of Eastern Kentucky migration will not, of course, be wholly applicable to studies of migration in all other areas, the frame of reference developed in this paper, which systematically links kinship structure and migration process, suggests, we believe, a conceptual approach that has wider application. Almost by definition folk cultures are characterized by strong familistic bonds that unite kin members in cohesive family groups and fit individual desires into a framework of family needs.[4] The Eastern Kentucky sub-culture, a part of the Southern Appalachian regional complex, has been, and still is, an area dominated by traditionally sanctioned particularistic value orientations; even today, in Eastern Kentucky, the *extended family* plays a highly functional role. Understanding the functions performed by kinship groups in the process of migration in the case of Eastern Kentucky migration should be useful in understanding the pattern of migration and the transitional adjustments of persons who move to urban areas of industrial opportunity from similarly strong familistic folk cultures in other parts of the world.[5] Furthermore,

[3] This paper is based on materials from: (1) demographic studies of the entire Southern Appalachian Region, of which Eastern Kentucky is a part; (2) a number of studies of migrants from Eastern Kentucky; (3) an intensive study of a three-neighborhood cluster (Beech Creek) by the senior author in 1942–3; (4) continuous field observations of migration from these neighborhoods during the last 20 years; (5) preliminary field work this past year in preparation for an intensive follow-up study (called The Beech Creek Study) of people who have migrated from these three neighborhoods; and (6) a series of discussions of the adjustment of migrants from Eastern Kentucky involving professional sociologists, economists, psychologists, anthropologists, and extension workers.

[4] See, for example, Pitirim A. Sorokin, Carle C. Zimmerman, and Charles J. Galpin, *A Systematic Source Book in Rural Sociology*, Minneapolis, The University of Minnesota Press, 1931, vol. I, ch. 4, pp. 186–259.

[5] For example, in India thousands of Malayalees, caught by a very high population density and limited employment opportunities, migrate from their homes in Kerala (Malabar Coast) to such urban areas as Bombay and New Delhi. They live in these cities in close proximity to one another, forming a

the general problem with which this paper is concerned arises from a serious deficiency in studies of migration elsewhere, namely, the superficial treatment of the part played by the family structure in migration and in the adjustment phase of the migration process.[6]

In this article we will be concerned with:

(1) The pattern of migration of Eastern Kentuckians, reviewed briefly to establish the general demographic characteristics and to put the problem in its broader setting.

(2) Various aspects of migration during a 20-year period from a three-neighborhood cluster in Eastern Kentucky, described as a case example of the part played by kinship in migration.

(3) Finally, certain modifications of Frédéric Le Play's conceptualization of family types, especially that of the stem-family (*famille-souche*), which we have found useful

---

cultural island within the local society. Their interaction with life in New Delhi, for example, is only segmental, being primarily in their occupational roles. The rest of the time they live a life of their own, their conduct being governed by the norms of the local world of their origin. They send money "home" for the support of their stem-families; they go "home" for marriage; and they are instrumental in bringing streams of Malayalees to New Delhi and in performing supportive functions for the newly arrived Malayalees, both as individuals and families. This is a pattern very similar to the pattern of out-migration from Eastern Kentucky to Ohio.

[6] One notable exception is found in Conrad M. Arensberg and Solon T. Kimball, *Family and Community in Ireland*, Cambridge, Massachusetts, Harvard University Press, 1940. They discuss the relationship of family structure and migration, as follows: Viewed in the light of this family structure, the decline of population becomes interpretable not as a flight from intolerable conditions, though economic distress had a powerful effect, not as a political gesture, though political disturbance took its toll, but rather as a movement arising from the effect of all these causes upon a family system whose very nature predisposed it to disperse population and which could, therefore, accommodate itself to that dispersal when it occurred. Emigration, no new thing in 1845, appears as the logical corollary of this dispersal. It derives much of its character, such as assisted passages and remittances, from the social forces at work in the family (pp. 155–6). Another exception, which will be discussed more fully later, is the Zimmerman and Frampton study of the Ozark Mountain family. (Carle C. Zimmerman and Merle E. Frampton, *Family and Society: A Study of the Sociology of Reconstruction*, New York, Van Nostrand, 1935.)

in studying the functions of kinship structure both in (a) the processes of migration and (b) in the adjustment of individuals within a migration system.

1. The Pattern of Migration of Eastern Kentuckians

Without going into extensive detail, let us draw from more complete demographic analyses of regional population trends a few pertinent observations about the patterns of Eastern Kentucky migration:[7]

(a) In the last 20 years the population of the part of Eastern Kentucky which is primarily a subsistence-agricultural area and in which our case-study area lies (State Economic Area 8) declined 19%, largely due to heavy migration from the area. During the 1940's the net loss through migration was the equivalent of 34% of the 1940 population, and during the 1950's the equivalent of 25% of the 1950 population.

Eastern Kentucky is a chronically depressed area with limited economic opportunities for its people. From 1940 to 1960 many more economic opportunities were available in the more prosperous urban areas nearby, and tens of thousands of Kentucky Mountain people have moved to take advantage of these opportunities.

(b) The pattern of the streams of migration from the area has been remarkably consistent over the years.

For example, the proportions of migrants moving (1) within Eastern Kentucky (that is, to other counties within State Economic Areas 5, 8, and 9), (2) to contiguous areas, or (3) to noncontiguous areas are very similar for both the periods 1935–40 and 1949–50 (Table 1), though there is a

[7] See James S. Brown and George A. Hillery, Jr., The great migration: 1940–1960, a chapter in *The Southern Appalachian Region: A survey*, now in press, University of Kentucky Press; see also George A. Hillery, Jr. and James S. Brown, Some conclusions on migratory streams from a study of the Southern Appalachians, a paper presented at the annual meeting of the Population Association of America, May 1961.

discernible trend for a higher proportion to go longer distances and for a lower proportion to go to contiguous areas.

TABLE 1. OUT-MIGRATION: INTRA-AREA AND TO CONTIGUOUS AND TO NON-CONTIGUOUS AREAS, 1935–40 AND 1949–50, EASTERN KENTUCKY[a]

| | 1935–40 | | 1949–50 | |
	Number of migrants[b]	%	Number of migrants[b]	%
Total	107,487	100.0	50,445	100.0
Intra-area	37,524	34.9	17,615	34.9
Contiguous area	32,741	30.5	12,500	24.8
Noncontiguous area	37,212	34.6	20,330	40.3

[a] "Eastern Kentucky" in 1935–40 includes Kentucky State Subregions 5 and 9. For the counties included, see Donald J. Bogue, Henry S. Shryock, Jr., and Siegfried A. Hoermann, *Streams of Migration Between Subregions*, vol. I of *Subregional Migration in the United States, 1935–40*, Scripps Foundation Studies in Population Distribution No. 5, Oxford, Ohio, Miami University, 1957. "Eastern Kentucky" in 1949–50 included Kentucky Metropolitan Area C and State Economic Areas 5, 8 and 9. For the counties included, see Donald J. Bogue, *State Economic Areas*, US Bureau of the Census, Washington, DC: US Government Printing Office, 1951.

[b] A "migrant" is defined as a person who has moved his residence across county lines. Intra-area migration is migration among the counties of Eastern Kentucky. Contiguous area migration is migration to areas adjacent to Eastern Kentucky. Noncontiguous area migration is migration to areas not adjacent to Eastern Kentucky.

(c) The great stream of out-migration from the subsistence-agricultural area of Eastern Kentucky (SEA 8) to non-contiguous areas has been to areas in Ohio and secondarily to areas in Indiana. Out-migration from Eastern Kentucky other than in these well-established streams has been to widely scattered destinations (Table 2).

(d) Countercurrents of in-migration, which generally accompany all streams of migration out of an area, exhibit a pattern almost identical with that of the out-migration. In other words, the proportion moving *to* a particular area "outside" is practically the same as the proportion coming *from* that specific area although more people move from, than move to, the Eastern Kentucky area during a specified time period (Table 2).

TABLE 2. PERCENTAGE OF OUT-MIGRATION TO AND IN-MIGRATION FROM STATE ECONOMIC AREAS NOT CONTIGUOUS WITH KENTUCKY STATE ECONOMIC AREA 8, 1949–50

	Out-migration[a]		In-migration[b]	
	Number	%	Number	%
Total number of migrants to and from noncontiguous areas	(6130)	100.0	(4410)	100.0
Kentucky, total	(590)	9.6	(330)	7.5
Kentucky A (Louisville)		3.3		1.9
All other Kentucky		6.3		5.6
Ohio, total	(2410)	39.3	(1800)	40.8
Ohio C		10.0		6.8
D		6.4		6.5
K		6.8		9.0
3		5.4		2.8
4		4.5		4.2
All other Ohio		6.3		11.6
Illinois, total	(150)	2.4	(90)	2.0
Indiana, total	(945)	15.4	(540)	12.2
Michigan, total	(305)	5.0	(355)	8.0
All others	(1690)	27.6	(1295)	29.4

[a] The total number of out-migrants during this period was 10,815, of whom 43.2 percent moved to contiguous areas.

[b] The total number of in-migrants during this period was 8,115, of whom 45.6 percent came from contiguous areas.

These data from demographic studies of Eastern Kentucky migration have led us to some basic questions, in the answering of which we find knowledge of the kinship structure relevant:

First of all, why has the directional pattern of out-migration from Eastern Kentucky been so consistent over the years that we could almost say the streams of out-migration were running in well-worn riverbeds?

Certainly widely accepted factors are important in understanding these streams of migration: Eastern Kentucky is an area of underemployment, and its people tend to migrate toward areas where more job opportunities are available. This generalization, that labor tends to flow in the direction of greater economic opportunity, is well founded.[8] However, geographical, historical, and other factors must be considered too. Stouffer's hypothesis of "intervening opportunities"[9] helps explain certain deviations from what might be considered a "normal" pattern for this area, e.g., the "leap" over the largely agricultural counties of Central

[8] One might begin with this thesis as developed by Goodrich and his colleagues. See Carter L. Goodrich *et al.*, *Migration and Economic Opportunity*, University of Pennsylvania Press, Philadelphia, 1936. See also (a) Donald J. Bogue, Henry S. Shryock, Jr., and Siegfried A. Hoermann, *Subregional Migration in the U.S., 1935–40, vol. I, Streams of Migration between Subregions*, Scripps Foundation Studies in Population Distribution No. 5, Miami University, Oxford, Ohio, 1957. (b) Donald J. Bogue, *Components of Population Change, 1940–50: Estimates of Net Migration and Natural Increase for Each Standard Metropolitan Area and State Economic Area*, Scripps Foundation Studies in Population Distribution No. 12, Miami University, Oxford, Ohio, and Population Research and Training Center, University of Chicago, Chicago, 1957, especially pp. 24–29. (c) Donald J. Bogue, *The Population of the United States*, Free Press, Glencoe, Illinois, 1959, ch. 15: "Internal Migration and Residential Mobility," pp. 375–418, especially pp. 416–18. (d) Everett S. Lee *et al.*, *Population Redistribution and Economic Growth U.S., 1870–1950, vol. I, Methodological Considerations and Reference Tables*, American Philosophical Society, Philadelphia, 1957. (e) K. M. George, *Association of Selected Economic Factors with Net Migration Rates in the Southern Appalachian Region, 1935–1957*, unpublished MA thesis, University of Kentucky, June, 1961.

[9] See Samuel A. Stouffer, Intervening opportunities: a theory relating to mobility and distance, *American Sociological Review*, **5**, 845–67.

and Northern Kentucky to the industrial counties of Southern Ohio.

But we believe that kinship also is a factor of some importance in the explanation of this consistency in the directional pattern of out-migration. For, as Lively and Taeuber point out, the "evaluation of relative opportunities is essentially a subjective matter."[10]

The kinship structure provides a highly persuasive line of communication between kinsfolk in the home and the new communities which channels information about available job opportunities and living standards directly, and most meaningfully, to Eastern Kentucky families. Thus, kinship linkage tends to direct migrants to those areas where their kin groups are already established.[11]

This effective line of communication among kin (which is, in our experience, overwhelmingly more important than that of State employment offices) helps also to explain the fact that the rate of

[10] C. E. Lively and Conrad Taeuber, *Rural Migration in the United States*, Research Monograph XIX, Works Progress Administration, US Government Printing Office, Washington DC 1939, p. 79.

[11] Bogue and Hagood note in their study of differential migration in the Corn and Cotton Belts that: "This examination of the household status of migrants of each age group in comparison with the household status of the populations of the same ages in the area of origin and of destination yields indirect evidence that the detailed form which migration takes is a response to a wide variety of factors many of which are only incidentally economic. Rural youth may choose a particular destination because they have relatives living there rather than because it offers the most opportunities." (Donald J. Bogue and Margaret Jarman Hagood, *Differential Migration in the Corn and Cotton Belts: A Pilot Study of the Selectivity of Interstate Migration to Cities from Nonmetropolitan Areas*, Scripps Foundation Studies in Population Distribution, No. 6. Miami University, Oxford, Ohio, 1953, p. 37.) (They also say that "streams of migration between two particular points tend to be self-perpetuating by virtue of the fact that the first migrants to arrive influence their relatives to migrate to that place, and provide housing and other assistance to the relatives who follow them. This appeared to have been particularly true of migrants whose origin had been in a rural area." pp. 28–30.) In their valuable study of rural migration in the 1930's Lively and Taeuber found: ". . . In the Kentucky areas more moved to adjoining states than to counties adjoining the survey areas. . . . Actually selective forces, such as the location of relatives and friends and employment opportunities, were active in determining the distribution of the migrant children." Lively and Taeuber, *op. cit.*, pp. 99–100.

out-migration is so immediately responsive to fluctuations in the rate of unemployment in migratory target areas.[12]

Because of ascribed role obligations, kinship structure also serves a protective function for new migrants to an area—a form of social insurance and a mechanism for smoother adaptation during the transitional phase of adjustment.

Secondly, why do streams of in-migration exhibit patterns that are practically identical to the patterns of out-migration from this area?

Individuals' reasons for moving back are of many kinds, as Peter Rossi observed in his study of "Why Families Move".[13] Knowing that Eastern Kentucky has long been an area with heavy net losses through migration, that it has not, especially in the last two or three decades, attracted many outsiders, and knowing also from much observation over more than twenty years that most persons migrating into the area are former residents, we can assume, until more systematic data are available, that most in-migrants to Eastern Kentucky are former residents and their spouses. Some of them could not adapt themselves to "outside" circumstances and decided to move back to their "home" areas. Others are persons who are of retirement age or are drawing pensions of one sort or another and feel they can live better and at less expense in their "home" areas. Most persons who migrate into the area, then, have "roots" in Eastern Kentucky, among which

[12] T. W. Schultz notes that the "post-war behavior of the economy clearly indicates that the *rate* of off-farm migration is highly sensitive to changes in unemployment that have characterized these post-war booms and recessions in business. . . . When 5, 6 or 7 per cent of the labor force is unemployed, the adjustment process under consideration is brought to a halt; on the other hand, when unemployment declines to 3 or 4 percent off-farm migration becomes large." (T. W. Schultz, *A Policy to Redistribute Losses from Economic Progress*, University of Chicago Office of Agricultural Economics, Research Paper No. 6008, Oct. 31, 1960, pp. 13–14.)

[13] An excellent abstract of Rossi's study of residential mobility is found in Peter H. Rossi, "Why families move," section V, ch. 8 in *The Language of Social Research*, edited by Paul F. Lazarsfeld and Morris Rosenberg, Glencoe, Ill., Free Press, pp. 457–68.

kinship ties are very important.[14] This suggests that kinship ties attract former residents to a specific area from areas to which they migrated in approximately the same proportions as have migrated to these outside areas.

These questions, posed by the analyses of demographic data, suggest a specific problem for research:

What influence do kinship ties have on the destination of migrants? Although our case study of an Eastern Kentucky neighborhood will focus primarily on this problem, the more general (and certainly the more theoretically significant) problem is:

What function does the kinship structure perform in the process of migration? In the exploration of the specific problem we shall attempt to shed some light also on the general problem. However, the latter, more fundamental problem obviously requires far more attention than we can give it either in this paper or in any one research project. Perhaps some indications of how we conceptualize various facets of the general problem may help to point out its theoretical significance as well as its scope and potential for students of migration.

Does, for example, the particular kinship structure characteristic of Eastern Kentucky encourage heavy out-migration? We believe it does and have found Habakkuk's discussion of the effects of rules of succession upon population growth in nineteenth-century Europe suggestive. Habakkuk points out that "the single-heir system tended to retard population growth and [the system of equal] division to promote it."[15] Eastern Kentucky has had a system of equal division of property among heirs, and here too this system seems to have promoted great population growth, so much so, indeed, that equal division of land seemed to be becoming somewhat less common and alternative plans were becoming more widespread (e.g. one heir's buying the shares of other heirs

[14] In this sense, we would also regard individuals whose parents, in-laws, spouse, children, or other close kin are or have been residents of that area as having "roots" there.

[15] H. J. Habakkuk, "Family structure and economic change in nineteenth-century Europe," ch. 13 in Norman W. Bell and Ezra F. Vogel, *A Modern Introduction to the Family*, Glencoe, Ill., Free Press, 1960, p. 167.

or of all the heirs giving up their shares to one, often the youngest child, on condition that he take care of the old parents until they die).

Another of Habakkuk's findings is pertinent to this discussion— the rules of equal division of property in Europe tended to pro- mote long-distance migration for seasons or short periods, such migration being "not an escape from the peasant family but a condition of its survival. The peasant went, not to acquire a new occupation in a different society, but to improve his position in the old. . . . [But] the inhabitants of division areas were not likely in the absence of . . . severe pressure to respond readily to demands for permanent industrial labor in regions distant from their homes."[16] From a study of the history of an isolated neighborhood cluster in the Eastern Kentucky Mountains and less systematic observations of Eastern Kentucky's agricultural areas as a whole, this same pattern seems to have been common until recently when pressure became so great as to sweep out whole families and almost whole neighborhoods. The earlier pattern of a man's leaving his family in the home neighborhood while he worked in "public works" out in Ohio has become much less common as whole families have migrated.

Another function or set of functions performed by the kinship structure in the process of migration is that surplus population has been drained off which if allowed to "dam up" might well have brought such strain that this society dominated by the family- kinship system would have broken up completely. Actually the gradual migration characteristic of Eastern Kentucky for decades has led to the formation of patterns enabling it to absorb the shock even of very heavy loss. The situation is similar to that Arensberg and Kimball found among the small farmers in Ireland where ". . . the forces operative within that structure are of such a nature as to allow the society of which they are a part to continue to function in essentially similar fashion through the welter of economic, political, and other events which have impinged upon the human beings who have successively filled the structure.

[16] *Ibid.*, p. 168.

Likewise, the structure is capable of continued and virile existence in the present, governing the lives of its component individuals and modifying itself to take in 'new influences.' "[17]

A crucial aspect of the Eastern Kentucky situation, confronting any student of this social and cultural area, is the importance attached to kinship relations in the everyday life of its people. Since familism, as a value-orientation, permeates the society and stamps all institutions with its mark,[18] to know the significant effects of heavy out-migration on the social institutions in the area, one would certainly want to begin by exploring the influence of out-migration on the family.

2. Beech Creek Migration and Kinship

Let us turn, now, to a case study that permits us to examine, in greater detail, the relationship of the kinship structure to the process of migration. Throughout this paper, we shall mean by "Beech Creek" a three-neighborhood cluster located in a relatively isolated area of Eastern Kentucky that was studied intensively in 1942, with family, class, and value patterns as the main foci.[19] We have the unique opportunity, then, of using our knowledge of Beech Creek to interpret the migration pattern from that area since 1942.

Beech Creek was, and still is, a family-centered neighborhood. Kinship units tend to be culturally insular groups, kinship relationships the most meaningful interactional patterns, and familistic norms the most important mechanisms of social control. In the sociocultural system of Beech Creek, familism as a traditional-value-orientation has been, and still appears to be, dominant.

[17] Arensberg and Kimball, *op. cit.*, pp. 156–7.

[18] Sorokin *et al.*, vol. II, p. 41.

[19] See James S. Brown, "The Social Organization of an Isolated Kentucky Mountain Neighborhood", Ph.D. thesis, Harvard University, 1950. *The Family Group in a Kentucky Mountain Farming Community*, Kentucky Agr. Exp. Sta., University of Kentucky, Bulletin 588, June, 1952; and *The Farm Family in a Kentucky Mountain Neighborhood*, Kentucky Agr. Exp. Sta., University of Kentucky, Bulletin 587, Aug. 1952.

Loss through migration is an old pattern for the Beech Creek area. During the last two decades, however, the loss has been unusually heavy.[20] Of the persons living in the Beech Creek area in 1942, 318 are still living (as of July 1, 1961), but only 25% presently reside in the original neighborhoods. About 17 per cent have moved to nearby neighborhoods. Fifty-seven per cent have

TABLE 3. PERSONS LIVING IN BEECH CREEK AREA ON JULY 1, 1942, BY RESIDENCE ON JULY 1, 1961

			Number of persons	%
Total Beech Creek residents 1942 still living July 1, 1961			318	100.0
Residence as of July 1, 1961	Number of persons	Percent of total		
A. IN KENTUCKY, TOTAL			156	49.1
1. Beech Creek area	80	(25.2)		
2. Nearby neighborhoods	54	(17.0)		
3. Other parts of Eastern Kentucky	2	(0.6)		
4. Kentucky outside of Eastern Kentucky, total	20	(6.3)		
B. OUTSIDE KENTUCKY, TOTAL			162	50.9
5. Ohio, total	133	(41.8)		
6. Indiana, total	17	(5.3)		
7. All other states, total	8	(2.5)		
8. Armed forces	4	(1.3)		

[20] The migration data reported here were obtained as the first phase of a 1961 follow-up study of those who in 1942 were living in the Beech Creek area. During the summer of 1961, these people were interviewed either at their present residences or in the case of migration to areas too distant for field interviewing, their present residences were verified by interviews with close kin.

established residence outside of Eastern Kentucky (Table 3).[21] About three-fourths of the migrants to areas outside of Eastern Kentucky now live in Ohio (Table 3).

Two southern Ohio towns (here referred to as X-town and Y-town) which are close to each other and their immediate vicinity have drawn about 42% of the Beech Creekers who have migrated from Eastern Kentucky; about 16% live in a big city nearby (referred to as City A) and another 16% are residents of a smaller city (referred to as City B). The rest of the migrants tend to form smaller clusters in rather widely scattered towns in the Ohio Valley.

These data show the tendency of out-migrants from Beech Creek to cluster in certain areas of destination. Now, let us explore the part that kinship ties have in this clustering. We will do this in several ways:

(a) *Members of the same family group in 1942 tended to migrate to the same places.*

The earlier study of Beech Creek (1942) established the existence of "family groups" in these neighborhoods.[22] The concept "family group" as used here is roughly synonymous with the concept "extended family". In the main, "family groups" consisted of families of old parents and their adult children or of adult siblings and their grown children's families. The composition of these groups was determined, however, not merely by ascertaining kinship relationships but by considering also the groups of kin which had the closest social relationships.[23] Thus, a conjugal family related by

[21] If we define migration as the ecological movement of people, involving residential changes that (1) remove them from the immediate interactional systems of which they have been a part and to which they are accustomed, and (2) places them in new interactional systems with which they are not accustomed, then those Beech Creekers who have moved to places outside Eastern Kentucky are the "true" out-migrants.

[22] See Brown, *The Family Group in a Kentucky Mountain Farming Community*.

[23] Pearsall made a similar observation in her study of a small isolated neighborhood in the Tennessee area of the Southern Appalachians: "An important feature of the kinship structure is the sense of closeness not only between a couple's family of procreation and their families of orientation but

blood to a number of other families in the neighborhood was considered to belong to that family group with which it, as a family, had the strongest social bonds.

Of the 58 persons who in 1942 were in the Andrews-Barnett family group, five had died and 53 were still living as of July 1, 1961. About one-half of the original members of this family group still live in the old neighborhood or in nearby neighborhoods. The out-migrants, as our data show, clearly tend to concentrate in two specific areas: (1) City B, a small city in Southern Ohio has drawn 12 members, or nearly half of the migrants, and (2) a small metropolitan area in Kentucky has drawn 6, all members of one family (Table 4).

Similarly, other examples can be noted of this tendency for

TABLE 4. PERSONS WHO CONSTITUTED THE ANDREWS-BARNETT FAMILY GROUP
IN BEECH CREEK ON JULY 1, 1942
By residence on July 1, 1961

	Number
Total, of the 58 persons in the Andrews-Barnett family group 1942 still living July 1, 1961	53
Residence as of July 1, 1961	
A. IN KENTUCKY, TOTAL	35
1. Beech Creek area	(23)
2. Nearby neighborhoods	(4)
3. Kentucky, outside Eastern Kentucky	(8)
B. IN OHIO, TOTAL	15
1. City A	(2)
2. City B	(12)
3. X-town	(1)
C. ALL OTHER STATES, TOTAL	3

also between these and all collateral lines. In other words, Parsons' 'inner circle' combines with his 'outer circle' to form one large kinship group—this is reminiscent of the early American family." (See Marion Pearsall, *Little Smoky Ridge*, University of Alabama Press, 1959, p. 94.)

migrants of the same family group to cluster. Our analysis of the migratory distribution of five family groups revealed: (1) Of the 76 living members of these five family groups as originally delineated, 32 still live in Beech Creek or nearby neighborhoods, (2) thirty-six now live in "X-town" a small town in Southern Ohio, and (3) only eight live elsewhere. (See Summary Statement A.)

(b) *Another way of showing the clustering of migrants who are kin is to analyze the kinship relationships of migrants in a given town or city.*

We find, for example, that Beech Creek migrants in City B (a small city in Southern Ohio) were predominantly from two family groups, the Andrews-Barnetts and the Preston Johnsons. Only 5 of the 24 Beech creek migrants in this smaller city were *not* members or had not married members of the original family groups. And of these 5, only 2 were *not* attached to these families by close kinship ties.

In X-town, Ohio, the situation, though somewhat more complicated, reveals a similar pattern. Of the 35 Beech Creek migrants now living there, 22 are members, or have married members, of two family groups, the Lambert-Snows and the Barnetts. Nearly all of the other 13 Beech Creek people there are related in some way to the Barnetts or to the Lambert-Snows, and, in a number of cases, to both.

Here we are perhaps being a bit "archeological", sticking too closely to statistical bones. For actually we *know* from many observations that members of a family "peel off" as they get old enough and join their kinsfolk who have previously migrated.

(c) *Finally, we observe the same clustering phenomenon when we analyze the distribution of out-migrants by present residence and according to their 1942 social class positions[24] in Beech Creek (Table 5).*

[24] For a definition of the "class schema" employed and a description of the class structure in Beech Creek (1942), see James S. Brown, Social class, intermarriage, and church membership in a Kentucky community, *American Journal of Sociology*, **57** (3) (Nov. 1951), 232–42.

TABLE 5. OUT-MIGRANTS: PERSONS IN DESIGNATED SOCIAL CLASS POSITIONS,
BEECH CREEK NEIGHBORHOODS, 1942 BY RESIDENCE OUTSIDE
EASTERN KENTUCKY, AS OF JULY 1, 1961

	Total out-migrants still living July 1, 1961 $(N = 182)$							
	High class		Intermed-iate		Low class		Unranked	
	No.	%	No.	%	No.	%	No.	%
Total, all residence categories	38	100.0	72	100.0	53	100.0	19	100.0
Residence, as of July 1, 1961								
A. Kentucky, outside Eastern Kentucky	9	23.7	4	5.6	6	11.3	1	5.3
B. Ohio								
1. City A, a big city in Southern Ohio	3	7.9	8	11.1	12	22.6	0	
2. City B, a smaller city in Southern Ohio	19	50.0	4	5.6	1	1.9	0	
3. City C, northern smaller city	0		2	2.8	5	9.5	2	10.5
4. Two smaller towns in Southern Ohio (X-town and Y-town)	1	2.6	34	47.2	20	37.7	10	52.6
5. Other Ohio	1	2.6	7	9.7	3	5.7	1	5.3
C. Indiana	1	2.6	7	9.7	4	7.5	5	26.3
D. All other states	4	10.6	2	2.8	2	3.8	0	
E. Armed forces	0	0.0	4	5.6	0		0	

SUMMARY STATEMENT A. Examples of the tendency of members of the same family group to cluster when they migrate.

(Based on persons who constituted five family groups in Beech Creek on July 1, 1942, by residence on July 1, 1961)

1. The Barnetts (16 still living):

    5 in Beech Creek and nearby neighborhoods

    10 in X-town, a small town in Southern Ohio

    1 elsewhere

2. The Carters (15 still living):

    5 in Beech Creek
    7 in *X*-town, a small town in Southern Ohio
    3 elsewhere

3. The Cundiffs (10 still living):

    5 in Beech Creek
    5 in *X*-town, a small town in Southern Ohio
    0 elsewhere

4. The Lamberts-Snows (22 still living):

    7 in Beech Creek and nearby neighborhoods
    11 in *X*-town, a small town in Southern Ohio
    4 elsewhere

5. The Smiths (13 still living):

    10 in Beech Creek
    3 in *X*-town, a small town in Southern Ohio
    0 elsewhere

Total, of all five family groups (76 still living):

    32 in Beech Creek and nearby neighborhoods (42.1%)
    36 in *X*-town, a small town in Southern Ohio (47.4%)
    8 elsewhere (10.5%)

Half of all the "high-class" out-migrants now live in and around City B, a small city in Southern Ohio. Only one "high-class" out-migrant lives in *X*-town.

On the other hand, nearly half (48.6%) of all those out-migrants previously designated as "intermediate class" live in *X*-town while only four live in City B.

The "low-class" pattern is much the same as that of the "intermediate" except that "low-class" migrants tend to concentrate less in any one area.

These observations are in the expected directions when one recognizes that class lines in Beech Creek tend to follow kinship lines very closely. To a great extent, the family group is the basic social class unit in the stratification system of Beech Creek as is the conjugal family in American Society.[25] Furthermore, inter-class marriages are not common in Beech Creek, especially between persons of the "high" and "low" strata; the social classes, therefore, tend to be networks of kinship relations. Thus, the available migration data reveal a pattern that is probably more a kinship than a social class phenomenon.

3. Le Play's Stem-family[26]

On the basis of these exploratory efforts discussed above, we conclude that kinship ties do, indeed, influence the destination of migrants from Beech Creek.

For a long time we have been aware of the similarity of Eastern Kentucky and the Ozark Mountain area, as reported by Zimmer-man and Frampton.[27] In particular, the structure of the Ozark family, which the authors call "an uncodified variety of the stem-family,"[28] resembles in many respects the structure of the Beech Creek (Eastern Kentucky) family, as described by Brown.[29]

Their imaginative use of Le Play's model in studying the Ozark family has increasingly influenced our thinking and has led us to consider carefully Le Play's discussion of the stem-family (*famille-*

[25] Talcott Parsons, An analytical approach to the theory of social strati-fication, *Essays in Sociological Theory*. Glencoe, Ill., Free Press 1949, p. 173,

[26] The following sources will be helpful for further study: Frédéric Le Play. *Les ouvriers européens*, 2nd edn., 6 vols., Paris; Tours A. Mame et fils, 1878. Frédéric Le Play, *The Organization of Labor*, translated by G. Emerson, Philadelphia, Claxton, Remsen & Haffelfinger, 1872. Carle C. Zimmerman and Merle E. Frampton, *Family and Society*, New York, Van Nostrand, 1935. Pitirim A. Sorokin, *Contemporary Sociological Theories*, Harper and Brothers, New York and London, 1928, ch. 2 on "Frédéric Le Play's School," pp. 63–98. For Le Play's biography, see Dorothy Herbertson, *The Life of Frédéric Le Play*, Le Play House Press, Ledbury, Herefordshire, England, 1950, which is a reprint of Section 2, vol. 38 (1946) of the *American Sociological Review*.

[27] Zimmerman and Frampton, *op. cit.*

[28] *Ibid.*, p. 272.

[29] Brown, *op. cit.*

souche) and its pattern of emigration as well as other aspects of his work.[30]

Let us, then, note briefly some of the main features of Le Play's conceptual model of the *famille-souche*, the stem-family, emphasizing of course what has been most useful to us.

Le Play considers the family the elementary and basic social unit.[31] He held that there was only one general family type though fluctuations in the strength of the main form accounted for three major subtypes of families—the patriarchal, the unstable, and the *famille-souche* or stem-family.

The *patriarchal-type* has as its theme the principle of continuity; emphasis is on keeping the family group intact and preserving traditional family boundaries rather than on encouraging individual initiative. Members are loyal to family tradition and the established social order: strong familistic, religious, and moral beliefs are maintained. All property and savings in this type of family are controlled by the household head. Married children reside near the parental homestead and remain under the dominance of the family. If, however, economic conditions become difficult, the patriarchal family either migrates *as a unit* or begins to break up under the strain.

The *unstable-type* of family, on the other hand, has as its theme the principle of change; a high degree of individualism is encouraged by freeing children from family obligations. Members of the family have no particular attachment to the parental homestead; family history and traditions have little importance. This type,

[30] Though Le Play's contributions to social science were many and important and the interplay of Le Play's inquisitive mind, his many interests, and the social and historical circumstances in which his ideas evolved is fascinating, we will discuss only a few of his ideas which are most relevant. We should, however, emphasize that Le Play lived in a period when urbanization and industrialization were bringing about great social changes (born 1806, died 1882). Both the period of transition in which Le Play lived and his attempts to understand the social and economic phenomena of his day make his work particularly relevant to the problems undertaken in this paper.

[31] Sorokin, *op. cit.*, p. 39, notes that Le Play realized "an isolated individual cannot constitute a social phenomenon." This is precisely why we contend that a great deal more could be learned about the process of migration if we focus our attention on the family as a basic social unit in that process.

according to Le Play, is found primarily in new, growing, and unstable industrial orders. The individual member of an unstable family, write Zimmerman and Frampton, "depends more upon himself for a standard of living, and, in case of serious accidents, unemployment, or other calamities, he suffers unless some extra-family agency, such as the government, takes care of him, or unless he has accumulated sufficient property to take care of himself."[32] Cyclical periods of unemployment and economic recession can, therefore, cause much physical and psychological hardship.

Finally, the *famille-souche,* which Le Play conceived as the type *best* able to adjust to the changing conditions of an industrial society, incorporates some of the characteristics of both the patriarchal and unstable types, emphasizing both the principles of change and of continuity within the same structural framework. Zimmerman and Frampton describe this type, as follows:

> This stem-family consisted of a parent household (*the stem*) which preserved the organic basis of society, and of a number of individuals (*the branches*) who leave the parent household in order to fit into industrial organizations and urban environments where high but fluctuating money incomes were produced. The stem of the family helps to preserve the society and to insure that the branches which fail in their adaptations to contractual relations have havens of safety to which they may return. Thus, the stem part of the family reduces to a minimum the needs for public charity for the unemployed. At the same time, the successful branches contribute to the embellishment of society by their rapid adjustment to new opportunities, by the development of industrial areas, and by the increase in new types of production.[33]

In his conceptualization of the structure and functions of the *famille-souche,* Le Play, we must emphasize, was describing an "ideal type", deriving this abstraction from his studies of concrete families. Zimmerman and Frampton note this in saying, "The stem-type form is only a common manifestation of many strong families and does not necessarily appear in all or in most families of an area predominantly familistic. In the Ozarks it is far from being manifested in all families."[34] Consequently, we would not

[32] Zimmerman and Frampton, *op. cit.,* p. 98.
[33] *Ibid.,* p. 47.   [34] *Ibid.,* p. 286.

expect all Beech Creek families to manifest the characteristics of the stem-family form.

Though our purpose here is not to examine exhaustively the *famille-souche* type, in order to show its usefulness we will discuss certain essential elements of Le Play's conceptual model in relationship to what we have learned about the Beech Creek migrants and migration.

The *famille-souche*, as described by Le Play, maintains a homestead for its immediate members and sends other members elsewhere to make their own living. The ancestral home, built by the founder, is maintained by an heir, thus guaranteeing a continuous head to the family and assuring the preservation of family traditions. In the case of Beech Creek, a family homestead ("the homeplace") in the very broad sense of the term, is maintained by the family. This is usually the parental household. However, often it may be simply a piece of land, a presently abandoned or temporarily rented house, or close kinsfolk in the old neighborhoods who offer migrants a "haven of safety" in time of need. The Le Play *homestead concept* appears in the Beech Creek case as a configuration of elements blending land, neighborhood, parental household, kinsfolk, and the like, into, as one Ohio migrant put it, "a *place* to go back to if things get rough out here." Zimmerman and Frampton hint at this point when they suggest, "It seems that the spirit and not the form, the strength and not the mould, is the dominating characteristic of this family."[35]

Family headship in this Beech Creek case, however, is *not* automatically ascribed to an heir who maintains the ancestral home. Nor is there a formal pattern of succession of the family leadership role, although on an informal level family leaders can be identified. Migration from the area has been so great over the years that family leadership is often held by one of the branches rather than by the stem. In this respect, the branches may, then, have as much to do with preserving family traditions and continuity as does the stem.

In case of misfortune, according to Le Play, the branches may

[35] *Ibid.*, p. 286.

secure temporary subsistence and aid from the stem or may draw back to the protective cover of the parental homestead. Thus, serving as a "haven of safety", the stem-family reduces to a minimum the need for public charity for the unemployed. Numerous examples from the Beech Creek case suggest this protective function of the kinship structure during the process of migration. Often migrants who have lost their jobs in Ohio, for instance, move back to their home neighborhoods until employment opportunities are again favorable in the Ohio area. Le Play, however, could not foresee such broad governmental programs of assistance for the unemployed as we have in the U.S. today, and these programs have done much to modify the stem-family form as found in Eastern Kentucky.[36]

Le Play's central concern was with the stem of this type of family and what it does for its branches in two ways: on the one hand facilitating and encouraging migration when conditions demand it, and on the other hand providing "havens of safety" to which the branches could return during crises such as unemployment. *This is our point of departure from Le Play's model*, though we should note at once that the variation described here is implicit in Le Play's schema.

The stability of the directions of migratory streams from Eastern Kentucky, discussed in Part I, and the clustering of class-oriented family groups in certain areas during migration, described in Part II, are *both* suggestive of the supportive role played by the "branch-families" (that is, the migrant's family and kin in the new communities) within the migration system. Numerous researchers have noted that the new migrant is not necessarily alone or a stranger in the new community,[37] and indeed most Beech Creek migrants have many kinsfolk in the communities to which they

[36] Nevertheless, although the protective function of the stem-family system so far as the economic aspects are concerned may not be as important as during Le Play's time, the social-psychological aspects, especially in terms of the migration process in a complex society, may be even more important.

[37] Bogue and Hagood, *op. cit.*, p. 37, note: "This concept of the lonely migrant in the city, living in a single room in a large rooming house and slowly suffering personality deterioration because of isolation, could apply to only

go. To extend Le Play's model, these kinsfolk form a network of "branch-families" which serves important supportive functions during the transitional period of adjustment. Our preliminary field observations of the Beech Creek migrants indicate, for example, that kinsfolk in the areas of destination often provide the newcomers with temporary housing, help in finding jobs, and assistance of many other sorts during difficult times.[38] Furthermore, it seems reasonable to expect that these networks of branch-families function as a socio-psychological "cushion" for the migrants during the transitional phase, and it is this cushioning function of the branch-families that will be our concern during the remainder of this paper.

For purposes of clarity, let us briefly explain two notions that we have used in the body of this paper without elaborating their

---

a very small part of the migrant population, and probably to rather select part. If the data for the present study are at all typical of migration generally, the much more usual pattern is that the young migrant sets up his own household at an earlier age than non-migrants of his own age, both in the population at the place of origin and at the destination, that he lives with a relative, or that he is a lodger in a private home." In support of this conclusion, see also Albert J. Reiss, Jr., Rural–urban and status differences in interpersonal contracts, *American Journal of Sociology*, **65** (2) (Sept. 1959), 182–95, and Lyle L. Shannon, Effects of occupational and residential adjustment of rural migrants, a paper read at the Conference on Labor Mobility and Population in Agriculture, Nov. 8–10, 1960, Iowa State University, Ames, Iowa, p. 7.

[38] Sharp and Axelrod, for instance, found that mutual aid among friends and relatives is widespread in Detroit and, though there is a difference in this phenomena between natives and migrants, 66% of their migrant sample reported help given or received from friends or relatives. Harry Sharp and Morris Axelrod, Mutual aid among relatives in an urban population, in *Principles of Sociology*, Freedman *et al.*, New York, Henry Holt, 1956, pp. 433–9.

Smith, in his study of migrants in Indianapolis, concludes that "one of the primary functions performed by friends and relatives involves the dissemination of information about urban opportunities". (Eldon D. Smith, Migration and adjustment experiences of rural migrant workers in Indianapolis, unpublished Ph.D. thesis, University of Wisconsin, 1953, p. 284.)

This observation has been made also about southern white migrants in Chicago. See William R. Simon, The southern white migrant in the metropolis, a paper read at the Social Science Research Institute, University of Chicago, May 1961.

meanings, first, our use of "migration system" and secondly, our use of "adjustment".

A migrant[39] is here defined as a person who has moved spatially from one system of interaction to another. The interaction system in which a migrant originates is called his "donor sub-system". The implication is that the two sub-systems (the donor sub-system and the recipient sub-system) together form the interaction system in which we wish to consider the adjustment of a given group of migrants, individually and collectively. As presented in our preceding discussions, we have then *one migration system* to consider, namely the Beech Creek-Ohio migration system.[40]

Secondly, what do we mean by "adjustment"?[41] From our definition of a migrant it follows that migration means the shifting of an individual, or a group of individuals, from one relatively stable set of normative patterns of behavior (norms governing institutionalized ways of acting in a given specific social situation) to another. This shift necessarily entails stresses on individuals and on groups. The strains thus produced have psychological, sociological, and cultural dimensions. The resolution of these strains in a manner that enables individuals and groups to function adequately in terms of the demands of the interaction (migration system) is what we are calling adjustment, without restricting its meaning to any *one* of the three dimensions. As we conceptualize it, it is a holistic notion, defined as "a dynamic state in which individuals in a given society are able to live in relation to the members of their significant membership groups, satisfying their

[39] See footnote 21.

[40] We recognize that Beech Creek itself is comprised of a number of interaction subsystems and so, even more obviously, is Ohio (or Indiana or some other place of destination). The point we are trying to make, however, is that we are not dealing with the adjustment of a given group of migrants, just in the place of destination; instead we are also concerned with the adjustment of a given group of migrants, collectively and individually, in relation to two subsystems of interaction in which they are forced to participate in the normative sense.

[41] A second working-paper for our study will deal with this concept and will advance arguments in support of the definition that we merely present in this paper.

basic needs, fulfilling the responsibilities of their major roles, and maintaining the identity and integrity of their individual selves."

Having thus somewhat clarified the notions of "migration system" and "adjustment" let us return to consider the relationship between our modified notions of Le Play's *famille-souche* and adjustment in the migration system.

According to Le Play the stem-family encourages individual initiative while at the same time exerting moral control over its members. The individual who is unhappy with his present circumstances and wishes to advance socially and economically is offered an "escape mechanism" through the family structure.[42] He is both assisted in his quest for opportunity, and also encouraged to go out "on his own". Further, branches that are already established in the areas of destination, as well as the stem at "home", provide a supportive structure and socializing agency for the individual during the process of migration. This support facilitates his adjustment to new circumstances in the migration system and helps to stabilize the migrant, in whom two interactional sub-systems meet during the process of migration.

The foregoing arguments have led us to an over-all working hypothesis as the basis for our study of the Beech Creek migrants out of Eastern Kentucky:[43]

> The greater the functional adequacy of the stem-family (modified to include the network of the associated "branch-families") of the Beech Creek sociocultural system in responding to the changing needs of the

---

[42] It has been suggested by Slotkin and others that a necessary precondition for migration to occur is a "cultural inadequacy" of the source culture. Slotkin emphasizes the idea of migration as an "escape value" for those individuals who find their own sociocultural system inadequate for their own role expectations. With this perspective, we tend to look upon migration as an "unnormal" event—that is, the deviant behavior of an individual relative to the normative structure of his society. However, regional migration statistics and an examination of the pattern of migration from the Beech Creek area lead us to believe that the migration process is an adaptive mechanism somehow tied in with the sociocultural system, and functional in maintaining the Beech Creek family structure. James Sydney Slotkin, *From Field to Factory*, Glencoe, Ill., Free Press, 1960.

[43] Migrants, that is, to such places as listed in Table 5.

Beech Creekers, the more adjusted the migrants will be, both as individuals and as families, under certain conditions.

In conclusion, let us put the whole problem which we have been discussing in a somewhat larger setting of social and cultural change.

Bell and Vogel have made the helpful suggestion that in analyzing family functions and changes in family functions it is necessary to make clear whether, for instance, the reference point is the nuclear family or the extended family. As they point out, "In some primitive and agrarian societies, the family is said to have (or have had) major economic, political, religious and educational duties, but in many cases these are (or were) functions of the extended family, not the nuclear family. In more complex societies, these functions are performed not by the extended family, but by specialized institutions organized on other bases than kinship; the nuclear family's relationship with these institutions has become more important, while the relationship with the extended family has been less important."[44]

Obviously when we have been saying that kinship ties have much to do with a Beech Creek migrant's destination, his ways of finding a job and a place to live in the new community, and his general social and personal adjustment, we have been emphasizing the continuing importance of the extended family. As time goes on the importance of the extended family will probably decrease and the broader pattern of the American kinship structure will be approximated both in Eastern Kentucky and the areas to which the migrants go, notably in that the nuclear family will be much more emphasized. This change, the strains and stresses connected with it, and the process of change in the stem-family itself form another major focus of the Beech Creek Study.

As a subsidiary point we should say that though our general hypothesis is that extended family relationships help cushion the shock of moving from Eastern Kentucky, to Ohio for example, and thus help the migrant to make a better personal and social adjustment in the new community, we recognize that the kinship

[44] Bell and Vogel, *op. cit.*, p. 6.

structure may also be an actual deterrent to more rapid assimilation. In the "little Kentuckies", e.g., migrants' social relationships tend to be exclusively among themselves. This limits their contacts with native Ohioans and lessens their opportunity to learn and accept new patterns.

Finally, Parsons points out that it

> is above all the presence of the modern occupational system and its mode of articulation with the family which accounts for the difference between the modern, especially American, kinship system and *any* found in non-literate or even peasant societies. . . . This means essentially, that as the occupational system develops and absorbs functions in the society, it *must* be at the expense of the relative prominence of kinship organization as a structural component in one sense, and must also be at the expense of many of what previously have been functions of the kinship unit.[45]

The general American family type, it should be noted, has gradually changed to meet the changing needs of the occupational and other institutions (and of course has changed these other institutions too). The Beech Creek family has remained much more of an extended family, not the least reason being that it met the needs of that society better than other familial forms. Now that the mountain family has been more or less abruptly moved into modern American society, it will be interesting to see how and how fast it is changed by (and perhaps changes) the "outside world".

[45] Talcott Parsons and Robert F. Bales, *Family, Socialization and Interaction Process*, Free Press, Glencoe, Ill., pp. 11–12.

Great Britain

The Motivation and Characteristics of Internal Migrants: A Socio-Medical Study of Young Migrants in Scotland

Part I

R. Illsley, A. Finlayson, and B. Thompson

Immigration control has been a boon to international demographers. For students of internal migration the periodic census has provided a partial substitute, especially for those concerned with the volume and direction of movement. For those, however, who are interested in the motives and characteristics of migrants, or in the effect of migration on the individual or community, the census provides only a numerical framework and a set of hypotheses. The very mobility of the migrants makes them hard to study. It is difficult in any community to identify in advance those who are likely to migrate from it and, hence, to determine their motives and characteristics prior to migration. Identification of people who have migrated to a given area is much easier, but in the meantime the very process of migration may have changed their socio-economic position, their family life, their habits and health and even their own view of why they migrated.

In 1938 Thomas, [21] in a comprehensive review of earlier work, concluded: "Our examination of researches bearing on these differentials led us to almost no acceptable generalizations about the strength and direction of selective internal migration." The scope of migration research has widened considerably since then. The United States, no longer preoccupied with the effect of mass

123

immigration, has turned its attention increasingly to other aspects of population movements—the migration of Negroes from the southern states,[11, 12, 13, 15] the growth of conurbations,[2, 8, 22] the continuous flow of inter-state migration,[3] the relationship of migration to industrial and occupational redistribution,[13] and the effect of residential movement on family and social relationships.[7]

In Britain, apart from census analysis, inquiry has been limited to a few studies of the volume of local movement[14, 16] of rural depopulation,[5, 17, 19] and of the social effects of housing programs.[23]

Lee,[13] in a preliminary revision of Thomas's 1938 review, was able to conclude: "Many gaps have been noted in the existing knowledge of mobility differentials, but it has been possible to arrive at a few generalizations which may have more than temporary validity." These generalizations, however, referred largely to such variables as age, sex, and marital status and hardly at all to motivation and personal characteristics. Very little information yet exists about the characteristics of migrants—the varied motives which prompt them to move, the number of moves they make, or the respects in which they differ from their static friends and relatives. It has long been assumed that migrants are superior in intelligence and physical health, but the evidence, with the exception of that on anthropometric measurements, is far from satisfactory,[21] and very little attempt has been made to relate the characteristics of migrants to the social context in which the migration occurred.

This paper documents the movement of young adults into and out of the city of Aberdeen in the post-war years. In Part I an attempt is made to distinguish sub-categories of migrants differing from each other in occupation, area of origin and reasons for migration; in Part II data are presented on stature and reproductive morbidity; and these "biological" characteristics are related back to the original social processes leading to migration. The analysis reveals a complex composition of migrant groups ranging from the professional man following his career round the country, through the rural–urban migrant, to the restless wandering of the socially unsettled. These groups differ systematically in their other characteristics.

Method

(a) SOURCES OF INFORMATION

The data on migration into Aberdeen were collected as part of a joint socio-medical study of reproduction in the city.[9] All primiparous women booked for confinement in the maternity hospital in the years 1951–9 (95% of all first pregnancies to married Aberdeen residents) were interviewed by a hospital almoner who, as part of the social history of the patient, took details of her place(s) of upbringing and, in particular, her place of residence at the time she left school. Similar details were collected for 75% of the remaining primiparae delivered in private nursing homes or in their own homes.

This information was supplemented during the years 1951–4 by detailed histories of a random sample of 430 married primiparae, who were studied intensively during the course of their first pregnancy by a team which included physicians, psychologists, and sociologists. The sample (every sixth patient booking for hospital or nursing home confinement) comprised women from all social classes, the only exclusions being women who delivered in their own homes (0.4% of married primiparae). Fuller data were collected from these sample patients, including data on the social and residential background of their husbands. The study was undertaken with the primary aim of discovering the interrelation between social factors and reproductive "efficiency"; migration was only one of many social, psychological, and medical variables considered relevant to the study. The design of the study makes it possible therefore to compare migrants and non-migrants over a wide range of phenomena.

Migration from the city is less comprehensively documented, being derived from two sources:

(1) a 5-year follow-up of the intensively studied sample of primiparae described above;

(2) a 5-year follow-up of all Aberdeen primiparae delivered in the year 1949, whether confined at home or in hospital.

Out-migration in this study relates therefore to couples at a later stage of family life.

(b) DEFINITIONS

Certain terms used throughout the paper require definition:

(1) *In-migrants* are those who, having resided outside Aberdeen at the age of 14, resided in Aberdeen at the birth of their first baby.

(2) *Out-migrants* are those who, having resided in Aberdeen at the birth of their first baby, left the city during the subsequent 5 years.

(3) *Areas* to or from which people migrated are classified as follows:
   (a) *North of Scotland*—the counties of Kincardine, Aberdeen, Banff, Moray, Nairn, Inverness, Ross and Cromarty, Sutherland, Caithness, Orkney, and Shetland.
   (b) *South of Scotland*—all other areas of Scotland.
   (c) *Elsewhere*—places outside Scotland.

(4) *Social class* is based on the occupation of the husband classified according to the system used by the General Register Office (1950):
   Class I   Professional.
   Class II   Intermediate, including managers, proprietors, and highly qualified technical workers.
   Class III Skilled manual and clerical workers.
   Class IV   Partly skilled.
   Class V   Unskilled.

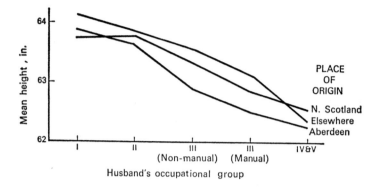

FIG. 1. Mean height of female in-migrants and Aberdeen natives
classified by husband's occupation.

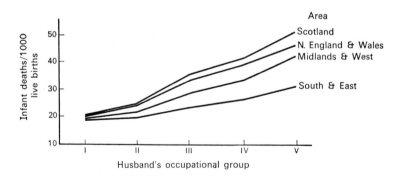

FIG. 2. Infant mortality according to husband's occupation for
different geographic regions of Great Britain.

Results

A. IN-MIGRATION

Geographical Origin

Of the 7643 married primiparous women resident and delivered in the city in the years 1951–9 whose place of origin was known,* 5907 (77%) were resident in Aberdeen at the age of 14. These include a small number (approximately 5–6%) who had spent some at least of their earlier years outside the city and had moved into Aberdeen some time during childhood. For the purpose of this paper, which is concerned with adolescent and adult migration, they are regarded as native Aberdonians. Of the remainder, 952 (12%) were brought up in the north of Scotland,

* In the period 1951–9 the number of Aberdeen women having a first pregnancy totaled 9203. Place of upbringing was known in 7643 cases (83%). Two reasons exist for lack of information about upbringing in the remaining cases:

(i) For a period of about a year, in the middle years of the survey, it was decided, for administrative reasons, to omit the question about place of upbringing from the interview with hospital patients. There is no reason to suppose that in this period the social background of patients differed from other years. Their omission is therefore of little statistical or interpretative significance. These constitute the great bulk of the excluded cases.

(ii) A small proportion of patients (approximately 270) "slipped through" the routine administrative machinery. Since they amount to only 2.9% of the population their exclusion does not materially affect the results. Moreover subsequent identification of migration among 162 of these patients showed that, within each class, they did not differ from the population used in the study. On the other hand, since the not-stated group was drawn disproportionately from the professional classes, who have the highest rate of migration, their exclusion will slightly understate the overall rate of migration and the proportion of the total volume contributed by the professional classes.

Data on the occupations of the wife or her father (Part II) were not known or not classifiable in a further 3.2% of cases. Again the percentage of not stated was rather higher in the upper social groups. Information on education (Part II) refers only to the hospital population in which the professional groups are under-represented.

None of these exclusions apply to the sample population which is a strict random sample or to the data on out-migration where 100% of the population was investigated.

415 (5%) in the south of Scotland, and 369 (5%) outside Scotland.

For many years the northern counties of Scotland have been the major source of migrants to Aberdeen which is the only large industrial city (population 189,000) in this scattered and sparsely populated rural area. Apart from its major industries—fish, granite, shipbuilding, engineering, paper, and textiles—Aberdeen has important docks and is the commercial and transport center of the North-east. In addition to the university and several institutions concerned with research or vocational training, it also contains regional and local government offices and the only teaching and specialist hospitals in the area. For all these reasons it is the first natural focus for rural out-migrants looking for occupational opportunities and the amenities of urban life. Moreover, for many decades, these rural northern counties have exported their population either to overseas countries or to more southerly areas of Britain. Banff County for example, lost 14.5% of its 1911 population by net migration in the decade 1911–20, an additional 13% between 1921 and 1930, and another 10% in each of the two decades from 1931 to 1950. Most of the other northern counties had a similar experience. Many of these rural migrants passed through Aberdeen on their way south, but others stayed and provided a substantial proportion of the city's growing population. Their numbers have, however, been falling in recent years. In 1931 one quarter of Aberdeen's population had been born in the eleven northern counties; by 1951 this proportion had fallen to 21%. The rate of 12% among young married women in our sample population reflects a continuing decrease in rural migrants to the city.

Class composition. Compared with the northern rural migrants, the increasing number of in-migrants from southern Scotland and elsewhere represent a quite different type of migration in that they have moved against the familiar north-south current. This difference is clearly reflected in their social class distribution.

Table 1 shows that, compared with native Aberdonians, in-migrants from all three areas contained a higher proportion of

TABLE 1. SOCIAL CLASS DISTRIBUTION (%) OF IN-MIGRANTS AND NATIVES BY AREA OF ORIGIN

Wife's area of origin	Husband's occupational Class[a]							All classes
	I	II	III Non-manual	III Manual	IV	V		
Aberdeen	3	8	15	51	11	12		100 (5907)
Northern Scotland	4	12	17	51	8	8		100 (952)
Southern Scotland	13	26	19	30	5	7		100 (415)
Elsewhere	15	21	15	36	6	7		100 (369)
All areas	4	10	16	49	10	11		100 (7643)

[a] See definitions on p. 126.

TABLE 2. INTERNAL MIGRATION: STAGE OF MIGRATION

Husband's place of upbringing	Wife's place of upbringing				All places
	Aberdeen	Elsewhere			
		Settled in Aberdeen		After marriage	
		Before marriage	On marriage		
Aberdeen	275	32	27	2	336
Elsewhere					
Settled before marriage	34	12	13	—	59
On marriage	12	2	—	—	14
After marriage	6	—	—	15	21
All places	327	46	40	17	430

non-manual workers and a lower proportion of semi-skilled and unskilled workers. Sharper, however, than the contrast between in-migrants and *sedentes* is the difference between long distance migrants from southern Scotland and elsewhere, taken together, and the remainder of the population, whether rural in-migrants or Aberdeen natives. The preponderance of non-manual, and particularly of professional, occupations among the long distance migrants conforms to previous findings[1] on the relationship between social class and distance of migration.

Stage of migration: sex, age, and marital status. Previous demographic research has demonstrated convincingly the comparative youth of migrant populations and the preponderance of females, particularly from rural areas. Less is known about the various stages, in their careers and in the growth of their families, at which people become migrants, and about the motives prompting migration at different stages. The detailed information available for the 430 couples who form our random sample is appropriate for the study of some of these problems, and, although single persons and couples who remained childless are, of course, excluded by the nature of the sample, the data on the sample couples include retrospective material on moves made when they were single and childless.

Table 2 shows that in 275 couples (64%) both husbands and wives were native to Aberdeen. In 42 cases (10%) both spouses were in-migrants. Among the remaining 113 couples an Aberdeen husband married an in-migrant wife in 61 instances and an Aberdeen woman married an immigrant husband in 52. The preponderance of 9 female in-migrants occurred as a result of the movements of wives to Aberdeen to join their husbands on marriage, 40 wives but only 14 husbands arriving in Aberdeen at the time of marriage. On the other hand, 59 husbands migrated to the city before marriage compared with 46 wives. In eight cases the move to Aberdeen after marriage was a return to the native city for one of the spouses. The various stages at which migration took place and the characteristics of the migrants at each stage are considered in detail below.

Women Migrants

Migration before marriage. Nearly half the women migrants (46 out of 103) came to the city between the age of 14 and marriage. Three main groups may be distinguished: those who accompanied their parents when the family moved, those who came independently as adolescents or young adults to take a job, and those who first came to the city to take a professional training. The great majority in all three categories were short-distance migrants—39 out of the 46 came from the rural northern counties surrounding Aberdeen. Because of its nearness, these girls already had some knowledge of the city; some had friends or relatives living there, and in a few instances, the family or one of its members had lived there at an earlier stage.

Twelve girls came when their families settled in the city. For a few of these a change in the father's job had prompted the move, but in eight cases the move represented the resettlement of the family after the father's death; his job no longer anchored the family in the countryside where jobs were few and limited in both variety and prospects, particularly for women and girls.

Eighteen girls came to enter employment in the city, two motives predominating. For many of the girls the move meant escape from uncongenial features of their home life; they wanted to leave a broken or insecure home, to achieve independence after having been brought up by a sister or a guardian or to relieve congestion in an overcrowded and unproductive croft. Much of this movement was of a drifting rather than a purposeful character. A history typical of many was given by Mrs. *X*.

She had had a hard life at home as one of a large family brought up on a small croft by a stern father who expected a good deal of heavy work from his children. In her early teens she went to work as a shop assistant—cum-domestic servant at a shop in a small local town where wages were low and the hours long; she left to become a resident domestic and her later history shows a series of job changes bringing her gradually nearer to the city; eventually she arrived there as a resident ward maid and shortly afterwards, having settled in the city, began work at the woollen mills, became pregnant and married a laborer of rural origin.

For all eighteen, however, whether happy or unhappy in their home backgrounds, an important factor was the lack of suitable local employment in a sparsely settled agricultural region with few towns and not many large villages. Apart from a strictly limited demand for such professionally qualified persons as teachers and nurses and a rather greater demand for shop assistants, the majority of local jobs for girls involve some form of domestic work. Many parents look to the nearest city for alternative jobs for their children and there they must find not only a job but accommodation suitable for an adolescent girl. Against a city background, domestic work often seems more attractive, especially when residence is provided. Thirteen of the eighteen took resident jobs in the catering and domestic trades and, whilst a few transferred later to factory work, the majority remained in these trades until marriage.

Training facilities, as well as jobs, are concentrated in the large cities and five girls came to train in nursing, a much respected profession in which the provision of residential accommodation generally counts as an attraction for country girls. The remaining 11 out of the 46 girls who came to the city before marriage came originally as students to the university, the teachers' training college, or the commercial college. Before they married, eight became teachers, two clerical workers, and one a physiotherapist.

In general, therefore, the main features of this pre-marital migration are its predominantly short distance rural–urban nature, discontent with occupational opportunities and social life in rural areas, and the attractive power either of relatively light and clean town jobs, mainly residential, or of facilities for higher education and vocational training. Behind these features which form part of the structure of the rural–urban relationship, there lie, of course, individual differences in personality and family cohesion which tend to make the city appear more attractive for some individuals than for others, and, among these, one major influence is the disturbing effect of parental loss or of a broken home.

Migration on marriage. There were four different ways in which marriage brought women as in-migrants to Aberdeen: country women who had previously commuted daily to the city met and married Aberdeen men there; other country women married men whom they had known in their home area before the latter had migrated to Aberdeen; women from a greater distance married professional men who had already migrated to Aberdeen or who were about to take up an appointment there; the largest single category consisted of women who had met and married Aberdeen men outside Aberdeen, mainly during service with the forces.

Of the 40 women comprising these four groups, 11 had previously lived within a 15 mile radius of the city and had travelled daily to work. Marriage to Aberdeen men caused no great change in their mode of life or in their social or family circle.

For the second group of 7 rural in-migrants the motivation and the character of the move were rather different. The husbands, (all but one of whom were craftsmen) had themselves migrated to Aberdeen to obtain work or to take a better job and after an interval had married girls from their home area and brought them to the city. Both partners were now out of daily contact with their families and former friends.

The third group of 6 in-migrants resembled the second in that the move meant that both spouses were now out of daily contact with their families and friends; they differed from the previous group, however, in coming from long distances and in the fact that the husbands were all professional men—lawyers, administrators, and students whose entry into and progress up the professional hierarchy often entails distant and sometimes repeated movement.

The last group consisted of 16 long distance migrants most of whom met their Aberdonian husbands while the latter (and occasionally the women themselves) were serving in the armed forces; this is reflected in the widespread of their pre-marital homes —Malta, Danzig, Aldershot, Warrington, etc. The husbands who married on their travels and brought their wives back to the city were drawn disproportionately from the upper social groups. It is an interesting commentary on the city's relatively isolated position

that these were the only Aberdonian men in the sample who met
their wives outside the city and its immediate countryside; and this
was largely the result of wartime and conscription conditions. As
Table 2 shows, a total of 61 Aberdonian men married non-
Aberdonian women but, except for the 16 mentioned above, the
meetings took place after the wives had arrived in Aberdeen
either with their parents or independently.

Male Migrants

Migration before marriage. Fifty-nine husbands had come to
Aberdeen before marriage. Of these, 10 came with their parental
families as dependent adolescents. As with the pre-marital
migration of women two distinct reasons are discernible: (1) the
father's promotion, change of job or retirement, (2) family
migration consequent on parental death or marital breakdown.

Most of the others came to Aberdeen independently as adolescents or young adults. Four came to study at the university
and afterwards took work locally; the others came straight to a
job, but for some of these young men, particularly those in technical and highly skilled occupations (e.g. pharmacist, agricultural
engineer, nursing assistant) the availability of training facilities
in the city was a major attraction.

The composition of this group of young job-migrants clearly
reflects the relation between migration and the structure of
professional and managerial careers. For example, 32% of this
group of pre-marital in-migrants had class I or II occupations
(i.e. professional or managerial), compared with 13% in the whole
sample. Two promotion mechanisms are apparent, each involving
migration and each of roughly equal importance. On the one hand,
are those who move within the same organization: bankers,
insurance officials, industrial managers, salaried employees of
large-scale organizations with many branches, for whom promotion means a larger branch, often in another town; unwillingness
to move in these circumstances is often tantamount to withdrawal
from the promotion race. For the other group, promotion is

obtained by a move from one organization to another, each move representing a step up the professional ladder. In our sample this group included university lecturers, teachers, local government officials, newspaper reporters, lawyers, and some industrial and commercial managers. It might be said that since migration for these men generally involved formal application for a job, it has more of the character of a voluntary act than it has for those who move within an organization; nevertheless, disinclination to move often means losing opportunities of promotion and, consequently, migration has become a generally accepted part of the way of life for many in these professions.

There are notable exceptions where the son follows the father in the business or practice and where "promotion" is obtained by building up a successful enterprise in one place; examples are found in industry, commerce, law, medicine, finance; but they represent a diminishing aspect of modern business and professional life. The way in which migration is built into the structure of the professions in contemporary society is also evident if we look at the migration status of the 19 men out of the 430 in the sample who had occupations in class I. Of these only 4 were born and brought up in Aberdeen and one of the latter had already left the city 5 years later. The remaining 15 were in-migrants and of these 8 had left the city within 5 years.

Thirty of the pre-marital in-migrants were routine non-manual or manual workers. For these occupations transference within an organization is less common and only 6 men followed this pattern; they were all working in rail and road transport or civil engineering, enterprises which, by definition, are regional or even national in their scale of operation. Eighteen others came from the surrounding counties to look for a job in the town, and their migration reflected either dissatisfaction with rural conditions and opportunities or the positive attraction of urban facilities. The remaining 6 came from longer distances. One, an Irishman, came to Britain to look for work, as did also his father and brothers, although the mother maintained the family home in southern Ireland. The remainder were motivated by personal factors rather than work. One, who had some association with Aberdeen in childhood had returned here after a nervous breakdown and a crisis in his career; his stay was temporary, a respite from a distressing experience. The general impression in the other four cases is of rootless men, often without parents, not anchored to one place by home and family, drifting to Aberdeen and settling there because they found a substitute home to which they could attach themselves. Mrs. *Y*, for example, told the story that her husband had lived in lodgings on his first arrival in Aberdeen to work at the shipyards and "once he started coming to our house, we all (the family) liked him so much that he used to come over every night".

The impulse towards migration is regulated by two factors, the pulling power of the new place of residence and the strength of ties with the old. In this type of survey and analysis the positive element is easy to detect; men say "I came here because I was transferred by my office", "because I was appointed as a lecturer", or "because there were plenty of jobs in my line in Aberdeen." Very rarely, however, do they put it negatively, e.g. "because I was unhappy or unsettled with my family", "because my parents were dead", "because I had a broken home and unhappy childhood and felt no love for my place of upbringing". It comes to the surface occasionally—as with these men—when compelling motives for migrating to Aberdeen are absent ("I came to Aberdeen on a holiday and liked it, and when my mother died I came to live here"), but personal and family factors which weaken the tie with the home town also underlie many other instances in which there is at the same time a good and sufficient reason for migration. These factors cannot adequately be studied in a retrospective inquiry carried out in the place to which migrants have moved, since the home background, the cultural setting and the events, and sentiments leading up to migration cannot be examined. Whilst such personal or negative factors receive little direct attention in this study it should be remembered that they, as much as the positive attractions of training, a job, or a spouse, contribute towards the decision to move.

Migration on marriage. It is customary, largely because of occupational reasons, for the wife to join her husband at his place of residence at marriage. In the present sample 40 wives came to join husbands in Aberdeen while only 14 husbands took up residence with their Aberdeen wives. In these fourteen marriages many factors might contribute to this reversal of customary behavior, for example, family ties so strong as to make the wife more than usually reluctant to leave home, lack of an adventurous spirit on her part, poor employment prospects or housing difficulty in the husband's home town, or, more negatively, lack of any family or other emotional ties binding the husband to his place of origin. Our data are not sufficiently rich or immediate to investigate many of these hypotheses; certainly the wife's reluctance to leave Aberdeen and her initiative in obtaining a flat in the city dictated the decision in one case. On the whole, however, the wives in this group were neither unadventurous (after all, they did marry a "foreigner") nor reluctant to move. A high proportion of these women met their future husbands when they were working in other parts of the country or serving in the women's forces.

The major factor in most of these cases seems to have been the unsettled nature of the husband's work. Five of the 14 husbands had jobs which took them from one place to another; before marriage they had based themselves on their parental home, but the nature of their occupations (merchant seamen, regular soldiers, commercial traveller, itinerant boxer) weakened their ties with home; it was simpler, after marriage, to base themselves on the wife's parental home, thus avoiding her isolation in a strange place, with a strange family and a new job. In a further five cases the marriage occurred while the husband was in the forces and the wife continued to live in her parental home and to work at her usual job. Again, this was the arrangement which caused least inconvenience. The willingness of the husband, after demobilization, to continue this arrangement depended largely on his civilian job. Most of these men had jobs which were as readily available in Aberdeen as elsewhere (craftsmen, laborers); none were in social classes I and II.

The general factor common to these cases was the absence of a compelling occupational reason for basing a home in one place rather than another. In such cases the choice of a home base can be determined on other grounds, such as the wife's job, family and social ties and personal preferences.

Migration after marriage. For 75% of the population the interval between marriage and birth of the first child is less than one year. Thus only a small number of couples move into the city during this time and out of 93 in-migrant husbands in our sample only 21 came in then. To understand the motivation and characteristics of post-marriage migrants on a larger scale it is necessary to analyze the couples who left Aberdeen after their first baby (see below, section on out-migration); in the meantime, however, certain informative conclusions may be drawn from this small group of 21 couples in which the husband was a post-marriage in-migrant.

They fall into two groups: 13 couples in which neither spouse had any previous connection with the city, and 8 in which the move was, for one partner at least a return to a previous home and often to their family of origin.

Husbands in the first group were primarily professional or business men who, like the pre-marital migrants in these occupations, came in pursuance of their careers. Of the 4 men not classifiable to social classes I and II, 3 were non-manual workers (commercial traveller, compositors) and the other a railway worker, and all were transferred within their organization.

In the other group the wife had either been brought up in Aberdeen or had worked there previously. The move to Aberdeen brought her back to familiar associations and in most cases occurred at her insistence or as a result of her unhappiness away from Aberdeen. Only two of these husbands were in social class I and II occupations; both had jobs involving much travelling and residence away from home (army officer, time and motion engineer) and the wife came to Aberdeen during pregnancy because it represented a firm base and sure support during a difficult period; both left again and rejoined their husbands elsewhere shortly after delivery.

B. Out-migration

Migrants out of an urban area differ in many ways from in-migrants. In-migrants include rural residents as well as inter-city migrants; few out-migrants go to live in rural areas, the majority being inter-city migrants and people following the main migration current to growing urban areas. At the 1951 census the Aberdeen population included 39,000 people born in the northern Scottish counties: these counties, however, contained only 18,600 born Aberdonians. Slightly more Aberdonians by birth lived in the rest of Scotland, particularly the cities, than such areas contributed to the Aberdeen resident population (15,600 against 13,200). A total of 10,000 Aberdeen residents were born outside Scotland; the corresponding number of Aberdonians living outside Scotland cannot be enumerated but estimates based on the city's natural increase and net migration statistics suggests a figure of 30,000 or more. Aberdeen, therefore, receives population from the rural north and exports population to England and countries overseas.

These movements of population are clearly reflected in our own data, which also point to important social differences between in-migrant and out-migrant groups. The findings are based on a 5-year follow-up of two populations (described above).

In both series we know whether the couple was in the city 5 years after the birth of their first child. In the smaller, intensively studied series we also know whether the out-migrants were originally in-migrants, and what their destination was on leaving the city. As in the earlier part of the paper, the detailed information available on the sample population will be used to illustrate trends revealed in the larger population.

Volume and Destination of Out-Migration

Out of a total of 1500 couples, 305 (20.3%) had left the city within 5 years of the birth of their first child. The destination of out-migrants from the sample population is compared in Table 3 with the area of origin of in-migrants. The main differences between in- and out-migrants are similar to those revealed by the census data described above. The in-migrants came predominantly from other parts of Scotland, particularly the rural northern counties; only 16% came from England and Wales and 4% from overseas, whereas these areas attracted 26% and 24% respectively of out-migrants. Aberdeen in this respect conforms to the classic pattern of an urban area in a declining rural setting—a receiver of rural migrants and an exporter to more distant, predominantly urban, centers.

Table 3 also shows that the destination of out-migrants differs according to whether they were originally in-migrants or natives. Native Aberdonian couples, when they leave the city, tend to travel long distances and thus make a sharp break with their environment; indeed, nearly three-quarters leave Scotland and almost half go overseas—for the most part to Commonwealth countries where friends and relatives have preceded them. In contrast, in-migrants to the city, when they leave, tend to return to the area from which one or both spouses came; 20 of the 35 in-migrant couples who left the city returned to the town or area with which at least one spouse had been previously associated.

We have seen that some of the in-migrants to Aberdeen later became out-migrants, thus swelling total migration statistics. In 155 couples of our sample population, one or both spouses was an in-migrant. The rate of out-migration in these couples was particularly high—16% where the wife alone was an in-migrant, 25% where the husband was an in-migrant, and 45% where both were in-migrants. The equivalent rate among Aberdeen-born couples was 11%. The rate of out-migration is therefore closely tied to the rate of in-migration.

Turning now to the origin of these repeat migrants, the rate of out-migration was least (13%) where both spouses came from the rural North or one spouse came from Aberdeen and the other from the North. A higher rate (22%) occurred where the husband was from Aberdeen or the North and where the wife came from further afield, but this in turn was lower than the converse situation where the husband came from further afield (41%). The

TABLE 3. ORIGIN AND DESTINATION OF MIGRANTS

Area	Origin of in-migrants				Destination of out-migrants (couples)					
	Male		Female		Previous In-migrants		Natives		Total	
	No.	%	No.	%	No.	%	No.	%	No.	%
North of Scotland	46	49	62	60	12	34	5	19	17	28
Southern Scotland	28	30	21	20	11	31	2	8	13	21
England and Wales	17	18	15	15	9	26	7	27	16	26
Overseas	3	3	5	5	3	9	12	46	15	24
	94	100	103	100	35	100	26	100	61	99

highest rate occurred where both spouses came from the south of Scotland or elsewhere (72%).

It emerges from these findings that a considerable part of the movement at this age and family stage is not movement to new territory but return to the familiar. If this is general, it suggests that true migration, in the sense of the move to unfamiliar settings, is even more restricted to very young people than present statistics suggest.

The findings also reveal differences between repeat migrants (i.e. those in-migrants to Aberdeen who then moved out again) and migrants who settled in Aberdeen. Both groups, it should be remembered, originally migrated from their community of origin and it is in their role as out-migrants that we are now considering them. It seems that:—

(1) The initial movement is most stable where either:

    (a) only one spouse is an in-migrant (20% out-migrants). In these circumstances one spouse at least has roots in the local community, local kinship ties and, in the case of the husband, a job. Out-migration for these couples means that only one spouse has to cut his or her link with a life-time environment; or

    (b) one or both spouses arrived with the migration current from the rural hinterland (17% out-migrants). For these people the original incentive to migrate sprang largely from lack of social and occupational opportunities, re-inforced by poor living conditions. The move to Aberdeen for the most part achieved these limited objectives. Further movement would entail return to the conditions which gave rise to discontent or the expansion of their original objectives by movement away from the northern region. Apart from the cutting of emotional ties, this presents practical difficulties as most such couples have limited knowledge of, and few connections in, other regions. The great majority therefore stay in Aberdeen, and the few who migrate return to their place of origin.

(2) The initial movement is least stable where both partners have arrived together or separately, against the migration stream, from areas further south (72%). Emotional and cultural factors are again involved, for most of these out-migrants return to the general area from which they came, but the major influence seems to be occupational. They moved to Aberdeen for promotion, and for the same reason they left. All the husbands, both those who stayed and those who left, were non-manual workers, the great majority being professional men, in contrast with the more settled group discussed above which contained only 29% non-manual workers and only 5% who were professionally qualified.

(3) Where the husband is local (Aberdeen or north) and the wife a distant migrant, the couple is more likely to remain than in the reverse situation of an in-migrant husband and a local wife. Again, this seems to have an occupational basis because the in-migrant husband is likely to be a professional man whose career may demand repeated movement.

With out-migration, as with in-migration, the motives are complex and we are aware that a broad sociological analysis gives only part of the picture. The factors, however, which emerge as important at this level of analysis are: the social and industrial geography of the area; the places of origin of husband and wife; and the husband's occupation. This last factor is discussed more fully below.

Occupation and the Rate of Out-migration

The data on out-migration in this study refer to the 5-year period following the birth of the first child. At this stage most wives are not employed outside the home and the wife's job or career has little bearing on family decisions. The husband's occupation automatically assumes greater importance in that he is the sole wage-earner and the family's standard of living is directly dependent upon him. Many young middle-class men are still at the beginning of a career which may entail further geo-graphical and hierarchical moves; most manual workers, on the other hand, have reached the peak of earnings in their occupation and further advance may be obtained only by change of occupation or by moving to an area with higher wages. The occupational basis of migration was still very evident in our population at this stage. The highest rate of out-migration occurred in social class I —63% within the 5 years; the rate fell sharply with decreasing status—to 33% in class II, 19% in class III, and 10% in classes IV and V. Broad class differences, however, conceal some of the most interesting industrial and occupational differences which are detailed in Table 4.

Two of the highest rates occurred in "occupational" groups which are intrinsically mobile—university students and members of the armed forces; they assume prominence in this study only because Aberdeen is a university city and because military con-scription was in force at the time. The high rate among university-trained or professionally-qualified workers, however, has a more general relevance, for it indicates a way of life and a career struc-ture current in a large and increasing section of society. It is in sharp distinction to the rate among men in managerial occupations, the group most similar in income and responsibilities; within this latter group the migration rate is high only among the employees of large-scale national organizations; it is lowest in the peculiarly local industries such as fishing, fish handling and granite working which require skills unprized in other centers, or in small businesses (catering, retail distribution) in which success depends on a stable clientele or a local reputation. Somewhat similar considerations apply to clerical workers whose rate of out-migration is identical, for here, too, it is the employees of large organizations (banks, insurance companies) who are most likely to move.

Among manual workers in our population the most mobile were skilled mechanics, fitters and electricians, their rate of out-migration in fact exceeding that of the remaining non-manual workers. This is probably in part a local phenomenon, stemming from the relatively limited outlets for their skill compared with

TABLE 4. OCCUPATIONAL AND INDUSTRIAL DIFFERENCES IN THE RATE OF OUT-MIGRATION

Occupational group	Total cases	Per cent out-migrant	Occupational group	Total cases	Per cent out-migrant
University students	20	85	Railway workers	48	19
Professional	72	54	Other non-manual	94	18
Armed forces	70	49	Other skilled	254	13
Managerial	63	25	Road transport	173	12
Clerical workers	95	25	Other semi-skilled and unskilled	246	11
Fitters and electricians	193	23	Other skilled engineers	60	10
Shop assistants	54	19	Fishing and fish handling	63	8

the opportunities available to them in larger industrial centers in England and abroad. Educationally, socially, and physically, however, these engineers are the aristocrats of local manual work and they may be particularly susceptible to the attractions of a higher standard of living elsewhere when they find their occupational pathway blocked locally. They are very largely Aberdonian in origin, not earlier in-migrants from the countryside. They differ sharply in their rate of out-migration from other skilled engineers in the city, many of whom are employed in shipbuilding, an industry which is stationary or declining throughout the country and which is not conspicuously more prosperous in other areas than in Aberdeen. The engineering industry thus provides an excellent example of the impact of both local and national conditions on rates of migration, of the push–pull forces which have received so much attention in migration research.

The other manual-worker industry experiencing relatively high rates of migration in Aberdeen is transport, particularly railway transport. Here again the national character of the industry is important, for transference within the organization is possible and may be the quickest method of obtaining promotion; the habit of long-distance travel, cheaper and easier communications and familiarity with other centers may possibly help to break down resistance to geographical movement.

The lowest rate of out-migration occurs in the fishing industry, which is largely manned by local workers. Employment in the same industry or occupation is available at only a few British ports, so that the incentive to move is low. It is probably relevant that this industry has had a low status locally and has not been attractive to workers with high social and economic aspirations. In terms of education, housing, and various aspects of reproductive behavior and health, the members of this industry tend to rank lower than social class V and it seems likely that limited cultural outlook and aspirations heavily influence the low rate of migration.

The net occupational effect of inflow and outflow is shown in Table 5. The native population which still remained in the city at the time of follow-up contained remarkably few professional or

TABLE 5. OCCUPATIONAL CLASS OF IN-MIGRANT AND OUT-MIGRANT MALES

Migration category	Occupational class (% distribution)				
	I and II Professional and managerial	III Other non-manual	III Skilled manual	IV and V Semi-skilled and unskilled	All classes
Natives					
In city 5 years later	7	14	50	29	100 (302)
Left city	16	8	60	16	100 (38)
In-migrants					
In city 5 years later	25	16	48	11	100 (64)
Left city	48	13	30	9	100 (33)

managerial persons but a high proportion of semi-skilled and unskilled workers and in these respects differed strikingly from all other categories. Natives who left the city closely resembled in-migrants; both contained a high concentration of professional workers. The in-migrants who had left at the time of follow-up contained by far the highest proportion of professional and managerial workers; the in-migrants who stayed, largely rural in-migrants, were similar to the native-born in the high proportion of skilled workers, but they contained a relatively low percentage of semi-skilled or unskilled workers and a corresponding excess of professional persons.

The out-migration material confirms the earlier analysis based on in-migration statistics in showing that mobility is part of the way of life of young professional people. Mobility is less common in the lower white-collar occupations where skills are less specialized and where local candidates are more readily available. At lower occupational levels, the position is more complex and the volume and character of occupational migration is relatively more affected, not only by personal and family factors, but also by the relationship between opportunities at the local and national level. Knowledge of the local context is consequently crucial to an understanding of the occupational drives towards migration; analysis on a national or even regional scale may, by an averaging process, conceal motivation.

Comparison with other sources on the relation between occupation and migration is complicated by differences in the way in which migration information is collected. Douglas,[6] in his sample drawn from children born throughout Great Britain in 1946, found that 4.5% of the families had emigrated (i.e. left the country) during the first 4 years of the inquiry; in a high proportion of these the parents were overseas nationals and others were members of the armed forces. Of the professional and salaried workers' families 6% emigrated compared with 1% of semi-skilled and unskilled workers. Excluding the emigrant families and an approximately equal proportion where children had died, he found that 32% of the remainder had made local moves which did not involve crossing administrative boundaries and 15% had crossed local boundaries (although only 4% had crossed regional ones). Those making local moves came more often than would be expected from among unskilled manual workers and agricultural workers and less often from the professional and salaried; the latter, however, were much more likely to move across local boundaries.

Jefferys, [10] in a survey of job-changing in Battersea and Dagenham restricted to men engaged in a manual, clerical or supervisory capacity in industry, found that in all the occupations covered, job-changing most frequently involved a change of working district. "Among skilled workers, who changed their occupation only infrequently, the object of district changes would appear to have been the desire to obtain work in which acquired skills would be of use; but among semi-skilled workers and, to an even greater extent, among laborers, willingness or ability to change the industry in which they worked and the type of work on which they were employed was greater than their readiness to change their district of work." She points out, however, that changes of working district in a conurbation such as London did not necessarily mean change of residence.

A report by Social Survey on depopulation and rural life in Scotland [19] published in 1949 which covered a sample of people who wished to migrate from three rural areas, including the North-east, found a markedly higher proportion of potential migrants in professional, white collar, and clerical occupations. Industrial classification revealed a rather higher than average proportion of potential migrants in national and local government, the building industry, and personal service industries, and a significantly lower proportion in agriculture.

Somewhat similar findings are provided by the Eire report on vital statistics for 1959 [4] which shows that 14% of the couples marrying in Eire during the year intended to live outside the state. The proportion varied from 30% for husbands classified as higher professionals, 21% for skilled manual workers, 15% for clerks, to 3% for farmers. It is also noted that average ages for both men and women intending to migrate were appreciably lower than for all marriages.

The Effect of Age on Class Migration Rates

The more educated upper and middle-class couples postpone marriage and child-bearing several years beyond the age customary among manual workers. At the time of interview, i.e., when expecting their first child they were, therefore, older, and had had, on the average, several more years in which to migrate. Does the higher migration rate of the upper social classes in this survey merely reflect their greater age or do they in fact move more than other groups of comparable age? Table 6 demonstrates that, in all except the youngest age groups, the class gradient in the percentage of in-migrants remains steep and consistent; in other words the higher migration rate of the upper social classes is not purely a function of their greater age at interview.

Within each class the percentage of in-migrants rises with age. The increase with age, however, is not due solely to the extra number of years at risk. Within each social class women having their first baby at different ages differ in other social respects so that to some extent each age-at-delivery group represents a class within a class. In each social class for example, women aged under 20 at delivery rank lowest in respect of their class of origin and educational level whilst those aged 25 or more rank highest. The effect of age *per se* is therefore over-stated to some extent in the rates given in Table 6.

The independent significance of occupational class is also demonstrated in Table 7 which shows, for each age-at-delivery group, the percentage of couples leaving the city within the subsequent 5 years. Again it is evident, that, within each age group, the higher the social class, the greater was the rate of out-migration. Among professional workers, and to a less extent the managerial, executive and technical groups, movement continued at a high, although declining, level among women aged 30 or more at delivery (35 or more at the time of follow-up). The higher total rate

TABLE 6. PER CENT IN-MIGRANTS IN EACH SOCIAL CLASS AND AGE-AT-DELIVERY GROUP

Husband's occupational class	Wife's age at first delivery				All ages
	16–19	20–24	25–29	30 and Over	
	Per cent in-migrant				
I	—	43	48	48	46 (315)
II	—	36	36	49	39 (733)
III Non-manual	19	20	28	34	24 (1196)
III Manual	12	18	24	30	20 (3762)
IV	9	14	22	21	15 (795)
V	12	13	19	24	15 (841)
All classes	13 (883)	19 (3951)	28 (2008)	36 (800)	22 (7642)

TABLE 7. PER CENT LEAVING CITY WITHIN 5 YEARS OF FIRST DELIVERY

Husband's occupational class	Wife's age at first delivery					All ages	
	16-19	20-24	25-29	30 and Over			
	Per cent out-migrant						
I	—	70	61	58		63	(75)
II	—	40	34	26		34	(134)
III Non-manual	—	18	22	20		19	(197)
III Manual	17	19	20	17		19	(717)
IV & V	8	13	6	13		10	(377)
All classes	13	19	23	24		20	(1500)
	(180)	(730)	(396)	(194)			

of out-migration among the older women reflects, of course, the higher representation of upper class groups at such ages. Even within the other classes, however, the rate does not fall with age despite the fact that one might expect older people to move less. It seems probable that this maintenance of the out-migration rate at a high level in classes I and II and at a constant level in classes III and V reflects, within each class, increasing social selection in that, as mentioned above, women having their first baby at later ages form a selected group atypical of their class.

In general, it is clear that the higher in-migration rate of the upper occupational groups does not merely reflect their older age-at-delivery, but is a true class difference. The rate of out-migration also increases with class irrespective of age.

References

1. BOGUE, D. J., *A Methodological Study of Migration and Labor Mobility in Michigan and Ohio in 1947*, Oxford, Ohio, Scripps Foundation Studies in Population Distribution No. 4, 1952.
2. BOGUE, D. J., *Population Growth in Standard Metropolitan Areas 1900–1950*, Washington, DC, Housing and Home Finance Agency, 1953.
3. BOGUE, D. J., and HAGOOD, J. M., *Subregional Migration in the United States 1935–1940. Differential Migration in the Corn and Cotton Belts*, Oxford, Ohio, Scripps Foundation Studies in Population Distribution No. 6, 1953.
4. CENTRAL STATISTICS OFFICE, *Report on Vital Statistics*, 1959, Dublin, Stationery Office.
5. DEPARTMENT OF HEALTH FOR SCOTLAND, *Depopulation in Rural Scotland*, HMSO, 1951.
6. DOUGLAS, J. W. B. and BLOMFIELD, J. M., *Children Under Five*, Allen & Unwin, London, 1958.
7. GOLDSTEIN, S., *Patterns of Social Mobility 1910–1960: The Morristown Study*, Philadelphia, University of Pennsylvania Press, 1958.
8. HAWLEY, A. H.: *The Changing Shape of Metropolitan America*. Free Press, Glencoe, Illinois, 1956.
9. ILLSLEY, R., Social background of first pregnancy, Ph.D. thesis, University of Aberdeen, 1956.
10. JEFFERYS, M., *Mobility in the Labour Market*, Routledge and Kegan Paul, London, 1954.
11. KISER, C. V., *Sea island to City: A Study of St. Helena Islanders in Harlem and Other Urban Centres*. New York, Columbia University Studies in History, Economics, and Public Law, No. 368, 1932.

12. KLINEBURG, O., *Negro Intelligence and Selective Migration*, New York Columbia University Press, 1935, Stillwater, Oklahoma Agricultural and Mechanical College, Agricultural Experiment Station Circular No. 88, May 1940.
13. LEE, E. S., Migration Differentials: Preliminary Revision of Research Memorandum (Prepared for Committee on Migration Differentials, Social Science Research Council, Unpublished, 1953).
14. NEWTON, M. P. and JEFFERY, J. R., *Internal Migration*, London, HMSO, 1951.
15. PRICE, D. O., Distance and direction as vectors of internal migration 1935 to 1940, *Social Forces*, **27** (Oct. 1948), 48–53.
16. ROWNTREE, J. S., *Internal Migration: A Study of the Frequency of Movement of Migrants*, HMSO, 1957.
17. SAVILLE, J., *Rural Depopulation in England and Wales, 1851–1951*, Dartington Hall Studies in Rural Sociology. Routledge and Kegan Paul, 1957.
18. SHRYOCK, H. S., The efficiency of internal migration in the United States, *Proceedings of the International Population Conference, Vienna, 1959*.
19. SOCIAL SURVEY, *Depopulation and Rural Life in Scotland* (Reports on Aberdeen and Banff, Tweed Valley, Solway Counties and Summary Report), HMSO, 1949.
20. THOMAS, B., *Migration and Economic Growth: A Study of Great Britain and the Atlantic Economy*, National Institute of Economic and Social Research, Economic and Social Studies XII. Cambridge, Cambridge University Press, 1954.
21. THOMAS, D. S., *Research Memorandum on Migration Differentials*, New York, Social Science Research Council Bulletin 43, 1938.
22. THOMPSON, W. S., *The Growth of Metropolitan Districts in the United States 1900–1940*, Washington, DC, Government Printing Office, 1947.
23. YOUNG, M. and WILMOTT, P., *Family and Kinship in East London*, London, Routledge and Kegan Paul, 1957.

Movements of the Population in the Birmingham Region

C. MOINDROT

IN THE 10 years between 1951 and 1961 the Midlands region, comprising Staffordshire, Warwickshire, Worcestershire, Herefordshire, and Shropshire, was the scene of large-scale movements of population. In the first place there was an influx of people from other regions of the British Isles and from overseas. Secondly, there was a levelling of densities inside the whole vast conurbation which spreads into the three eastern counties (Fig. 1) and takes in the City of Birmingham, the two huge urban districts to the east of the city—Solihull and Sutton Coldfield, and the Black Country, some twenty-one localities of varying administrative status to the north-west of Birmingham. Lastly, complex exchanges took place between the conurbation and the rest of the region, and between various districts in the region. All these movements are evidence of an active redistribution of people and their employment, a break in the demographic and industrial equilibrium inherited from the nineteenth century, and the pursuit of a new equilibrium.

1. Movements into the Region from Outside

In 10 years the population of the Midlands rose from 4,425,000 to 4,750,000. This is an overall increase of 7.2%, which is far higher than the national average of 5.1%. Only the south and east of England showed a higher rate. The adjoining North Midlands region, around the centres of Leicester and Nottingham, was much the same. The high rate is in part due to natural increase which

157

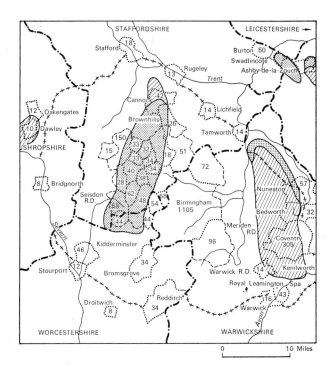

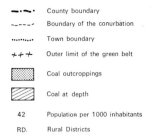

—·—··	County boundary
――――	Boundary of the conurbation
··········	Town boundary
+++	Outer limit of the green belt
▓	Coal outcroppings
▨	Coal at depth
42	Population per 1000 inhabitants
RD.	Rural Districts

Fig. 1. Birmingham and its environs.

also is higher than the national average on account of the immigration of young adults. The average decennial birth rate is relatively high—16.5/1000 (against 15.9/1000 in England and Wales)—and the mortality rate relatively low—10.6/1000 (England and Wales 11.5/1000). The difference between overall increase and natural increase is attributable to the net immigration of

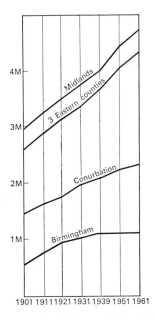

Fig. 2. Growth of the population, 1901–61.

60,000. This growth is not spread evenly over the five counties (Fig. 2). The three most populous and most industrialized counties have been growing fastest since the start of the century, and they now account for 91% of the population occupying 56% of the area in the region. The population of Warwickshire, now over 2 million, increased 8.7% in 10 years despite the levelling of the Birmingham curve. By contrast, the two rural counties, Shropshire and Herefordshire, have difficulty in maintaining their rather scanty population. Herefordshire, with 130,000 inhabitants, has a smaller population than the town of Wolverhampton, and density of population is no more than 23 per square mile—only 16 per square mile if the one town of any size, Hereford, is excluded. Its fine agricultural land has remained intact.

In actual fact immigration only affects the three eastern counties. People throng there in search of work. They may come from other parts of England, particularly the north, from Scotland, from Wales (following a tradition established several centuries ago), and from Ireland. Or else they may be citizens or dependents from the Commonwealth, especially West Indians. The latter number perhaps 80,000 when all children born in the region after their parents' arrival are included. Yet a shortage of manpower continues to be a permanent feature of the labour market. Whilst the population in the region rose by 7.2% between 1951 and 1961, the number of jobs rose by 10.2% (against the average for Great Britain of 7.1%). The number of unfilled jobs, therefore, is constantly higher than the number of unemployed. The demand for immigration continues to be renewed without constituting a threat to full employment—the very opposite, in fact, since the new industrial workers require services such as public transport, hospitals, restaurants, which in turn create jobs, while their children need additional schools. The shortage of teachers in Birmingham is so serious that the City Council has had to advertise in the national press. Since 1955 the regional rate of unemployment has fallen as low as 0.4%. The highest figure of 2.2% occurred only during the economic recession, in the autumn of 1958, which had a particularly serious effect on the car industry. The 1960 average was less than 1%. In England and Wales as a whole the rate varied between 0.9% and 2.8%, with a 1960 average of 1.6%. In Scotland and Northern Ireland figures are much higher.

Owing to the abundance of mechanical industries, wages in the region are above the national average. The attraction of high wages to a large extent compensates newcomers for the recognized difficulty of finding accommodation. In addition, far-sighted parents take into consideration the fact that Birmingham has a large number of technical schools of all levels where their children will get a sound education, perhaps even an engineering degree. It is only after they arrive that they discover that the few vacancies in overcrowded schools are keenly contested. Furthermore, Birmingham is reputed to be a city where hard work leads to success. This belief is strengthened by the memory of Joseph Chamberlain and by sayings learnt in childhood, such as "Birmingham's a city of a thousand and one trades"; "With courage and £10 in the pocket you can make a fortune in Birmingham"; "Go and try your luck in Birmingham, my lad".

There is one basic reason for this reputation and the high wages, low levels of unemployment and long columns of "situations vacant" in the local press: that is the exceptionally wide range of industries in most of the towns within the conurbation. Wise[1] notes that among "towns of about 1,000,000 population" Birmingham probably holds the world record for the diversification of its industries. By way of example the following is a partial list of products manufactured in the town of Wolverhampton (population 150,000): aeroplanes, trolleybuses, automobile parts and chassis, lorries, bicycles, wagons, landaus; cisterns, tanks, boilers, baths and cans; metal hangars, cranes and lathes; garden tools, dairying equipment, household tools; screws, bolts, nails, springs; bedsteads; bronze objects; corrugated iron; refrigerators, lamps, radio-sets; safes; toys; cement, tiles, bricks, pipes, enamel ware; furniture; tyres; straps, shoes; soaps, paints, oxygen; medicines; animal feedstuffs; artificial eyes. Moreover, this range of industrial products does not cover such local specialization as locks, keys, and safes at Willenhall and Wednesfield; marine chains and anchors at Cradley, Rowley Regis, and Dudley; carpets at Kidderminster; crystal at Stourbridge; jewellery and guns in Birmingham, etc. The Ministry of Economic Affairs is well aware of the close connection between business prosperity, full employment, and immigration, on the one hand, and industrial diversification on the other. In their drive to revitalize other regions hit by unemployment and depopulation (South Wales, Scotland, Northumberland, Northern Ireland), they are endeavouring above all to introduce industries that are foreign to the local industrial traditions.

One further factor contributes to the prosperity of the region and its attraction to immigrants. This is the large number of companies offering jobs to both sexes, to suit all tastes and skills, and with good chances of re-employment should a crisis hit a particular sector of the economy. Seeing the profusion of small businesses, the newcomer can visualize the day when he, too, will set up on his own. In a study published in 1958, but based on the registers of HM Factory Inspectors dating back to 1948, Johnson[2] records 10,097 workshops and factories in the conurbation alone. Of these 9183 employed fewer than 100 workers, while accounting for more than 30% of the labour force of 570,000. Only 187 factories had more than 500 workers and eight more than 5000. The highest figure is for the Austin car factory, at Longbridge in the extreme south of Birmingham, which employs 20,000. At the other end of the scale, Wise refers to a "firm" in the jewellery district of Birmingham which at the time of the survey consisted of two old ladies engaged in contract work. In fact, the small business is the rule in the two long-established specialized trades of central Birmingham. Of the two, the jewellery trade is still flourishing, but the manufacture of sporting guns has almost ceased. There is, of course, less information available about the structure of industry outside the conurbation. The average size of business there is naturally somewhat larger, but the small workshop still has its place. For example, in the Rural District of Meriden, between Birmingham and Coventry, numerous small workshops have started up since 1945, mostly to manufacture automobile parts and precision instruments.

Except in large companies such as Austin, Rover, Singer (automobiles), or Cadbury (cocoa and chocolate), vertical integration is not well advanced. Factories and workshops are therefore extremely interdependent. A new business has an excellent chance of finding a ready supply of raw materials or semi-pro-

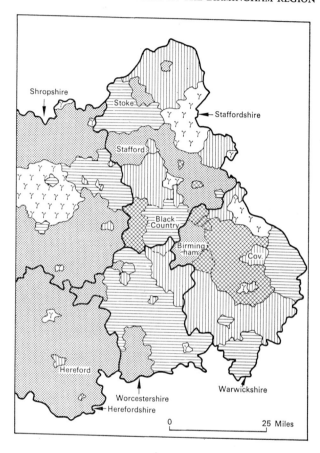

Approximate growth 1951-1961

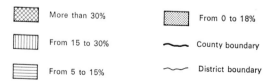

	More than 30%		From 0 to 18%
	From 15 to 30%		County boundary
	From 5 to 15%		District boundary

FIG. 3. Approximate growth, 1951–61 (by counties).

cessed materials and often even a market for its finished products or components. While the region is a magnet for all types of workers, it is equally attractive therefore to employers. New arrivals create new jobs in their turn, and so it goes on. Most of the employers, who are new to the region and are thinking of setting up in business there, express a preference for Birmingham. As we shall see later, this preference is less and less likely to be satisfied. Instead they are having to be content with a neighbouring town or village. Birmingham, therefore, is static (-0.6% in 10 years), the conurbation as whole is increasing gradually ($+4.5\%$), while the three eastern counties are developing more rapidly ($+11.8\%$). All but one of the districts on the periphery of the conurbation have gained more than 15% in 10 years (Fig. 3). This is because they are at the meeting point of two converging population flows. One is moving in from outside to get as close as possible to the conurbation, while the other is leaving the conurbation in search of a less densely populated suburb. The three eastern counties, therefore, are benefiting from Birmingham's prestige and expansion, but to the other two counties, which are too far away, this same attraction is proving to be a drawback.

2. Movements within the Conurbation

Of the seven British conurbations defined in the 1951 census, the Midlands is the only one to record any appreciable increase in population, rising from 2,237,000 in 1951 to 2,344,000 in 1961. Glasgow, Newcastle, Yorkshire, Manchester and Liverpool remained static and London declined. Natural increase is roughly the same as for the entire Midlands area, 6/1000 as against 5.9/1000, and exceeds the total increase. The conurbation thus follows the general trend whereby emigration exceeds immigration by 32,000.[3] According to Eversley and Jackson,[4] 80,000 people have left Birmingham and a further 40,000 the Black Country, in particular Wolverhampton and Smethwick. This suggests an inward migration to the conurbation of about 90,000 in 10 years —an uncomfortable situation for the local authorities since it means that slum clearance and the acute housing shortage are failing to discourage immigrants.

Population densities are very unevenly distributed (Fig. 4). Along the industrial north-west–south-east axis from Wolverhampton to Birmingham densities exceed 12 and sometimes 15 to the acre. The highest figures are in Smethwick, with 27, and in certain isolated districts of the central Birmingham area, with 40 per acre. In sharp contrast are the outskirts in the south-west,

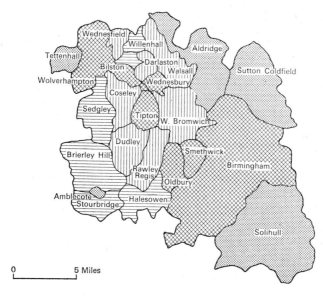

0   5 Miles

Densities in 1961

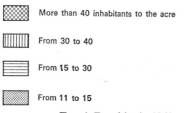

More than 40 inhabitants to the acre

From 30 to 40

From 15 to 30

From 11 to 15

FIG. 4. Densities in 1961.

north-east, and south-east where, in places like Amblecote and
Solihull, densities are as low as 5 per acre. The areas to the south of
Solihull and east of Sutton Coldfield have retained their semi-
rural landscape, which has resulted in their inclusion in the urban
green belt. Visitors accustomed to continental levels of urban
density find nothing discreditable in such figures. To them the
streets seem wide and straight, the houses low, and open-space
provisions excellent. They are seldom conscious of any overcrowding. The Department of the Seine, for example, covers an
area of 185 square miles, whereas the Birmingham conurbation,
with only half the population, occupies 269 square miles. On the
other hand, what will be noticed are the monotonous rows of
brick houses, the scarcity of trees and parkland, except in a few
wealthy residential districts like Edgbaston in Birmingham, the
sight of quarries in the middle of towns (marl at Oldbury, dolerite
at Rowley Regis), and, lastly, the presence in industrial zones of
dwellings, workshops, and traffic routes. Yet a big effort has been
made to achieve a more balanced distribution of population
within the conurbation. Figures 4 and 5 show clearly that the
population of the towns with the heaviest densities—Birmingham,
Wolverhampton, Tipton, Bilston, Wednesbury, Smethwick—
declined between the last two censuses (by 7.6% in Wolverhampton and more than 10% in Smethwick). In contrast the low
density peripheral towns are gaining rapidly—Solihull by 41%,
Sutton Coldfield 51%, Aldridge 75%, Wednesfield 89%, Tettenhall 91%. But a balance has not yet been reached (see Fig. 4).

The merging of relatively overcrowded towns can be explained
by the large-scale development projects, in particular the Birmingham schemes, which will certainly prove to be one of the main
attractions at the 20th International Geography Congress. As
the chief town of the region Birmingham has a triple task to
perform. First, to speed up motor traffic—two wide, concentric
boulevards will cut through the central area. The inner one, the
inner ring road, was started in 1957 and, when completed in 1969,
will be nearly 4 miles long and will have cost about £24 million.
The first stretch of nearly 900 yards has been in use since March

1960. It has three lanes in each direction and parking space on either side. Construction of this arterial route involved the compulsory purchase of 80 acres of built-up land and demolition of numerous premises, some of them still in good condition, in which 8000 people were housed. In the same way many acres of built-up land will have to be sacrificed to the outer boulevard. Naturally the City of Birmingham and its enterprising chief architect, Sir Herbert Manzoni, are anxious to find accommodation outside the town for the population overspill so that road construction work need not be held up.

The second task facing the city is the clearance of five small blocks erected before 1870 just outside the central area and within a radius of 1–2 miles of the Anglican Cathedral. Densities exceed 40 to the acre, and industry and housing are too closely interwoven, not just in the same district, but often in the same building. In some cases up to four craft industries are carried out in the same three-storey house; or else workshops and dwellings face each other across a small courtyard, which is not much better. Work is already well advanced in the Newton block near the jewellery quarter where well-spaced apartment blocks of varying heights are being built to the standards laid down for "new towns". Even the network of roads has been completely redesigned. For these schemes about 160 acres will have to be evacuated.

Finally, slum clearance is going ahead in other areas as, for example, to the north-east of Snow Hill station, where the ancient gun quarter is shortly to disappear. In the town as a whole 1000 slums are cleared each year, but in 1961 25,000 still remain. In 10 years' time the entire centre will have been completely redeveloped. By then the old Birmingham will be the ring built between 1870 and 1914, which lies between the remodelled centre and the peripheral districts developed for the most part between the wars.

The decrease in acreage allotted to housing has a further cause. Conscious of the fact that it owes its prosperity to industry and that the general tendency is to increase the amount of floor space per worker, the city agreed to a 25 % increase in land for industrial use, but the Ministry of Economic Affairs later intervened and reduced this figure to 18%. Slum workshops as well as decayed houses are currently being demolished. Johnson[2] refers to an area of about 250 acres in the jewellery quarter which houses no less than 923 undertakings, some of them occupying what used to be the maid's room. To rehouse them the municipal authorities are buying up all vacant industrial property and putting up new buildings. None of this is, however, available to new immigrants. The same situation arises in all big towns, especially in London, since it is thought better to lose population, which is a source of expenditure, than to lose industries which are a source of revenue for the local accounts.

The authorities have succeeded in rehousing part of the over-spill forced out by new development, either in barely finished apartment blocks in the city centre, or in those shooting up rapidly on the outskirts, such as the group of twelve-storey blocks at Erdington. Tall buildings, though rare before 1950, now form a considerable part of the skyline. It is possible for the badly housed in districts not affected by reconstruction to obtain other accommodation. Except in cases of emergency, however, they have to wait an average of 8 years. In 1956 the city opened an Overspill Housing Register where those prepared to leave the city may put down their names and seek advice on housing con-ditions in the Black Country or elsewhere in the Midlands. By 1960 some 4600 people had left the city under the scheme, while there were still 6200 names on the register. New tenants quickly took over the accommodation left vacant, but it is only a stop-gap solution.

The problem can be reduced to the following terms: land set aside for housing is diminishing; land for workshops and factories has got to increase; on the other hand, although the population is declining slightly, the number of jobs has risen by 10% in 10 years. Along the inner ring road and the districts under recon-struction large blocks are already going up to provide office space for banks, insurance companies, official organizations, administrative services for industrial firms, etc.

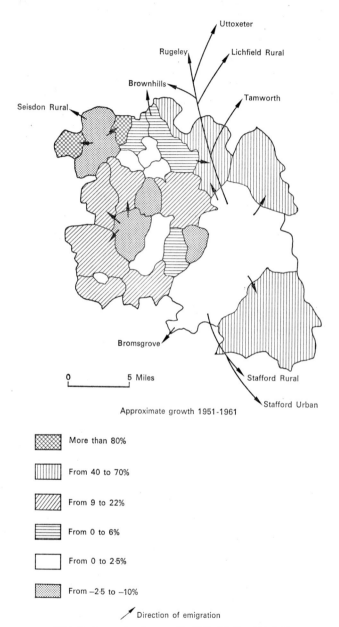

Uttoxeter

Rugeley

Lichfield Rural

Brownhills

Tamworth

Seisdon Rural

Bromsgrove

Stafford Rural

Stafford Urban

0 5 Miles

Approximate growth 1951-1961

More than 80%

From 40 to 70%

From 9 to 22%

From 0 to 6%

From 0 to 2·5%

From −2·5 to −10%

Direction of emigration

FIG. 5. Approximate growth, 1951–61 (by districts).

In Birmingham alone it is forecast that between 1961 and 1971 an additional 40,000 office jobs will be created. The only solution lies in lengthening the journey to work and accepting the commuting which this entails. The highest paid workers have solved the problem by moving out to Sutton Coldfield, Solihull, and the Rural District of Meriden, and driving to and from work. They are encountering stiff resistance, however, from the Staffordshire County authorities who wish to preserve the green belt separating Coventry from the conurbation and are very reluctant to grant building permission. [5] Nevertheless the population of the Meriden district has increased from 38,000 to 57,000 in 10 years.

For those not so well off, Birmingham is either building dwellings on land owned by other authorities (e.g. on the Kingshurst Hall Estate in Meriden), or else it is offering financial aid to such authorities to build for them (Aldridge, for example). In much the same way workers from Wolverhampton are moving towards Tettenhall and Wednesfield, and workers in Dudley towards Coseley, Sedgley, or Brierley Hill, where they occupy dwellings newly erected by the local council or by private enterprise (Fig. 5).

3. Movements Between the Conurbation and the Rest of the Region

From an early stage the large councils were obliged to look beyond the boundaries of the conurbation for a solution to their problems. They made use of facilities afforded under the Town Development Act of 1952 under which a receiving authority and an exporting authority reach agreement, the Government will pay 50% of removal and installation costs. Negotiations between the two councils are often quite tough. It is useless for the small receiving district to say "Your overcrowding and your large works are proof of your prosperity". In its turn the large exporting town can merely appeal to regional solidarity. More often than not it is Goliath who must accept David's terms and pay the interest on loans obtained for the construction of the dwellings and also pay a subsidy for a number of years on each unit completed. Birmingham City has had to set up a miniature "Ministry of Foreign Affairs" to handle negotiations with more than a hundred different authorities, some of them, like March in the Fen District, a fair distance away. By 1960 only thirty-three of them had agreed to build a total of 8000 dwellings by 1966. Of these the most co-operative were Tamworth (1700 dwellings), Lichfield (1200), Brownhills, Cannock, Rugeley, and the rural districts of Stafford, Uttoxeter, etc. Wolverhampton has entered into similar agreements with Seisdon Rural District, for example, which has promised 1500 dwellings, and likewise Walsall has made an arrangement with Brownhills. However, it often happens that months of discussions lead to the construction of no more than ten dwellings. Here, again, results seem to fall far short of requirements.

As far as the problem of overspill is concerned the Midlands conurbation ranks third in England, after London and Manchester. It is estimated that 300,000 dwellings will be needed between 1961 and 1981, two-thirds to cope with present overspill and one-third with immigration, which cannot be halted, and with the children born of British and West Indian parents just after the war who are now reaching adulthood. No doubt it will be possible to build 200,000 dwellings within the conurbation, particularly on the north-east and south-west fringes, but a further 100,000 will still be needed, either inside or, better still, beyond the green belt. Planners are therefore convinced that the Conservative Act of 1952 is inadequate. They prefer Labour's New Towns Act of 1946. They will soon win their case, of course, when the first New Town in the Midlands is built at Dawley in Shropshire. Its benefits will be twofold: it will absorb part of the overspill from the conurbation and will help to revive a declining county. The regional branch of the Town and Country Planning Association has been studying other potential sites for further new towns.

One of the main causes of the poor results obtained to date is the lack of co-ordination in schemes to reduce densities and to decentralize industries. The one is the responsibility of the local authorities, the other—at least where factories and the larger workshops are concerned—that of the Ministry for Economic Affairs. Yet some progress has been made since 1955. The councils of three industrial counties and Birmingham City Council have formed a joint consultative committee to examine the overall problem posed by overspill to the extent that it affects the movement of population and industry, and to adopt appropriate methods to solve it and allied problems. The county councils are taking stock of industrial land at their disposal, whilst Birmingham is endeavouring to steer to such land those industrialists from other regions who are wanting to set up in the city. Birmingham claims to have turned away over 2,900,000 square feet of industrial accommodation between 1956 and 1960, and, since 1945, by this and other similar means, the city has heroically turned away 25,000 jobs.

Businesses, however, are not enthusiastic about moving away from the conurbation. They may decide to move for a variety of reasons—the scarcity or exorbitant price of building sites, unsuitability of old premises for modern machinery, traffic congestion which hinders loading and unloading of lorries, lack of manpower, or disappearance of their premises at the hands of demolition gangs in redevelopment zones. Some of them are tempted by the advantages offered by the Minister for Economic Affairs to those willing to move to development districts,* that is to regions with a high level of unemployment. In a survey of 200 firms which have left Birmingham or plan to do so shortly, Loasby found only thirteen had selected South Wales, inadequate communications and distance from the markets being severe handicaps. Two of these were forced to close down and one has returned in part to the Midlands. The majority prefer to move only a short distance: 64 chose Staffordshire, 22 Warwickshire, 21 Worcestershire, thus ensuring that they would retain close contact with clients, suppliers, bankers, etc. Aldridge, right on the doorstep of Birmingham, has taken twenty-one firms. Fre-

* The "development districts" have been known as "depressed areas", "special areas", "development areas", before assuming their present name in 1960.

quently these companies avoid moving to the other side of town—
those in the northern districts move north, those in the south
move south. Unfortunately, key workers, and especially their
wives, are loath to follow their companies if they like the house
they are living in. These firms are so afraid of losing them that
they continue to pay them full wages during periods, admittedly
short and infrequent, of economic recession. And in order to
retain them after the firm has moved, they organize coaches to
fetch them from town in the mornings. These coaches meet the
public transport buses taking people into town from the suburbs.
Generally speaking the growing use of cars, combined with a
higher standard of living and the keen interest which workers in
industry have in car engines, and the longer journey to work,
create serious traffic and parking problems. At the moment parking lots are large and numerous, but they will shortly have to
yield to building construction. For the future the answer seems to
be to construct more multi-storey car parks, like the new one
along the inner ring road, near the Bull Ring.

Both workers who are persuaded to leave the conurbation and
new immigrants looking for work, try to find a home not too far
from their job. This is why the greatest increase in population has
been in close lying districts (Fig. 3), notably the rural districts of
Warwick (+ 33%), Meriden (+ 51%), and, above all, Seisdon
(+ 70%). The increase is less marked in Worcestershire the further
one goes from the conurbation. Coventry's influence in Warwickshire has not been very considerable, since reconstruction of
the town has made large numbers of new dwellings available.
Staffordshire has a central band declining demographically, with
emigration southwards to Birmingham and northwards, though to
a lesser extent, to the Potteries. Finally, as we have seen, the
conurbation already exerts a negative influence on the two
western counties, particularly Herefordshire, which has few towns,
whilst part of Shropshire's rural population is moving toward
small local towns. Birmingham's image is that of a big capital,
like Paris and even London, attracting population from afar and
redistributing it in the immediate neighbourhood.

All these population movements make of the conurbation a real urban unity. Present administrative divisions appear more and more outdated and artificial. In the recent past Birmingham has annexed numerous villages in which the nucleus can still be recognized about the parish church, as, for example, Northfield or King's Norton. A commission set up to study local government reform in the Black Country recommended in a report published in 1960 that five county boroughs centred on Wolverhampton, Dudley, Walsall, West Bromwich, and Smethwick, should replace the twenty-one local authorities now in being. Local patriotism however dies hard, especially in Bilston (see *The Guardian*, 8 July 1961). However, it is long odds that the Government, which is currently studying the project, will adopt the majority of the commission's recommendations. Beyond the conurbation, Burton—which has had a maximum population of 50,000 since the start of the century, and Worcester which has only 65,000 inhabitants—are in danger of losing their county borough status and of being relegated to the more modest rank of municipal borough. As for Birmingham, it continues to play the leading role in an active conurbation. Its City Council is worthy successor to the one over which J. Chamberlain presided. In a few years' time, however, the juxtaposition of Victorian and Manzonian architecture in central Birmingham may not perhaps be to everybody's liking. The decline in Birmingham's population is not indicative of a crisis—on the contrary, its demographic and economic expansion into the Midlands region is growing and intensifying.

Note on the term "overspill". This word has now passed into everyday speech, although to many it sounds inhuman and is characteristic of the arrogance of planners. It creates an image of liquid overflowing from its vessel.

Borg has given the following definitions of the verb and noun:

> *to overspill:* to organize the movement of a significant number of people from territory under one planning authority to dwellings on that under another;

the overspill: the sector of the population thus treated or who hope to be so treated.

References

1. WISE, M. J., On the evolution of the jewellery and gun quarters in Birmingham, *Institute of British Geographers, Transactions and Papers*, 1949.
2. JOHNSON, B. L. C., The distribution of factory population in the West Midlands Conurbation, *ibid.*, 1958.
3. MOINDROT, C., Premiers resultats du recensement britannique de 1961, *Population*, 1961, p. 522.
4. EVERSLEY, D. E. C. and VALERIE JACKSON, Population, employment and housing trends in the West Midlands, *Town and Country Planning*, Aug. 1961.
5. MOINDROT, C., Un essai de planification du paysage, les zones vertes des villes britanniques, *Annales de Géographie*, 1961, p. 585.
6. BORG, N., Overspill—a short study of the essentials, *Journal of the Town Planning Institute*, May 1961.
7. *Census 1961, England and Wales, Preliminary Report.*
8. LOASBY, B., The experience of West Midlands industrial dispersal projects, *ibid.*, Aug. 1961.
9. RAWSTORNE, P., Report on Birmingham, *Architectural Design*, Oct. 1960.
10. *Report of the Ministry of Housing and Local Government, 1959.*
11. STEDMAN, M. G., The townscape of Birmingham in 1956, *ibid.*, 1958.
12. STEPHENSON, B. L., Planning of the Birmingham–Coventry green belt, *Journal of the Institution of Municipal Engineers*, Aug. 1959.
13. THE MIDLANDS NEW TOWN SOCIETY, *The Overspill Problem in the West Midlands*, 1958.
14. THE WEST MIDLAND GROUP, *Conurbation: A Planning Survey of Birmingham and the Black Country*, 1948.
15. TOWN AND COUNTRY PLANNING ASSOCIATION, The West Midlands region policy statement, *ibid.*, Oct. 1961.

France

The Growing Population of Paris

Regional Origin—Social Composition—Attitudes and Motivation

Presentation of a Survey by I.N.E.D. and the Préfecture de la Seine

G. POURCHER

THE growth of the population of Paris is a most striking development, full of implications. Opinions differ from the outset even as
to the desirability of this movement or of its present pace, and
biased and emotional viewpoints often prevail.

Moreover, when the complex problems of adaptation posed by
this growth come to be tackled, debates are too often inspired by
rough and ready ideas. As in so many other fields, grave errors are
committed or risked for lack of adequate knowledge of the subject.
It is only this knowledge which can render debates and decisions
fully effective.

INED has already published a full retrospective study of the
formation of the population of Paris.[1] This time we went on to
analyse the mechanism of concentration. As it was concerned for
the most part with individual decisions, this research required
first of all general qualitative information, as complete as possible,
on the migrants pouring into the capital from the provinces. We
were subsequently able to research into the motives which influenced the migrants, as well as their plans for the future, especially
any possible departures from Paris at the end of their working life.

---

[1] Louis Chevalier, *La Formation de la population parisienne au XIXe siécle*,
Travaux et documents de l'INED, No. 10, Paris, PUF, 1950.

Scientific knowledge on these various points was virtually non-existent. This is why we undertook an extensive investigation of representative samples. In this we had the collaboration of the Préfecture de la Seine, and financial help was accorded to us by the Conseil Municipal de Paris and the Conseil Général de la Seine.

A résumé of the entire report of the survey is published in the third number in 1963 of the review *La Conjoncture économique dans le département*, edited by the Préfecture de la Seine. This report provides the material for a book which is now in press and is due to appear within the next few months.[2]

In this article, M. Guy Pourcher, research director at INED, presents the main findings.

Objectives of the Research

In the course of the last 10 years more than 100,000 migrants from the provinces have flocked to Paris every year, creating problems of shortage everywhere: housing, various collective facilities, roads, water, and so on.

Independently of all other research, whether statistical measurement of the migratory flow towards Paris, or financial and economic assessments of the cost of growth, our object was to distinguish the various components of the migratory movement.

We wanted to know who the provincials were who were coming to settle in Paris, how and why they made the decision to come, their subsequent situation, and their plans for the future—in short, we wanted to build up a picture of their personal history. We tried equally to ascertain the migrants' impressions of their experience and the opinions they had formed of life in Paris.

The complementary aspect of emigration to the provinces was examined through the migrants' future intentions. As many people leave Paris on retirement, a study of plans being made in view of retirement is particularly significant here. This observation

[2] G. Pourcher, *Le Peuplement de Paris*, Paris, Presses Universitaires de France, 1964, 310 pp.

is really a continuation of the first; the question was whether the intentions of people who had come to Paris were the same in this respect as those of Parisians by origin.

Urbanization is a worldwide development which is far from complete. Nevertheless, our country of France provides an example of particular interest on account of its traditionally very centralized organization of space, and its agriculture, which has always occupied a position of prime importance in our national activity. While England and Germany possess a number of cities which act as metropolises, France has only one, and internal migration has been spontaneously directed towards Paris, which has thus drained a great part of the nation's vital force.

1. Carrying out the Survey

THE SAMPLE

Representative samples were taken from two distinct sectors of the population: on the one hand, the inhabitants of the greater Paris area, aged 21–60 and born in the provinces, thus excluding immigrants of foreign origin whose arrival in France involves special motives; additionally, in view of the projected study of intentions of moving away on retirement, the survey included persons living in Paris and its suburbs, aged 50–60, irrespective of their place of birth.

The sample was made up as follows: firstly, a random selection was made of 34 *quartiers* of Paris and 51 suburban *communes*, after a preliminary stratification based on the socio-professional character and rate of growth of each one of these districts. Secondly, a random selection was made of people inscribed on the electoral lists of the *communes or quartiers* being sampled.[3] This selection was confined to the sectors of the population to be studied, and was made in such a way that the ratio of the sample

---

[3] *Arrondissement* is a ward of Paris proper. *Quartier* also implies a district in the city of Paris. *Commune* is roughly equivalent to a municipality, and refers to the suburbs. A *département* is the largest administrative division of France, roughly equivalent to the English county.

was 1/175 for the migrant population and 1/350 for the population of people aged 50–60. In this way a sample was made up comprising 6,627 names.

A hundred interviewers were sent out in the second and third quarters of 1961 to visit the people on the sample list and submit to them a detailed questionnaire.

The interviewers were favourably received in 81 % of cases. Nevertheless, many of the migrants could not be located because of imperfections in the drawing up of the electoral lists, which only register changes of address after a time lag.

The definitive analysis deals with information contained in 4,442 documents, some of the questionnaires having been set aside to balance the different sample ratios.

THE QUESTIONNAIRE

A single survey document was drawn up which made it possible to reconstruct the biography of the people observed; it includes both factual questions, requiring simple answers, and more general questions, the answers to which, in simplified form, bring in more detailed and extensive information. A place was reserved for the examination of the opinions or judgements of those questioned, on their successive moves and on living conditions in Paris.

The text of the questions is given below. The questionnaire is reproduced *in extenso* and as set out originally, together with all useful indications for conducting the interview, in the full report of the survey.

1. FAMILY CIRCUMSTANCES
   Where were you born?
   What is your date of birth?
   What are your family circumstances?
   In what year did you marry?

2. CHANGE OF RESIDENCE
   Can you tell me the successive places where you have lived since your birth, and at what age or in what year you changed your residence?

3. ORIGIN

What is your father's occupation?
In what *département* were your parents born?
How many children were there in the family, including yourself?
What was your position in the family?

4. EDUCATION

What is the last school or teaching establishment which you attended as a pupil or student?
Was it a primary school, a higher primary school, or an establishment of technical, secondary, or further education?
How old were you when you left?
What are your qualifications?
Have you had specialized training, for instance in an apprenticeship centre, a factory or with a craftsman?
What form did this take, and how long did it last? Give details.

5. WORK

What, very precisely, is your present occupation?
Have you had others?
What were they, and when did you change your occupation?

6. ARRIVAL IN THE PARISIAN REGION

Can you tell me in a few words the circumstances and the reasons for your settling in the Parisian region?

7. CONNECTIONS WITH PARIS

Before settling in the Parisian region, had you already been to Paris?
How many times?
For what reasons?
Before settling there, did you know anyone there capable of helping you?
Who?
Were you advised to move to the Parisian region?
Who advised you? Give details.

8. EMPLOYMENT OR OCCUPATION IN PLACE OF ORIGIN

What did you do at . . .?
For those who had paid employment
Was your job well-paid, averagely paid, poorly paid or very poorly paid?
Were you in any way in danger of losing your job?
Could you have found another job at . . .?
What were your reasons for deciding to leave your job?
For those who had no particular fixed work or employment
Did you look for work or a job at . . . before coming to the Parisian region?
What type of work were you looking for?
Why did you not find any?

9. First Job in the Parisian Region

Did you take a job straight away on arriving in the Parisian region?
Were you certain of getting this job beforehand, or did you find it immediately after arriving?
How long were you looking for a job?
Did you choose this job from among others equally possible?
Give details of this first job.
Did you earn much more, a little more, as much as or less than at . . .?
Is life in the Parisian region dearer, as dear or less dear than at . . .?
What makes you think so?

10. Accommodation on Arrival and Electoral Enrolment

Where did you stay on your arrival in the Parisian region?—Give details.
How long did you occupy this first accommodation?
In what *arrondissement* of Paris or what suburban *commune* were you enrolled for the first time on an electoral list for the Parisian region after your first arrival?
In what year?

11. Connections with the Region of Origin

Do you return very often, sometimes, rarely, or not at all to your old part of the country?
Have you still got parents, family, friends, or a house there?
Did you spend your holidays there last summer?

12. Connections with Other Newcomers

Would you advise anyone from your region of France to leave it and come to the Parisian region?
Why?
Since your arrival, are there people among your circle of friends who have come, like you, to settle in the Parisian region?
Have you helped any to settle there or find work there?
Give some details of their motives for coming here, the way they are related to you, and, if applicable, the ways in which you helped them.

13. Motives for Coming

You have already explained to me the reasons for your settling in the Parisian region. But could you now indicate in a more detailed way, which of the following motives have contributed to your decision, and may also account for your coming here?
I. *Motives connected with the family*
    1. To marry somebody living in the Parisian region.
    2. To bring up the children: study, professional training, etc.
    3. As a consequence of some development within the family: death, divorce, a birth, illness, estrangement, etc.
    4. Wanted to be nearer to members of the family already living in the Parisian region.

5. No motive connected with the family played any part in the decision.

II. *Motives connected with living conditions*

6. Desire for change—boredom—no taste for life in the country or in a small town.
7. Attracted by Paris—by its opportunities for entertainment—by the more pleasant life there—wanted to meet interesting people.
8. None of these motives played a part in the decision.

III. *Motives connected with work*

9. Assigned, nominated, or transferred to the Parisian region.
10. Pursuit of studies—professional training.
11. Without work in the provinces—no job available—was unable to provide for his own or his family's needs.
12. Although not in danger of being out of work, wanted to improve his situation—earn more money—have better prospects for the future—take up a more important post.
13. No motive connected with work played a part in the decision.
Can you now tell me which of the above motives was the most important for you? The next most important? And the next after that?

14. DIFFICULTIES IN THE PARISIAN REGION

Did you get used to life in Paris easily?
Give some details of your first impressions.
Since being in the Parisian region, have you encountered any particular difficulties in connection with the following: accommodation, work or employment, shortage of money, isolation or loneliness, leisure pursuits or amusements, health, or other difficulties?
Give more details of the difficulties you have met with.
Lastly, do you think that your life in the Parisian region is better, the same, or not so good as if you had stayed in the provinces?
What makes you think that?

15. HUSBAND OR WIFE

Where was your husband or wife born?
What is his or her date of birth?
Where did he or she live before you were married?
What is his or her profession?
In what year and at what age did your husband or wife settle in the Parisian region for the first time?
What were the reasons and the circumstances? Give details.

16. CHILDREN

Have you any children?
How many?
Will you tell me their age, their sex, where they live, and, for children over 14, their occupation or present form of study?

17. ACCOMMODATION

In what capacity do you occupy your accommodation?
Since what year have you occupied it?
How did you obtain it?
When was the block of flats built in which you live?
Not counting the kitchen, how many rooms do you have?
Is there a separate kitchen?
Who lives in this accommodation?
In your opinion, is your accommodation satisfactory, acceptable, inadequate, or very inadequate?
Why?

18. FUTURE INTENTIONS

Do you intend to leave the Parisian region one day?

For those who intend to leave the Parisian region

What are your reasons, and when do you plan to leave?
In what place or region would you like to settle?
Have you already made arrangements for leaving?
What are they?
When you leave your present accommodation, who will have the use of it?

For those who do not intend to leave the Parisian region

Could you tell me exactly why you intend to stay in the Parisian region?
While remaining in the Parisian area, do you intend to move one day?
What are your reasons, and when do you intend to do so?
What suburban *commune* or quarter of Paris would you like to live in?
Have you already made arrangements for the move?
What arrangements?
When you leave your present accommodation, who will have the use of it?

19. RETIREMENT

When do you intend to retire?
On retirement, do you think you will continue with some sort of paid work?
What work? What are your reasons? Give some details.

20. DISPOSITIONS AND OPINIONS

Generally speaking, do you consider living conditions to be better in the country, in a small provincial town, in a large provincial town, or in Paris?
What are, in your opinion, the main advantages of life in the Parisian region?
What are the principal disadvantages?
In your opinion, which are more important all in all, the advantages or the disadvantages?

Is it desirable in your opinion that the population of the Parisian region should increase, decrease or stay the same?
In your opinion, what should be done to prevent the population of the Parisian region from increasing?

THE FIVE GROUPS STUDIED

The people whom we questioned were classsified in five groups.

1. *Recent Migrants*

These are residents in Paris or its suburbs who were born in the provinces and settled in the Parisian region after 1944, on their own, and not following their parents there, but being of an age to make a decision arising out of personal choice. Study of the migratory movement towards Paris is based essentially upon the information obtained from this group.

2. *Long-standing Migrants*

These also came to the Parisian area independently of their original family, but before 1945. Nevertheless, many migrants in this category who came to Paris at an advanced age have either died or have gone back to the provinces, thus escaping observation. Consequently, group 2 imperfectly represents the totality of provincials arriving before 1945, although it is fully representative of those migrants still present in the Parisian area at the time of the survey.

3. *Migrants Arriving in Childhood*

Many of those questioned came to Paris at an age when they were not in a position to decide their own future. Having arrived with their parents, they are usually unable to give precise information about the circumstances of their arrival. For this reason they were studied separately.

4. *People Aged* 50–60, *Born in the Parisian Area*

This group, like the following one, was originally intended to give information about projected moves to the provinces. But it has also made it possible to compare in this respect the situation of Parisians born in the provinces and Parisians by birth. In this way, further light is often shed on the study of the migratory movement itself.

5. *People Aged* 50–60, *Born in the Provinces*

For the most part, this group is made up of provincials arriving before 1945 or accompanied by relatives. A certain number of these people were also included in the sample of migrants.

To sum up, the analysis distinguishes the five samples represented in Table 1.

TABLE 1.

	Number of people
Recent migrants	1470
Long-standing migrants	726
Migrants arriving in childhood	934
Total number of migrants	3130
People aged 50–60, born in the Parisian area	497
People aged 50–60, born in the provinces	815
Total number of people aged 50–60	1312

EXECUTION AND ANALYSIS

The details of the carrying out of the survey are given in the introductory part of the work, which also contains a discussion on the implications of findings, leading on to an evaluation of the age structure at arrival of the migrants, and the intensity of the migratory flow. Further to these, a retrospective view of provincial migration to Paris, the work of Paul Clerc, helps to situate the migratory movement under consideration in time, and in relation to the various available sources of statistical information.

The numerical findings of the survey are derived from a punched-card analysis of the information gathered, transcribed into code. Extracts from replies in a simplified form sometimes illustrate the statistical tables and give them human content. Twenty-odd life stories of provincials who have settled in Paris are given in an appendix. They have been selected from among a great number of accounts, and serve to illustrate the fact that it is always particular and individual situations which, in the last analysis, form the basis of the work.

II. The Findings

Geographical Origin of the Migrants

The findings on geographical origin of the provincials who had settled in Paris,[4] confirmed the data of the censuses. There are people in the Paris area from every region of France.[5] Nevertheless, Britanny, the departments of the Centre, and the regions of the Loire have yielded the highest count, namely 15%, 8%, and 7% respectively of the sample of recent migrants. Next come the region of Basse-Normandie, and the Département du Nord (6% each). All in all, six out of every ten migrants were born to the north, to the west, or immediately to the south of the Parisian region.

The strength of the attraction of the capital is measurable by the number of migrants who leave to settle there compared with the total population of the region which they leave. A zone of high attraction surrounds Paris, stretching towards the east and

[4] In the following we define Paris as the whole built-up area which includes the Départment de la Seine and the nearest *communes* in the *départements* of Seine-et-Oise and Seine-et-Marne.

[5] All the geographical results were assessed in regions comprising from two to eight *départements*.

south, and comprising—as well as Britanny and Normandy—
more peripheral regions like Auvergne and Limousin. The present
situation of the regions which do the most to feed the migration
to Paris, results from a slow regional shift from east to west,
which began in the last century. Emigration from Britanny in
particular is a relatively recent development.

The survey provides some new findings on the comparative
influence of attraction on people from country regions and those
born in towns.

If we assign the value of 100 to the emigration rate[6] from the
rural communes towards Paris, we obtain the series of indices set
out in Table 2, measuring the attraction exerted by the Parisian
area.

TABLE 2.

	Index
Rural *communes*	100
Urban areas:	
Less than 5000 inhabitants	106
5000–20,000	91
20,000–50,000	89
50,000–200,000	79
Over 200,000	44

*Thus the pull of Paris is felt above all in the rural environment and
in small towns.* It is apparent also in medium-sized towns, although
to a lesser degree. On the contrary, in the very large towns the
attraction is reduced by more than half compared with the rural
areas. The conditions necessary to hold people and make newcomers stay on are found only in the sizeable urban concentrations,
and this is a very important factor brought to light by the survey.

There are, nevertheless, quite large regional discrepancies,
stemming from an uneven degree of urbanization. The pull of

[6] The emigration rate is the proportion of emigrants related to the total
population of the region which they leave.

the capital is strongest for the country dwellers of Britanny, Normandy, the Centre, and Limousin. On the other hand, the sphere of attraction is more of an urban nature in Aquitaine, in the Midi-Pyrénées region, in the Rhône-Alpes region, in Franche-Comté and Alsace. Generally speaking, the stronger the attraction of Paris the more it affects country dwellers; when, on the contrary, the attraction in the main is weak, it is above all the town dwellers who migrate.

THE ROAD TO PARIS

Fifty-five per cent of provincial settlers in Paris were born in rural *communes*. When compared with 49% of the population designated as living in the country in the census of 1954, this figure shows that the origin of the movement towards Paris is not exclusively rural.

In the last analysis the stages of the road towards Paris depend little on the rural or urban nature of the place of birth. Forty-one per cent of the migrants have made the transfer directly; the rest have stayed temporarily at one or two, rarely more, places on the way. Although they are not very numerous, these stopping-places are more markedly urban than the birthplaces. A quarter of the migrants were born in the country, and arrive directly from it.

Some regional differences are found in the degree of geographical mobility. Migrants from the north, the east, and the south-east have more stopping places than those coming from the west and the south-west before their arrival in Paris. Immigrants from Britanny and Limousin tend to come directly from the country, whereas migrants from Provence and the Rhone Valley come to Paris by stages, and more usually via the towns. But mobility also depends on occupation and age, increasing as age advances and as the social environment improves.

Migration to Paris from the provinces can be an individual or a family affair: 45% of migrants come to Paris alone, 28% are accompanied by their husband or wife and children, and 27% make the transition with their parents when very young. For every 100 heads of households coming to Paris, there is, in fact, an addition of 170 people to the provincials already settled in the area.

DISTRIBUTION BY AGE

People come to Paris at all ages, but especially between the ages of 20 and 25, as the structure by age on arrival for migrants as a whole demonstrates (Table 3).

TABLE 3.

Age groups on arrival	%
0–4	12.8
5–9	8.2
10–14	4.4
15–19	20.5
20–24	24.3
25–29	13.2
30–34	6.9
35–39	5.1
40–44	2.1
45–49	1.4
50–54	0.8
55–59	0.3

The corresponding age pyramid shows a dip between 10 and 15 years old; this is because the arrival of longer-established families with adolescent children is less frequent than the arrival of young couples with small children. Nevertheless, this irregularity eventually tails off because of the uninterrupted flow of migrants. It is still true that taken as a whole, the Parisian population born in the provinces is younger than the Parisian population by birth. The average age for migrants who come to Paris on their own account is 26. Age constitutes an important differentiating factor in migration. The total number of women (56%) who settle in Paris is slightly greater than the number of men (44%). But under the age of 19, girls make up two-thirds of the migratory flow.

Motives for Migration

Work, family, or private life, and the psychological attraction of the capital, are motives for leaving the provinces and settling in Paris, as Table 4 demonstrates. It shows the most important motive for recent migrants from the provinces.

Migration can be accounted for basically by factors relating to work: 60% of migrants come to Paris first and foremost because of their work. However, several reasons may contribute to the decision to move. All in all, 83% of the provincials explain their arrival by financial considerations. Unattached and family men alike come to Paris primarily to enter professional life or take a job, because the best wages and the best prospects for the future are in the capital.

However, different circumstances underlie the financial motives according to the social group. In general, provincials move to Paris to have better prospects of promotion (29%) rather than because they felt they lacked sufficient work and financial resources in the provinces (14%). Nevertheless, the analysis shows that the migrants do not constitute a homogeneous group.

It is possible, in fact, to distinguish two groups of more or less equal importance.

The first comprises white-collar workers, managerial classes, and the professions. Besides containing a high proportion of migrants arriving young to pursue their studies, this group is characterized by the great number of instances of professional appointments to Paris. The immigrants come to take up high-level jobs which are available in greater abundance in the capital than in the regional urban centres.

These men arrive at a later stage, when their career is more advanced. As a result, this type of migration has more of a family character, the migrant bringing with him his wife and children.

More modest categories make up the second group, which is mostly manual workers: artisans, workmen and service personnel. Here one finds, above all, migrants who wish to improve their situation or earn higher salaries. They come to Paris at the

beginning of their working life and they often come alone—not yet family men.

Contrary to what is happening in the less-developed countries, the effect of migration is not to set in motion a sub-proletariat in search of a subsistence livelihood. Most of the provincials are not directly threatened by unemployment in the area where they lived before coming to Paris, since 80% of the migrants think that they could have kept their jobs there.

Their move to Paris is part of an upward movement towards living conditions which satisfy ever-increasing requirements—above all, material requirements. The attraction of life in Paris and the prestige of the capital play what is at most a secondary role, acting in certain cases rather to reinforce a decision for which the primary motive is work, and especially the dual factors of availability of employment and social betterment.

RECEPTION

The provincials who have decided to undertake the migration to Paris are not going into the great unknown: 77% of them have spent holidays or paid visits to relatives in the capital, and 58% already know someone there who can assist them.

A favourable environment on arrival helps the settling process: 41% of the migrants find their first jobs through contacts or relatives. Furthermore, a third of the provincials are put up, to begin with, by their friends or family. Despite this the problem of accommodation is often mentioned as one of the main difficulties encountered by migrants. But the inconvenience of bad housing conditions is eventually accepted, counterbalanced as it is by the prospect of financial improvement.

All in all, adaptation is easy whatever the social level: 76% of the migrants think that they have adjusted easily to Parisian life, and they express their opinion in vivid and lively terms which show an accurate appreciation of the real situation in the capital in spite of an occasional feeling of isolation, of not fitting in, which rarely persists.

TABLE 4.

	Wish for promotion	Assigned, nominated, transferred	Without work or means of subsistence in provinces	Study, professional training	Marriage	Family reasons	Desire for change, attracted by Paris	Total
	%	%	%	%	%	%	%	%
Overall	29	16	14	9	14	12	6	100
Sex:								
Male	34	19	14	11	7	10	5	100
Female	26	14	14	6	20	12	8	100
Place of birth:								
Rural communes	32	15	16	7	11	12	7	100
Urban areas:								
Less than 50,000	27	19	13	9	17	10	5	100
50,000–200,000	21	20	11	13	17	11	7	100
Over 200,000	10	19	8	19	22	16	6	100
Age on arrival:								
Under 19	28	6	19	23	7	5	12	100
19–28	32	16	11	8	19	8	6	100
29 and over	23	27	18	1	5	23	3	100
Profession of head of family:								
Professions, managerial	17	27	4	22	20	6	4	100
Lesser managerial	23	20	15	10	15	9	8	100
Clerical workers	23	29	13	3	11	13	8	100
Tradesmen, artisans	38	2	13	5	16	21	5	100
Workmen	40	7	18	4	14	11	6	100
Service personnel	35	6	17	3	11	20	8	100

MIGRATION AND WORK

The shift of provincials to Paris includes at the outset all categories of the population. The social origin of the migrants is extremely varied, as the breakdown of migrants according to occupation of the father demonstrates (Table 5).

TABLE 5.

	%
Professions and managerial	7
Lesser managerial	4
White-collar workers	11
Tradesmen and artisans	18
Workmen	28
Service personnel	2
Farmers	19
Farm workers	7
Other professions	4
	100

Only a quarter of the migrants had a father engaged in agriculture. The substantial number of families in the clerical and managerial classes explains why the level of education of the migrants as a whole is higher than for the provinces as a whole. Migration to Paris involves quality as well as quantity.

Nearly a third of the migrants were not working before they settled in the Paris area but were at school studying or assisting their parents. The range of migrants' occupations in the areas they came from was wide, but workmen and white-collar workers predominated. Among the migrants who were working before they came to Paris, 10% were self-employed, 22% were public servants, and 68% in private enterprise.

For more than half of the migrants, their new job in Paris was guaranteed in advance. The others found work very quickly, half of them within a week. But it is remarkable that immediately upon arriving in Paris, more than one fifth of the migrants take on a higher-level job than they had in the provinces. Subsequently their career progresses along the same lines as those of Parisians by birth. The migrants are in no way reduced to the most humble and unremunerative jobs: on the contrary, they occupy positions which guarantee them the same prospects of promotion as the Parisians by birth. In terms of social mobility, the upward trend is manifest, especially for the children of farmers and the lower middle classes—tradesmen, artisans, white-collar workers. Thus there is very broad recruitment from the socio-professional classes of migrants. Their distribution is shown in Table 6.

TABLE 6.

	%
Professions and managerial	14
Lesser managerial	15
White-collar workers	15
Tradesmen and artisans	7
Workmen	34
Service personnel	6
Other professions	6
Non-active persons	3
	100

MIGRATION AND FAMILY SIZE

As one would imagine, it is, above all, children from large families who emigrate to Paris because of their economic effect on the family enterprise—farm, workshop, or trade. In these social environments migrants have more brothers and sisters than provincials in general. However, this finding does not extend to other social groups, where being one of a large family is not found to be more conducive to migration than belonging to a small one.

Once they have become Parisians, the migrants have less

children than provincials in the provinces. Their family size falls into line with their new environment. Migration to Paris is accompanied by a decrease in the number of children per family.

ACCOMMODATION OF PROVINCIALS IN PARIS

Interviewees were questioned about their first accommodation in the Parisian region as well as their residence and housing conditions at the time of the survey.

Just over half of the first "points of impact" of migration (52%) are located within the city of Paris. Changes of residence result in the migrants being spread fairly evenly and in proportion to the population, all over the Parisian area.

Migrants are subject equally with Parisians by birth to the accommodation situation in Paris. 73% of provincials who have moved there after 1945 live in houses or blocks of flats built before 1948. They are housed at an average of 1.32 persons per room, and 40% occupy accommodation in a state of critical or temporarily admissible overcrowding. Over a third of the migrants think that they are housed in unsatisfactory conditions.

FOR AND AGAINST MIGRATION

In the view of those involved, migration gives a strong net gain: the life of migrants in Paris is better than the life they would have had if they had stayed in the provinces. Above all, they have found higher salaries there and, as a consequence, their life has broadened. On arriving in Paris, 77% of the migrants earned more money than in the provinces straight away, and more than half of them did not judge the cost of living to be higher in Paris than in the provinces.

These main trends, and the balance of approval for migration to Paris, are apparent throughout, but they hold good especially for the younger age groups and the working classes. Manual workers, whose living conditions are the least satisfactory, appear to be more satisfied with life in Paris than the professional and higher managerial classes, who are nevertheless in a better position to benefit from the real or hypothetical advantages which the capital affords. This is a finding of great importance.

Table 7 shows the degree of satisfaction of the migrants.

The general satisfaction is corroborated by the future intentions. Only 10% of the migrants envisage returning to the provinces to take up active employment, and these are among the small number who are the least satisfied with life in Paris.

TABLE 7.

	Compared to the life they would have had in the provinces their life in the parisian region is:				
	Better (%)	The same (%)	Worse (%)	No opinion (%)	Total (%)
Overall	61	13	14	12	100
Sex:					
Male	63	10	13	14	100
Female	60	15	14	11	100
Age:					
21–29	68	12	11	9	100
30–39	62	11	14	13	100
40–59	53	16	16	15	100
Profession of head of family:					
Professions, managerial	50	13	19	18	100
Lesser managerial	62	10	13	15	100
Clerical workers	57	17	10	16	100
Tradesmen, artisans	62	16	16	6	100
Workmen	65	12	13	10	100
Service personnel	77	2	13	8	100
Place of birth:					
Rural communes	66	11	11	12	100
Urban centres:					
Less than 50,000	60	13	15	12	100
50,000–200,000	56	12	18	14	100
More than 200,000	43	21	22	14	100

Nevertheless, taking into account those who do not exclude the possibility of returning to the provinces, but on the condition of finding there a standard of living and a way of life comparable to those they had in Paris, and including in addition the migrants who intend to leave the capital when they retire, half the migrants envisage leaving the Parisian area one day. Only a third of the Parisians by birth, as their retirement approaches, make similar plans. But those who have made definite plans for leaving only constitute a small minority.

Accommodation conditions which are considered satisfactory are conducive to keeping the population in the capital. Similarly, the prospect of reduced income will tend to fix on the spot a great number of those who, when the time comes, will seek to make up their income by some part-time job in retirement.

The general feeling of satisfaction among the migrants is rational, and relates closely to the opinion which Parisians by birth have of the capital. Both groups are perfectly conscious of the inconveniences of Parisian life, such as noise, polluted air, stress, and transport and housing difficulties. The advantages, nevertheless, remain more important for all groups of the population studied, regardless of their origin or age, as Table 8 shows.

TABLE 8.

QUESTION: *In your opinion, which are more important all in all, the advantages or the disadvantages of life in Paris?*

	Advantages (%)	Dis-advantages (%)	No opinion (%)	Total (%)
Recent migrants	62	22	16	100
Long-standing migrants	56	28	16	100
Migrants arriving in childhood	57	28	15	100
People aged 50–60, born in the provinces	56	27	17	100
People aged 50–60, born in Paris	56	25	19	100

Nevertheless, 47% of the people questioned would like to live away from Paris, very often in a little provincial town, but on the condition of finding there the same advantages as in the capital regarding finance and prospects of social and cultural advancement. This wish is in conformity with the facts as they emerge in the survey. In fact, the provincials move in the first place activated by a wish to improve their work situation. Some stay in the large regional towns, some feel that it is only Paris which combines all the conditions for improvement. From that point, the disadvantages of Paris are accepted; nevertheless, the ambition to achieve an even better way of life remains, and in this respect the general opinion of the migrants concurs with that of the Parisians by birth, despite the fact that these have not had to move.

The contrast between manual workers and white-collar and managerial classes, apparent in connection with their reasons for moving, is also reflected in their attitudes. The former accept the disadvantage of life in Paris much more readily, because for them the essentials of life are secured, and they are very much aware of this. Non-manual workers, on the other hand, are less satisfied. Having reached a standard of living in which the mere essentials of existence have taken second place, they are more sensitive to the inconveniences of the Parisian area or would rather live in a provincial town.

Although the migrants themselves make a very substantial contribution to the increase in the population of Paris, they are almost unanimous (86%) in thinking that this increase should be checked. To this end it is essential to create work in the provinces, raise salaries there, or, alternatively, decentralize. This attitude appears very consistently: the migrant advocates the measures which, in his opinion, would have kept him in the provinces, and thus gives his support to an active policy in this direction.

III. Conclusion

The essential lesson of this research is to be found in the motivation of the provincials who have settled in Paris.

Prospects of promotion or increased income constitute, for six-tenths of the migrants, the activating factor in the migration. Their moving is part of a general movement towards living conditions more satisfactory than those in the provinces. This desire for improvement takes different forms according to the social group. For manual workers, service personnel, farmers, and clerical workers, Paris guarantees a decent standard of living. For higher civil servants and private managerial classes, and members of the professions, who also move in great numbers, coming to Paris sets the seal on a successful career. However this may be, the move from the provinces to Paris is accompanied by an improvement in social and professional status. This improvement in its turn gives rise to new needs which would not have arisen elsewhere. There is, so to speak, a dual upward movement: on the one hand, the upward trend in terms of material situation, giving rise to the other, psychological movement when it reveals glimpses of broader possibilities.

The movement towards Paris is general in its scope. People come there—at a varying rate, it is true—from all age groups, from all social strata, and from all parts of France. They come there drawn by an image of the capital which corresponds to deep aspirations.

Paris has come to correspond to the image which provincial immigrants had of their future because the underlying collective aspiration has a permanent nature and is transmitted from generation to generation. If it is true that, once they have settled in Paris, the great majority of migrants feel that coming to the capital has greatly contributed to their success, it is also true that by their own mobility they have created the conditions necessary for the continuation of a movement of upward mobility.

When contemplating action it is important to distinguish this overwhelmingly positive aspect of migration to Paris from the negative aspect of the tension set up by concentration of the population.

To relieve the tension presupposes economic and social measures for the better arrangement of the capital. But the creation of conditions which favour upward mobility, implies an ever-increasing degree of urbanization.

For only cities of a sufficient size are in a position to offer newcomers what they are looking for. In France, Paris is almost the only pole of attraction, and the disadvantages of this situation are all too well known.

In the light of the present study, one can, it is true, envisage partial measures which would tend to restrain the migratory flow towards Paris. But it is only the development of other urban concentrations which may finally divert the flow from Paris to other destinations.

Geographical Mobility and Urban Concentration in France: A Study in the Provinces

A. GIRARD, H. BASTIDE, AND G. POURCHER

The rural exodus in France and the concomitant growth of the urban area surrounding Paris is of great interest to the authors of this study.

But the growth of other urban centres is also of interest. A study has been undertaken in this area by Mols.[1]

Recent work on the population of Paris[2] shows in particular how the growth of Paris has been a response to strong psychological as well as economic pressures.

The conclusions presented in this article are the results of a study made in the provinces of France and are a continuation of the Parisian study mentioned above. Some new evidence is offered on the motives which control movements of population to the smaller French towns as well as to Paris.

Object of the Inquiry

During the course of an important study of the psychological and social aspects of migration from provincial areas to Paris, the Psychosociological Section of the INED conducted an analogous study within the provinces of France.

Although a large portion of the French population have moved to Paris in search of employment, better working conditions or accommodation, or for other reasons, many people, for similar reasons, have left their homes and not gone to Paris. Were the members of these two groups acting for the same or for different reasons? How did they accomplish their moves, and why did they go? Were their aspirations comparable?

The object of this study is to bring out the answers to these questions and to make a comparison between the situation in the provinces and that observed in Paris. We are dealing with a very well-defined subject; it proceeds from a definite group of the French population at a definite moment in time. It is not a study over a length of time, and does not include predictions about the future or comparisons with the past. A study of mobility over several generations would involve many new problems, and will be the subject of a future article oriented towards professional mobility rather than towards geographic mobility.

The Survey

This study concentrates on a representative sample of the adult population of France residing outside the greater Parisian area. It was conducted using the methods of proportional representation, and took place during January and February of 1961. Table 1 shows a breakdown of the 1989 subjects interviewed. They were drawn from the whole of France, questioned by 177 interviewers in 163 localities, and were chosen according to the several variables which served as a basis in establishing the outlines of the study.

The questionnaire, similar in several respects to the one used in our study of French immigrants to Paris, included questions about the relative sizes of the two communities involved in each subject's change of location and any changes of profession accompanying the move.

It also contained several questions about the family and social background of the subject and, in the case of married subjects, of their spouse also.

An examination of the motive behind the migration constituted an important part of the questionnaire as did an examination of the subject's intentions for the future.

A question about the subject's opinions about the relative merits of various types of residence and the attraction of Paris concluded the survey.

TABLE 1. CATEGORIZATION OF PEOPLE INTERVIEWED

| | Total sample | | France except Seine and Seine-et-Oise (%) |
	No.	%	
Total	1989	100	100
Sex:			
Men	980	49.3	47.4
Women	1009	50.7	52.6
Age:			
Under 30	367	19	20
30–39	475	24	21
40–49	315	16	16
50–59	376	19	18
Over 60	422	22	25
Unknown	34		
Residence:			
Population under 2000	886	45	44
2000–5000	196	10	15
5000–20,000	319	16	16
20,000–100,000	304	15	13
over 100,000	284	14	12
Region:			
North-east	687	35	33
North-west	466	23	23
South-east	485	24	25
South-west	351	18	19
Profession of the head of the family:			
Farm owners	353	18	19
Farm workers	112	6	8
Manual labourers	613	31	33
Clerical workers	358	18	12
Tradesmen, artisans	200	10	8
Businessmen, industrialists, professional workers	107	5	4
Retired people, annuity holders	246	12	16

Overall Results

Let us consider first the results in terms of geographic mobility. This term is meant to imply changes in the kind of residential area rather than moves from one area to a similar one, no matter how far away in miles. For instance, cities are generally agglomerations of several *communes*. So a person who has moved from Lyons to Villeurbanne or from Caudéron to Bordeaux, for example, or the inverse, is not considered to have made a bona fide change of residence. Similarly, houses used for war-time refuge, or residence taken up as a result of ties with the military, have not been considered.

The distance between residences has not been calculated. It is immediately evident from the data that the distance covered by rural migrants who have not moved to a city is less than that covered by urban residents who have moved from one city to another, or by people who have moved from the country to a city.

For the purposes of this study, moves undertaken after the age of 15 have been considered separately from those made before that age, as these latter cases are likely to have been the results of decisions made by the parents of the individual in question, whereas in the former case moves are more often the result of a decision taken by the subject. Throughout the study we will be dealing with those people who have made their own decision to move.

Table 2 shows all changes of residence made by the subjects, broken down in terms of the variables mentioned above.

The group that was studied can be broken down into three sections: those who had never moved (38%), those who had moved once (29%), and those who had moved more than once (33%). The number of times members of this last group had moved varied from 2 to as many as 4 or more times in the case of ten individuals.

In addition, 31% had also changed their residence at some time before they reached age 15. It was found that a fairly strict correlation existed between personal mobility later in life and the mobility

TABLE 2. CHANGES OF RESIDENCE

Number of moves	After age 15		Also one or more times before age 15		
	No.	%	No.	%	
None	762	38	148	19	
1	585	29	199	34	
2	318	16	131	41 ⎤	
3	154	8	51	33 ⎬ 39	
4	72	4	29	40 ⎦	
5 or more	98	5	47	48	
Average number of moves	1989 1.3	100	605 1.7	31	

5 moves = 2.5% or 50 cases   7 moves = 0.6 or 12 cases
6 moves = 1.4% or 27 cases   8 or more = 0.5% or 9 cases

of the family of origin, measured from the birth of the individual under study: only 19% of those who had not subsequently moved had changed residence with their family before age 15, while 34%, 39%, and 48% of those who had changed residence respectively once, 2–4 times, and 5 or more times had moved with their families in their youth. Again, the average number of moves was found to be 1.7 for those individuals whose parents had moved as opposed to an average of 1.1 moves for those whose parents had not moved. This correlation falls into the category of social origins. The degree of mobility will be shown to have varied greatly also among the different professional milieux.

Another similar correlation has been observed among the emigrants from the provinces who have established themselves in Paris. Among these people mobility—measured by number of changes of residence—is higher than among those who moved within the provinces without going to Paris. The probability for an individual to be "mobile" increased with the mobility of the family of origin. In other words, "He who has moved, will move", or, at least, "He who has moved is very likely to move".

Finally, 31% of the study group had never changed their residence.

Variations with Age, and Age at Change of Residence

The sample has been analysed according to age because, as one would expect, the number of changes of residence increased with the age of the subject.

Half the subjects under consideration under age 30 had moved by their own choice, and 16% had moved more than twice. Conversely, only a quarter of the group aged over 60 had remained in the same location, whereas half had moved 2 or more times. In the group between 30 and 60 years of age the degree of mobility rose continuously between these two levels (see Table 3).

TABLE 3. AGE AND CHANGES OF RESIDENCE (%)

Age (years)	Number of moves				Total
	None	1	2	3 or more	
Under 30	50	34	12	4	100
30–39	39	30	19	12	100
40–49	37	32	16	15	100
50–59	41	24	17	18	100
Over 59	25	27	16	32	100

As Table 4 shows, the distribution of ages at the time of a change of residence was fairly wide, but it tended to cluster towards the older subjects as it changed from a measure of the first move to one of subsequent moves.

The first move tended to come between the ages of 16 and 30, becoming more frequent towards age 30; the second move fell between ages 20 and 35; the third between ages 24 and 49; the fourth between ages 36 and 59, etc.

The first move took place at an average age of 24; subsequent moves occurred on the average at ages 29, 34, 35, 39, etc.

TABLE 4. AGE AT CHANGE OF RESIDENCE, RELATED TO NUMBER OF MOVES

	1st move	2nd move	3rd move	4th move	5th move	More than 6	Total	Cumulative total
Number of moves	1227	642	324	170	98	89	2550	
Age (years)								
16–17 (%)	5.8	0.5	—	—	—	—	2.9	2.9
18–19 (%)	14.9	3.8	1.3	—	—	—	8.3	11.2
20–21 (%)	24.3	11.8	2.9	1.2	2.2	—	15.1	26.3
22–23 (%)	16.4	12.4	8.5	6.6	5.3	—	12.6	38.9
24–25 (%)	13.2	17.4	11.4	8.4	15.9	—	13.0	51.9
26–29 (%)	11.6	18.1	21.7	19.2	18.9	4.8	15.0	66.9
30–34 (%)	5.8	13.6	20.3	18.8	18.9	20.2	15.5	78.4
35–39 (%)	3.7	7.2	10.4	16.3	22.0	13.1	11.5	85.6
40–49 (%)	2.4	9.9	11.1	12.6	11.5	25.0	7.2	93.3
50–59 (%)	1.1	4.0	6.7	11.5	3.2	23.8	7.7	97.7
Over 60 (%)	0.8	1.3	5.7	5.4	2.1	13.1	4.4	100.0
Total (%)	100	100	100	100	100	100	100	—
Unknown (%)	3.3	2.0	2.8	2.4	3.1	5.6	2.9	—
Whole sample (age in years)	24.1	29.5	33.9	36.3	39.3	45.5	—	—
Average age of those who moved:								
Once	26.0	—	—	—	—	—	—	—
Twice	22.9	31.9	—	—	—	—	—	—
3 times	23.0	29.7	38.4	—	—	—	—	—
4 times	20.7	25.4	31.5	40.2	—	—	—	—
More than 5 times	20.7	24.1	28.4	33.4	39.0	45.5	—	—

The first move can be seen to have happened earlier in cases where subsequent moves were undertaken, increasingly so as the total number of moves increased (see bottom of Table 4). The average age at the first move thus varied between 21 and 26, depending on the total number of moves undertaken in the individual's lifetime; the average age at the time of the second move ranged from 24 to 32 years. The third move almost always occurred after the age of 30.

Because several generations were present in the study group, moves undertaken early in life seemed to be much more frequent than those embarked upon later. This explains why, out of all recorded moves, one quarter were made before age 22, one half before age 26, and two-thirds before age 30. Only one quarter were made between ages 30 and 50, and only 7% after this, of which 2% were made after age 60.

Those who moved can thus be overwhelmingly classified as young adults.

Other Factors Contributing to Degree of Mobility

The degree of mobility of the modern French population appears from a geographic study to be the same at all levels of the social scale. The proportion of people who stayed where they were, as opposed to those who moved one or more times, was apparently the same in the country as in the small towns and large cities. (These statements do not apply to Paris as it was not part of this study.)

In each area studied, approximately 4 out of every 10 people have never moved, and 1 or 2 have moved at least 3 times. It is interesting to note that in the country, as in the largest cities, the degree of mobility is slightly higher than in the smaller towns (Table 5).

But this large-scale geographic homogeneity conceals variations linked to social milieu. A geographic study groups together all professional classes, from the agricultural workers at the bottom of the social scale to the more mobile members of the professional

TABLE 5. CHANGES OF RESIDENCE RELATED TO SEX, PROFESSION, AND RESIDENCE AT TIME OF STUDY

	No moves	1st move	2nd move	3rd or more moves	Total
Numbers	762	585	318	324	1989
	%	%	%	%	%
Sex:					
Men	40	27	15	18	100
Women	37	32	17	14	100
Residence at time of study:					
Population less than 2000	41	30	14	15	100
2000–5000	38	27	19	16	100
5000–20,000	34	30	16	20	100
20,000–100,000	35	29	18	18	100
more than 100,000	39	30	17	14	100
Profession of father:					
Farm worker	27	41	17	15	100
Farm owner	41	31	15	13	100
Labourer	43	27	18	12	100
Artisan, tradesman	44	23	15	18	100
Clerical worker	32	26	16	26	100
Businessman, industrialist professional worker	34	30	14	22	100
Profession of head of family at time of study:					
Farm worker	36	36	17	11	100
Farm owner	49	30	12	9	100
Labourer	39	30	18	13	100
Artisan, tradesman	46	26	14	14	100
Clerical worker	29	27	19	25	100
Businessman, industrialist, professional worker	27	30	14	29	100

bureaucracy. The necessity of considering the profession of the subject becomes immediately obvious from a comparison of the profession of the father of the migrant and the profession of the migrant himself as head of his own household.

Farmers, artisans, and shopkeepers—all attached to the soil or to a particular place of business—were among the least mobile sectors of the population, though not less so than manual workers who also experienced a sort of constraint (Table 5).

While men were found to be slightly less mobile than women (Table 5), at the same time those men who did move were found to do so on the average a little more frequently than did women. But women tended to move at a slightly earlier age than men.

This age difference was usually to the order of 2–3 years, i.e. about the same as the difference in ages between men and women at the time of their marriage. Indeed, marriage was found to be one of the most common reasons for change of residence, and undoubtedly accounts for this phenomenon (Table 6).

TABLE 6. AGE AT TIME OF MOVE AS RELATED TO SEX OF MIGRANT
(Average age in Years and Decades)

Number of moves	1st move	2nd move	3rd move	4th move	5th and subsequent moves
			Men		
1	29.5	—	—	—	—
2	23.4	33.4	—	—	—
3	23.4	29.8	39.4	—	—
4	20.6	25.9	32.5	41.6	—
5 or more	20.8	24.2	28.9	33.8	38.7
			Women		
1	24.6	—	—	—	—
2	22.2	30.4	—	—	—
3	22.6	29.6	37.4	—	—
4	20.7	24.8	30.1	38.1	—
5 or more	20.6	24.0	27.9	33.0	39.6

Motives for Moving

The motives which caused people to move without going to Paris are for the most part quite clear.

There were two principal motives—one of a professional nature, the other of a personal nature.

The former of these is the more usual, affecting half of those who changed their residence. These can be divided into three major categories: first, those who moved in order to find work—as farmer, labourer, or shopkeeper; second, those who moved in order to find a better job; and third, those who moved for reasons inherent in their career—transferral, advancement within a profession, or change of location of the firm (Table 7).

By far the most common personal motive is marriage; one quarter of the sample had changed their residence at the time of their marriage. As the location of a household is in most cases a function of the profession of the husband, this fraction applies more to the women in the study than to the men (3 out of 10 as against 1 out of 10); men moved much more often for professional reasons (54% as against 39% of the women).

Apart from this, 6% of the total moved at the end of their professional lives. We shall return later to moves which accompanied the cessation of activity.

Other motives, such as health, accommodation, or external events, only intervened in a minority of cases (1 or 2 people out of 10).

When we consider the objectives of the migrants of our study, that is to say their final localities, we find that the motives for moving were not generally the same for people moving within rural areas and people moving into cities of various sizes. Professional motives became more common with the increasing size of the urban areas; family motives, specifically marriage, diminished conversely.

In other words, although a professional motive seemed to underly most migrations, rural people tended to change residence at the time of their marriage, remaining in the country, whereas

TABLE 7. REASONS FOR MOVING

QUESTION: *(For people who have lived in their present location for 14–15 years.) In a few words, can you say under what circumstances you came to live in .., either by yourself or to be joined by your family?*

	Total sample	Men	Women	Residence at time of study		
				Country(Less than 5000 inhabitants)	Small town (5000–100,000)	Large town (More than 100,000)
Number:	1227	593	634	647	408	172
	%	%	%	%	%	%
Work:						
To find work, a farm, or a small business	50	59	41	44	55	59
To get better work, higher salary,	21	26	16	19	22	26
a larger farm	16	22	10	14	18	17
Appointment, transfer, advance within a company or a move of the company itself	13	11	15	11	15	16
Family:						
To marry	32	21	42	36	26	24
To move nearer to other members of the family	22	14	30	27	17	14
After a death or divorce	7	6	8	7	6	8
To move nearer to place of work or find	3	1	4	2	3	2
better accommodation	8	8	9	9	9	2
To retire	6	8	4	8	5	5
As a result of political developments (war, return of former colonial territories)	2	2	2	2	2	2
For reasons of health	2	3	4	1	3	5
Other reasons	6	8	4	4	7	9
Unknown	5	3	6	5	5	3
Total	111[a]	112[a]	110[a]	109[a]	112[a]	109[a]

[a] Total greater than 100% because of multiple replies.

people who moved to the city did so in order to better their professional situation.

The Parisian study showed this tendency also. The professional motive was operative in a large proportion of those who moved from the provinces to Paris (Table 8).

TABLE 8. REASONS FOR MOVING TO THE PROVINCES AND TO PARIS ACCORDING TO RESIDENCE AT TIME OF STUDY

	Less than 5000 inhabitants (%)	From 5000 to 100,000 inhabitants (%)	More than 100,000 inhabitants (%)	Paris (%)
Professional reasons	43	51	52	62
Family reasons	34	24	21	27
Marriage	26	16	12	10
Other reasons	23	25	27	11
Total	100	100	100	100

The question of motive underlying migration was put to the group in two ways. Subjects were asked to name their motive, giving a spontaneous expression, and they were asked to choose the motive nearest to their own from a list which included, besides professional reasons, improvement in living conditions and better accommodation.

Replies to the question put in these two ways uncovered practically identical results. Better living conditions or accommodation were named by only a minority as their prime reason; nor did these reasons appear much more frequently as less important motives (Table 9).

These results contradict the oft-repeated opinion (which will arise later in this study) that people who move to large cities, especially Paris, do so primarily to find better living conditions and the distractions of a large city. This is probably true to some

TABLE 9. REASONS FOR MOVING (MULTIPLE CHOICE)

QUESTION: *Of the following reasons, choose that which was most important in your decision to move. Which was second in importance? Were any others important?*
  In order to find better living conditions
  In order to get better work
  Family reasons
  In order to get work
  Transfer or advancement within a company
  Accommodation

	1st reason (%)	2nd reason (%)	3rd reason (%)	Total (%)
Work	46	27	12	87
To get work	22	11	4	38
To get a better job	15	12	6	33
Transfer, advancement	9	4	2	16
Family	29	15	5	49
Improvement in living conditions	12	14	15	41
Accommodation	8	12	13	33
No reason given	5	32	55	—
Total	100	100	100	210

extent; one could not deny that improved surroundings might sometimes be the real motive. But the decision to move, according to the migrants interviewed, with the exception of those cases where marriage was the motive, arose primarily from the necessity to find work or to improve on existing employment. Men move towards places which offer work, or, if already employed, towards places where they may find better employment. Geographic mobility is thus directly related to professional mobility.

Motives for Moving as Related to Age

Reasons for moving, thus related to profession and to important personal changes, vary in frequency with age (Table 10).

TABLE 10. REASONS FOR THE MOST RECENT MOVE, ACCORDING TO AGE

	Age (years) at most recent move						
	Under 20	20–24	25–29	30–34	35–39	40–49	50 or over
Numbers	97	328	274	150	106	112	136
	%	%	%	%	%	%	%
	50	45	52	55	72	59	21
Work:							
In order to find work, a farm or a small business	36	22	20	17	33	29	7
In order to find better employment, higher salary or larger firm	12	12	19	20	25	17	6
Appointment, transfer, advance within a firm, or firm itself moved	2	11	13	18	24	13	8
Family:	35	47	32	24	16	14	24
In order to marry	27	41	24	16	6	4	2
In order to move nearer to other members of the family	6	4	5	5	8	4	21
After a death or divorce	2	2	3	3	2	6	1
Accommodation:							
To be close to place of work, find better accommodation	5	9	10	9	10	6	5
Retirement:							
To retire	—	—	—	—	3	4	49
Political events: As a result of war the return of former colonial territories	3	2	1	3	2	3	1
Health: For reasons of health	1	1	1	3	3	6	4
Other reasons	5	5	5	11	7	4	4
Unknown	3	3	6	7	1	8	2
Total[a]	102	112	107	112	114	104	110

[a] Total greater than 100% due to multiple responses.

Motives derived from private considerations, particularly marriage, are most common between the ages of 20 and 24. During this period marriage explained changes in residence as often as did professional reasons.

At all other ages, professional reasons were the prime motives. However, the older the subject the more it became a question of improving on already established working conditions by transferring within a firm or moving up within an administrative hierarchy rather than moving in order to find employment.

Beginning at about age 50, this trend lost its vitality. Among those who moved after this age, 7 out of 10 had already retired (49% + 21% who were moving in order to rejoin a member of their family). This proportion represented 12% of the non-Parisian population of France over age 49 at the time of the study.

A most useful study has been made of this aspect of migration by using voting records.[3] An analysis by age showed that people of 60 years or older tended to move towards smaller communities.

Acquaintances in the New Location

In almost one half of the sample, people moved towards a place where they already knew someone (Table 11).

In many cases there were relatives nearby in the area to which the individual moved. In 18% of the sample these were relatives or parents-in-law, not a surprising fact in view of the high percentage who had moved away at the time of their marriage.

Where there was an acquaintance in the new location, in 3 out of 5 instances this person gave some sort of aid to the migrant family. This was usually in the matter of lodging rather than employment.

Migrants were more likely to know someone in a large city than in a smaller community. It was found that only 49% had acquaintances in the country, while 57% knew people in cities of over 100,000 inhabitants. Among people who moved to Paris, 58% had acquaintances there. These statistics indicate a very

TABLE 11. RELATIVES IN THE NEW LOCATION

	People who had moved	Residence at time of study		
		Country	Small town	Large provincial town
Numbers	1227 %	647 %	408 %	172 %
Already live there:				
Parents, parents-in-law, spouse	18	22	14	13
Friends	8	5	11	9
Parents and friends	11	8	13	15
Brothers, sisters, brothers-in-law, sisters-in-law	6	5	7	6
Uncles, aunts, nephews, nieces	4	3	4	5
Children	2	2	2	4
Other people	4	4	3	5
No acquaintances there	47	51	46	43
People who had moved	100	100	100	100
Have had help in finding:				
Accommodation	18	16	18	20
Work	5	4	6	9
Accommodation and work	6	7	5	7
Other	2	2	2	1
Have not been helped in the new location	22	20	23	20
	53	49	54	57

important aspect of the nature of internal migrations in contemporary France. In most cases it is not a question of adventure, nor of a leap into the unknown. Individuals, part of an already ancient current of which they are hardly aware, go often towards places where some part of their family is already established. Migration is less a rupture with the original location than it is a rejoining with relatives in the new location.

Direction of Mobility

In accordance with the general rural exodus to the cities, the net result of provincial displacements is the growth of the urban population (Table 12).

Comparing the birthplace and the actual place of residence of

TABLE 12. GEOGRAPHIC ORIGINS BY SIZE OF TOWN OF RESIDENCE

Birthplace	Residence at time of study					
	Under 2000 (%)	2000– 5000 (%)	5000– 20,000 (%)	20,000– 100,000 (%)	More than 100,000 (%)	Total (%)
Less than 2000 inhabitants	82	27	28	31	28	52
2000–5000	5	46	9	7	8	11
5000–20,000	5	7	45	11	8	13
20,000–100,000	3	12	7	38	7	10
Over 100,000	2	5	5	7	39	9
Paris	1	—	3	2	4	2
Outside France	2	3	3	4	6	3
Total	100 45	100 10	100 16	100 15	100 14	100 100

	Country (Less than 5000) (%)	Small town (5000– 100,000) (%)	Large town (Over 10,000) (%)	Total (%)
Country	85	37	37	63
Small town	10	51	15	23
Large town	2	6	38	9
Paris	1	3	4	2
Outside France	2	3	6	3
Total	100 55	100 31	100 14	100 100

the group under study we observe the distribution shown in Table 13.

TABLE 13.

Population	Birthplace (%)	Residence (%)
Less than 2000	52	45
2000–5000	11	10
5000–20,000	13	16
20,000–100,000	10	15
Over 100,000	9	14
Paris area	2	—
Born outside France	3	—
Total	100	100

According to Table 12, 8 out of 10 people living in rural areas were born in rural areas, whereas in all cities of the provinces, 3 out of 10 inhabitants were born in rural areas. The larger the town, the larger the proportion of people who were born in smaller towns or the country.

By contrast, only 2% of the people living in the provinces were born in Paris.

Although most moves are made towards urban concentrations, this trend tends to conceal some movement in the opposite direction. Table 14, showing only people who have changed residence, is a good measure of this complex phenomenon.

Eight per cent of the people now living in the country have spent some period of their life in a city. Conversely, 2% of the people considered as urban have spent some time in the country and then returned to the city. But the number who now live in a town, having moved there from the country, 25%, far outweighs the number of urban-born migrants who were at the time of the study living in the country (9%). This difference is exactly the same as that shown earlier between present residence and birthplace for the whole study.

TABLE 14. DIRECTION OF MIGRATION

People who had moved	1203
Had lived:	%
Always in the country	34
Always in towns	20
Country, then towns	25
Towns, then country	9
Country, towns, then country	8
Towns, country, then towns	2
Other cases	2
Total	100

Labour Market, Economic Conditions, and Urban Concentration

The tendency towards urban concentration is in any case a corollary of the economic situation or, more precisely, of the labour markets in the country, the smaller towns, and the larger cities. It was pointed out above that migrations corresponded in the large majority of cases to the need to find work or a better situation. The following observations put the professional character of migrations further into relief.

In the smaller towns of France it is obvious that young people are having difficulty in finding work. This is evident from responses to the question of Table 15.

Although living conditions have improved vastly in the last few years in the rural areas of France, further improvements are not anticipated there to any greater extent than elsewhere (Table 16).

The general trend of opinion, that conditions are improving, does not really have a bearing on the mobility of rural people. This trend does fit in with opinions observed in a study made several years ago, and shows a much more favourable attitude than that found 10 years ago,[4] but the general nature of our observation obscures distortions which occur in the different areas covered in the study. As is obvious from responses to the

TABLE 15.

QUESTION: *In your area, from what you have observed, do young people in general find it hard or easy to get work? If your answer is qualified, elaborate.*

	Total (%)	Population				
		Less than 2000 (%)	2000–5000 (%)	5000–20,000 (%)	20,000–100,000 (%)	over 100,000 (%)
Difficult	57	66	68	51	46	38
Depends on	17	13	17	19	24	24
Kind of work	*11*	*9*	*12*	*12*	*13*	*11*
Professional establishment	*3*	*2*	*3*	*3*	*5*	*5*
Level of training	*1*	*—*	*1*	*1*	*2*	*4*
Other reasons	*2*	*2*	*1*	*3*	*4*	*4*
Easy	20	18	11	19	22	29
No response	6	3	4	11	8	9
Total	100	100	100	100	100	100

TABLE 16.

QUESTION: *Still with reference to your area, do you think that living conditions are better than, worse than, or about the same as they were 10 years ago? Why?*

	Total Ensemble (%)	Population				
		Less than 2000 (%)	2000–5000 (%)	5000–20,000 (%)	20,000–100,000 (%)	Over 100,000 (%)
Better	38	41	29	36	39	31
Same	21	22	26	22	15	19
Worse	29	28	31	24	32	34
No reply	12	9	14	18	14	16
	100	100	100	100	100	100

Comments:

	Total
Better:	(%)
Higher incomes, more money	18
More comfortable life (cars, television)	6
Better accommodation	4
Higher production, development of machines	3
Important social progress	2
Modernization of the area	2
Other reasons	1
Worse or the same:	
Cost of living increasing more than income	24
Cost of living increasing with income	13
Other reasons	8
No opinion, no response	19
	100

question of Table 17, the feeling in rural areas is that conditions are not improving. There is consequently no braking action on the rural exodus.

TABLE 17.

QUESTION: *Do you think that in a few years conditions in your area will be better, the same, or worse?*

	Total (%)	Population				
		Less than 2000 (%)	2000– 5000 (%)	5000– 20,000 (%)	20,000– 100,000 (%)	Over 100,000 (%)
Better	26	23	20	31	33	24
Same	29	32	30	23	28	25
Worse	15	15	14	15	12	17
No reply	30	30	36	31	27	34
Total	100	100	100	100	100	100

The only area where the responses to this last question do have significance is in the medium-sized cities (5000–100,000 inhabitants), where optimism is the most marked. Public preferences for an urban home without the inconveniences of the most crowded urban areas explains this. [4]

Variations in Attraction Among the Regions

Although interior migrations tend towards areas of population concentration, they do not do so indiscriminately, but favour those areas which are being built up by industrial developments.

A regional analysis of degree of mobility shows this clearly (Table 18). For the purposes of this study the degree of mobility was defined as the proportion of people in each *département* born outside the *département* in which they were residing at the time of the study. The limited dimensions of the population sample

TABLE 18. PROPORTION OF PEOPLE BORN OUTSIDE THE DÉPARTEMENT IN WHICH THEY WERE RESIDING AT THE TIME OF THE STUDY

Residence at time of study	Total (No.)	People born in				Total
		Département in which they were residing (%)	Another département in the region (%)	Another region (%)	Outside France (%)	(%)
Franche-Comté	40	90	—	10	—	100
Bretagne	91	86	8	4	2	100
Limousin	50	82	2	16	—	100
Flandre-Artois	150	80	8	9	3	100
Alsace-Lorraine	85	80	8	6	6	100
Berry, Nivernais, Bourbonnais	12	76	8	8	8	100
Lyonnais	61	75	2	16	7	100
Lorraine (western)	119	75	7	17	1	100
Savoie-Dauphiné	103	74	14	9	3	100
Poitou	83	73	7	19	1	100
Normandie, région mancelle	162	72	11	15	2	100
Midi languedocien	85	72	5	21	2	100
Causses-Cévennes	60	72	3	20	5	100
Aquitaine (coastal)	108	69	9	18	4	100
Aquitaine (interior)	85	68	6	22	4	100
Bourgogne	68	68	1	25	6	100
Picardie-soissonnais	79	66	5	23	6	100
Parisian Region[a]	72	64	3	29	4	100
Normandie (eastern)	88	61	6	33	—	100
Loire country	101	61	10	28	1	100
Champagne	86	60	3	37	—	100
Midi provençal	137	60	5	28	7	100
Auvergne-Velay	64	58	13	27	2	100
	1989	71	7	19	3	100

[a] Eure-et-Loire, Loiret, Seine-et-Marne.

made it necessary to regroup the 87 *départements* (the study did not include Seine, Seine-et-Oise, or Corsica), into the twenty-three geographical areas listed in Table 18 and illustrated in Map 1.

It is well known that the mobility of the population as a whole increased greatly in the nineteenth century and the first half of

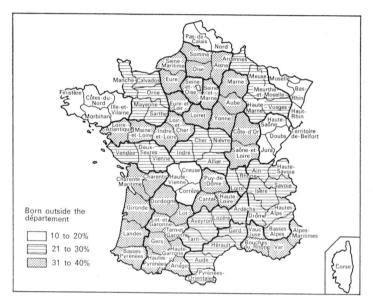

MAP 1. 1961 study – Proportion of people born outside the *Département* in which they resided.

the twentieth century. The most recent data available for the whole of France are from the census of 1946. The following figures show the proportion of people born outside the *département* in which they were living, from 1911 to 1946.

1911	21.4%	1936	26.2%
1921	24.2%	1946	28.1%

In order to make a comparison with the data of this study, it was necessary to exclude census material for the *départements* of

Seine and Seine-et-Oise, for in these areas the population is disproportionately mobile, and Corsica, as here the population is disproportionately immobile as well as being comparatively sparse. For 1946 this gives the overall proportion of 23.1 % of the population born outside the area in which they were residing at the time of the census.

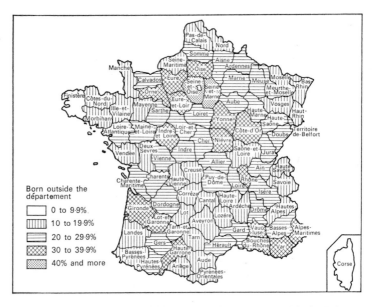

MAP 2. Census of 1946. – Proportion of Frenchmen born outside the *Départe-ment* in which they were recorded for the census.

In our study this proportion was found to be 29 % which, when we take into account a reasonable margin of error, shows the rise in mobility of the population between 1946 and 1961.

Regional variations are readily apparent. Regions where the proportion of people born elsewhere is highest, that is to say regions of most drawing power or attraction describe a circle around the Parisian area (Seine and Seine-et-Oise), spreading out in rays along the Loire Valley, the Seine Valley, and the Saône as far as Burgundy.

Other areas of attraction are the Midi, including the cities of Marseille, Toulon, and Nice; the Côte d'Azur; then Aquitania, including the Valley of the Garonne, Bordeaux, and Toulouse.

Auvergne-Velay also appears here, perhaps because of a fluctuation in the sample. Perhaps also for this reason the area around Lyon appears to have more than its share of drawing power.

This last statement is based particularly on a comparison with the map of the *départements*, taken from the 1946 census (Map 2). In all but these two regions, agreement is striking. The picture that the map presents is not as dramatic as the census data because it was compiled by region instead of by *département*, which allowed the "contamination" of certain *départements* by their contiguity with other *départements*, as, for example, those which surround Gironde, Lot-et-Garonne, and Haute Garonne. In other cases of disparity, the degree of mobility may easily have changed between 1946 and 1961.

The regions in which the highest proportion of the population was native-born were first the west, then the north, Alsace-Lorraine, and the central area. The regions which did not attract as strongly have several traits in common: higher birth rate, more established religious traditions, and Conservative or Popular Republican voting characteristics. All these factors, and doubtless others still to be researched, are internally correlated.

The Attraction of Paris

Apart from the "zones of attraction" that are thus spread unevenly over the French provinces, Paris exercises an attraction which elevates her high above all other urban concentrations in France. Tables 19, 20, 21 show this very clearly.

These tables were constructed on the basis of the information given in answer to the following question: *If a young man whom you knew was unemployed or wished to change his employment*

TABLE 19. SIZE OF AREAS CITED AS PROVIDING POSSIBILITIES FOR EMPLOYMENT

Residence	Number of replies	Paris, Seine, Seine-et-Oise (%)	Cities with over 100,000 (%)	Cities of 20,000–100,000 (%)	Cities of 5000–20,000 (%)	Country pop. under 5000 (%)	Outside France (%)	Total (%)
Parisian area[a]	85	40	8	10	40	—	2	100
Champagne	103	34	13	25	21	6	1	100
Picardie–Soissonnais	110	33	14	30	12	10	1	100
Limousin	75	32	19	21	8	19	2	100
Bretagne	123	32	49	14	3	—	1	100
Poitou	104	28	18	30	16	7	—	100
Causses–Cévennes	89	22	46	20	—	12	—	100
Normandie, region mancelle	174	20	35	20	11	12	2	100
Normandie (western)	83	20	35	18	17	4	6	100
Loire Country	132	20	20	37	10	11	2	100
Aquitaine (interior)	102	15	35	22	17	10	1	100
Bourgogne	70	13	44	26	14	3	—	100
Midi provençal	146	12	51	8	9	15	5	100
Flandre–Artois	181	12	24	45	13	6	—	100
Lyonnais	73	10	67	19	3	—	1	100
Savoie–Dauphiné	123	9	30	35	13	11	2	100
Midi languedocien	108	8	16	31	7	38	—	100
Aquitaine (coastal)	149	7	21	33	14	22	3	100
Lorraine (western)	154	5	13	29	30	21	2	100
Auvergne–Velay	90	2	51	16	28	3	—	100
Alsace–Lorraine	133	2	13	39	31	15	—	100
Franche-Comté	55	—	4	60	31	5	—	100
Berry, Nivernais, Bourbonnais	10	—	—	100	—	—	—	100
Total	2472	17	28	27	15	11[b]	2	100

[a] Seine and Seine-et-Oise excluded.   [b] Cadarache, Donzère, Lacq, Lavéra, Marcoule, Pierrelatte, etc., 3%.

where would you advise him to go in search of a better job? (give one or two places). Subjects were asked to give more than one location if they wanted to, and 2472 responses were recorded for the 1989 people interviewed.

In Table 19 the responses are broken down by region of residence, using the same twenty-three regions as in the preceding section. Paris or its outskirts was named in 17 out of 100 instances.

Paris was cited in all but two regions. In four regions, of which all except Limousin were near Paris, Paris was named more often than any other area. In all other areas the regional capital was named most often, usually with the other important regional urban centres, in proportions which vary from 2% to 32%.

Further, 72% of the replies cited cities of more than 20,000 inhabitants (Paris 17%; other cities of population greater than 100,000, 28%; cities of population between 20,000 and 100,000, 27%). This indicates that the public realize that work can only be found above a certain level of population concentration. Only 11% of the responses named a rural locale of less than 5000 inhabitants, and of these 3% were industrial centres recently formed in rural zones, for example, Donzère, Lacq, Lavéra, Pierrelatte, etc.

Table 20 shows these data in a slightly different light, listing by region the frequency with which each city was cited.

In eight regions, Paris was cited more often than any other city. In Brittany, for example, Paris was cited 39 times, Rennes 27, Nantes 12, and Brest 11. In the Loire area, Paris again was named more often than Tours or Nantes. In the Limousin, mentioned above, Paris was named 24 times, six other cities receiving 19 votes each, an effect which may be due to a certain degree of stagnation in Limoges at the time of the study.

Finally, Table 21 shows clearly the attractive force of Paris in relation to that of other cities, among them Lyon, Marseille, and eleven other large cities. This table shows the frequency with which each of these urban centres was named in each of the residential regions.

Paris was named more than 4 times as often as Lyon, which was

TABLE 20. LIST OF CITIES NAMED MOST OFTEN BY RESIDENCE

	Number of replies	Most frequently named towns (numbers)
Parisian Area	85	Paris 34. Meaux 16. Montereau 7.
Champagne	103	Paris 35. St-Dizier 11. Vitry-le-François 11. Troyes 9. Reims 7.
Picardie-Soissonnais	110	Paris 37. St-Quentin 13. Amiens 13. Lille 4.
Limousin	75	Paris 24. Lyon 4. Bordeaux 3. Clermond-Ferrand 3. Brive 3. Châteauroux 3. Limoges 3.
Bretagne	123	Paris 39. Rennes 27. Nantes 12. Brest 11. Lorient 5.
Poitou	104	Paris 29. Nantes 10. Poitiers 6. Tours 6. Thouars 6. Niort 5.
Causses-Cévennes	89	Paris 20. Toulouse 19. Marseille 11. Lyon 5 Alès 5.
Normandie, région mancelle	174	Paris 35. Laval 37. Rennes 34. Le Mans 18. Caen 16. Alençon 10.
Normandie (eastern)	83	Paris 17. Rouen 23. Le Havre 4.
Loire Country	132	Paris 26. Tours 20. St-Nazaire 12. Blois 11. Vendôme 8. Nantes 12.
Aquitaine (interior)	102	Paris 15. Toulouse 20. Bordeaux 12. Tarbes 10.
Bourgogne	70	Paris 9. Dijon 25. Montbard 9. Roanne 8. Lyon 7.
Midi provençal	146	Paris 17. Marseille 39. Lyon 12. Toulon 11.
Flandre-Artois	181	Paris 22. Lille 35. Dunkerque 15. Valenciennes 13. Denain 12. Armentières 11. Roubaix-Tourcoing 8. Douai 8. Cambrai 6.
Lyonnais	73	Paris 7. Lyon 29. St-Etienne 15.
Savoie-Dauphiné	123	Paris 11. Lyon 17. Grenoble 19. Annecy 12. Valence 17.
Midi languedocien	108	Paris 9. Marseille 9. Perpignan 10. Nimes 9. Alès 5. Montpelier 3.
Aquitaine (coastal)	149	Paris 10. Bordeaux 28. Bayonne 21. Biarritz 11. Pau 7.
Lorraine (eastern)	154	Paris 8. Méziêres-Charleville 17. Longwy 11. Nancy 10. Bar-le-Duc 9. St-Dizier 8. Metz 7. Sedan 7. Reims 6.
Auvergne-Velay	90	Paris 2. Clermond-Ferrand 33. St-Etienne 10. Issoire 21.

TABLE 20—*cont.*

	Number of replies	Most frequently named towns (numbers)
Alsace-Lorraine	133	Paris 2. Colmar 19. Hayange 17. Thionville 15. Strasbourg 13. Mulhouse 9.
Franche-Comté	55	Montbéliard Sochaux 12. Belfort 7. Besançon 6. Pontarlier 5.
Berry, Nivernais, Bourbonnais	10	Bourges 10.

second in popularity, $5\frac{1}{2}$ times more often than Marseille, and 8 times more often than Bordeaux, Toulouse, or Lille.

Furthermore, none of these cities was named in more than three regions except Paris, which was cited often in thirteen regions, and appears at some point in the responses of practically every region. In other words, the Paris attraction, although it varies with distance, is definitely of national importance. The attraction of the other large cities is only regional, spreading out to a distance related more or less directly to the size of the city.

It could be argued that these data would be different if the areas of intense study were altered. This observation is doubtless justified in the case of the less important towns, but not in the case of the large cities.

Map 3 shows the importance and the extent of the attraction exercised by Paris, as indicated in the responses to the question put above. The results showed that the more often a region named its own capital as offering promising conditions for employment, the more often it named Paris also as having this attraction.

The role of Paris as an attractive force is seen especially strongly in the Parisian basin, the west, and towards the Central Massif. The lack of attraction of Berry–Nivernais–Bourbonnais and Auvergne–Velay, compared to that of the neighbouring regions, can undoubtedly be explained as aberrations in the sample.

TABLE 21. ZONES OF ATTRACTION OF PARIS AND SEVERAL OTHER
LARGE URBAN AREAS

Most frequently cited towns	Frequency	Residential Region[1]
Paris	408	Bretagne 39. Picardie-Soissonnais 37. Normandie, région mancelle 35. Champagne 35. Parisian area 34. Poitou 29. Loire country 26. Limousin 24. Flandre-Artois 22. Causses-Cévennes 20. Midi provençal 1. Normandie (eastern) 17. Nine other regions 73.
Lyon	94	Lyonnais 29. Savoie-Dauphiné 17. Midi provençal 12. Fourteen other regions 36.
Marseille	73	Midi provençal 39. Causses-Cévennes 11. Midi languedocien 9. Thirteen other regions 14.
Rennes	67	Bretagne 27. Normandie, région mancelle 34. Three other regions 6.
Bordeaux	46	Aquitaine (coastal) 28. Aquitaine (interior) 12. Four other regions 6.
Toulouse	46	Aquitaine (interior) 20. Causses-Cévennes 19. Four other regions 7.
Lille	44	Flandre, Artois 35. Six other regions 9.
Nantes	39	Bretagne 12. Loire country 12. Poitou 10. Normandie-région mancelle 5.
Clermond-Ferrand	37	Auvergne-Velay 33. Two other regions 4.
Grenoble	31	Savoie-Dauphiné 19. Eight other regions 12.
St.-Etienne	31	Lyonnais 15. Auvergne-Velay 10. Four other regions 6.
Dijon	28	Bourgogne 25. Three other regions 3.
Rouen	27	Normandie orientale 23. Two other regions 4.
Le Mans	23	Normandie, région mancelle 18. Three other regions 5.

The number after the region indicates the frequency with which the corresponding town was cited.

Map 4 shows the distribution of places of origin of Parisian immigrants as recorded in the study of provincial emigrants there. The appeal of Paris is even stronger than is apparent in those regions where the number of migrants is high in proportion to the total population of the region of origin.

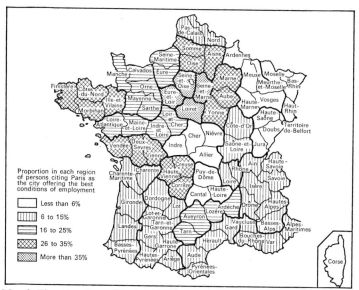

MAP 3. The attraction of Paris according to the study made in the provinces.

Proportion in each region of persons citing Paris as the city offering the best conditions of employment

Less than 6%
6 to 15%
16 to 25%
26 to 35%
More than 35%

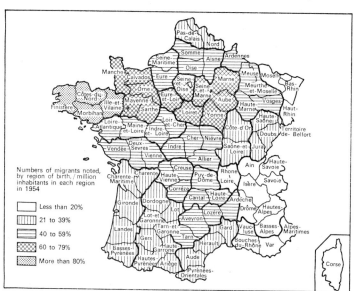

MAP 4. The attraction of Paris measured by emigrant polls according to the Parisian study.

Numbers of migrants noted, by region of birth, / million inhabitants in each region in 1954

Less than 20%
21 to 39%
40 to 59%
60 to 79%
More than 80%

As in Map 3, the zone of Paris's attraction does not include the north, but extends towards Brittany, on the one hand, and the Central Massif on the other. Excluding the regions of Berry–Nivernais–Bourbonnais and Auvergne–Velay, the similarity between the two maps is striking. This indicates that the attraction that Paris actually exerts on the various regions of France is almost identical with the attraction which people in the provinces who have not migrated there would accord it.

Migration to Paris

Migration to Paris is such a widespread phenomenon in France that more than three-quarters of the non-Parisian population (78%) number among their acquaintances people who have gone there to live. Almost half (44%) of these people are the relatives of those who have migrated there.

Persons agreed 5 to 1 that people were right to move to Paris, as living conditions are so much better there (Table 22).

But do people move to Paris because they expect to find a more agreeable way of life there or because circumstances force them to? (Table 23.) There was no general agreement on this point although there was a slight tendency towards the view that migration to Paris is the result of constraint imposed by circumstances.

Migration to Paris is from cities, towns, and villages of all sizes. Throughout the survey the proportion of people who had acquaintances who had moved to Paris was a constant. Opinions about this move were also constant throughout.

The Force of the Growing Urban Concentration

According to a study made a year prior to this one (December 1959–January 1960),[5] the actual distribution of the French population is not the same as the popular picture of its distribution. If the latter were a true picture, rural areas would be

TABLE 23.

QUESTION: *In your opinion do people go to live in or near Paris because they are more or less forced to or because they anticipate a better life there?*

	Total (%)	Population				
		Less than 2000 (%)	2000–5000 (%)	5000–20,000 (%)	20,000–100,000 (%)	Over 100,000 (%)
They are more or less forced to go there	48	48	40	42	53	51
Anticipate better life there	41	41	45	45	36	40
No reply	11	11	15	13	11	9
Total	100	100	100	100	100	100

appreciably less populated than they are, and the Parisian area would also lose some of its inhabitants. Towns of all sizes in the outlying areas would gain.

The question asked in the previous study was the following: *If you had absolutely free choice, and were promised the same income in any case, would you prefer to live in the country, in a town of medium size, in a large town, or in Paris?* (Table 24 shows the results of the replies.)

TABLE 24.

	Preferred residence (%)	Actual residence (%)
Country (less than 5000 inhabitants)	39	50 (of which 37 have under 2000 inhabitants. 13 have 2000 – 5000 inhabitants)
Small town (pop. 5000– 100,000)	34	28
Large town (pop. more than 100,000)	18	10
Paris (Département of Seine)	9	12
	100	100

The present study confirms these data to a certain extent and shows clearly how the attraction of Paris tends to undermine the attraction of the outlying cities.

In this study the question was slightly different. Inhabitants of areas other than Paris were asked to judge the relative merits of life in the country, in a small town, a larger town, and in Paris (Table 25).

As in the earlier study, where people showed an overall tendency to prefer the kind of area in which they were already living, in this study also a majority of the sample considered that conditions in the kind of town they already inhabited were optimal (Table 26).

TABLE 25.

QUESTION: *In general, do you think that living conditions are better in the country, in a small town, in a large town, or in Paris? Why?*

Better living conditions	Total (%)	Population			
		Less than 2000 (%)	2000–5000 (%)	5000–100,000 (%)	Over 100,000 (%)
In the country	27	40	22	15	16
In a small town	28	25	36	34	18
In a large town	25	17	22	29	44
In Paris	10	8	10	12	12
No opinion	10	10	10	10	10
Total	100	100	100	100	100

Comments	Total (%)	Better living conditions			
		Country (%)	Small Town (%)	Large Town (%)	Paris (%)
Higher income	24	19	23	29	46
Lower expenses	16	22	20	12	19
Quieter, calmer life	15	33	18	4	—
Better opportunities, employment	11	1	7	29	14
More agreeable life	9	11	10	10	8
Better accommodation	2	3	3	1	—
Better community services (sanitary, education, social, commercial)	2	—	4	3	2
Other reasons	5	6	8	6	5
No opinion	16	5	7	6	6
Total	100	100	100	100	100

TABLE 26.

	Area with best living conditions[a] (%)	Actual residence (%)	
Country (pop. less than 5000)	30	59	of which 44 have pop. under 2000 and 15 have pop. 2000–5000
Small town (pop. 5000–100,000)	31	29	
Large town (pop. over 100,000)	28	12	
Paris	11	—	
Total	100	100	

[a] After proportionate distribution of those who did not reply.

A slight inclination towards urban concentrations is evident at all residential levels. The reason for this is simply that the larger a city becomes the more people believe that individual incomes are high and that employment and opportunities are available. Whether or not this is, in fact, true, this opinion seems to be a source of motivation for people to move to larger and larger cities, including Paris, rather than to the smaller cities or the country.

As in the case above, if people moved to the areas which they favoured in this study, the urban concentration phenomenon would be even more marked than it is.

Thus the attractive force of the largest cities and of Paris shows clearly over and above other preferences and the attraction of the local provincial capitals. Whatever the cause of this, the resulting exodus from the rural areas conforms fairly well both to the preferences expressed by provincial inhabitants and to their judgement of living conditions.

The opinions of people who have actually gone to live in Paris, however, reinforce this tendency. Table 27 is a comparison of the opinions of migrants living in Paris with the opinions of people living outside the Parisian area.

TABLE 27.

Better living conditions	Provincial residents (%)	Migrants to Paris		
		Earlier migrants[a] (%)	Children of migrants (%)	Recent migrants[b] (%)
In the country	27	19	15	14
In a small town	28	20	22	23
In a large town	25	9	10	14
In Paris	10	36	37	35
No response	10	16	16	14
Total	100	100	100	100

[a] Pre-1945 arrivals.   [b] Post-1945 arrivals.

The very general agreement about quite diverse criteria shows the widespread tendency for urban areas to grow. Men and women, young people, adults and old people, settled people and migrants were in agreement in their judgement of living conditions in various types of environments as they were about migration to Paris and about their motives for this. Tables showing all these categories are not shown as they would not point out any differences.

The only criteria which obviously differentiated groups within the study were related to profession, the degree of familiarity of the subject with Paris, and the kind of life experienced in Paris.

Degree of Familiarity with Paris and Kind of Experience There

One quarter of the non-Parisian population of France has never been to Paris and 15% have been there only once. More than half have been there several times or often, and 8% have lived there (Table 27a).

TABLE 27a.

QUESTION: *Have you ever been to Paris?*

| | Total (%) | Population | | | | | | IFOP Study, 1951 (%) |
		Less than 2000 (%)	2000–5000 (%)	5000–20,000 (%)	20,000–100,000 (%)	More than 100,000 (%)	
Never	26	34	26	19	19	17	31
Once	15	15	16	13	12	17	14
Several times or often	53	46	53	62	61	57	47
Have lived there	6	5	5	6	8	9	8
Total	100	100	100	100	100	100	100

Changes of residence

| | (%) | Never (%) | Only before the age of 15 (%) | After 15 years | | | |
				1 (%)	2 (%)	3 or more (%)
Never	26	33	22	28	23	15
Once	15	18	17	13	17	8
Several times or often	53	49	56	54	50	63
Have lived there	6	—	5	5	10	14
Total	100	100	100	100	100	100

The proportion of people who were not acquainted with Paris increased as the size of the village in question decreased. In rural areas this proportion reached one-third.

For the non-Parisian group as a whole this proportion was 31 %, according to a study made in 1951 by the French Institute for the Study of Public Opinion (in *Sondages*, 1951, No. 2), and takes into account marginal fluctuations, and the development of public transport and automobiles, which have both added to the influx of tourists from the provinces to Paris.

Finally, acquaintance with and experience in Paris increased with mobility. It is obvious that those who moved least visited Paris least.

Profession, as was indicated above, underlies the more obvious variations in this respect. More than half the workers and 4 out of 10 farm owners had no acquaintance with Paris. Among professionals at most levels, this situation would be most unusual.

Opinions about living conditions are also more closely related to profession than to the size of the community of the subject. It is interesting to note that the majority of the population agreed in general that people who went to Paris did so because they were more or less forced into it (61 %) (Tables 28 and 29).

The better the subject knew Paris, the more he appeared to be satisfied with living conditions there. If the subject had actually lived in Paris this view was even more strongly expressed.

The Regrouping of Small Townships

The widespread migration to areas of urban concentration has not been accompanied by changes in the administrative structure. As a result there are in present-day France a large number of underpopulated townships. Out of 37,962 parishes, 23,962 (or 63.1 %) have less than 500 inhabitants. This is about 12 % of the population of France (Table 30).

It would therefore perhaps be advisable to proceed with a redivision of the *communes*, reuniting larger groups of inhabitants.

TABLE 28.

	Farm workers (%)	Farm owners (%)	Labourers (%)	Artisans and tradesmen (%)	Clerical workers (%)	White-collar workers (%)	Businessmen, industrialists, and professionals (%)
Have been to Paris:							
Never	54	38	30	15	17	9	3
Once	19	19	16	12	12	10	6
Several times or often	25	42	49	64	61	74	75
Have lived there	2	1	5	9	01	7	16
Living conditions are better:							
In the country	46	43	24	22	18	21	14
In a small town	25	23	26	29	32	32	35
In a large town	14	15	27	31	28	27	35
In Paris	7	7	13	9	11	10	8
Those who have lived in Paris:							
Were more or less forced to	44	45	46	51	47	61	48
Went in order to find a better life	41	42	41	41	43	36	38

TABLE 29.

	Have been to Paris			
	Never (%)	Once (%)	Several times (%)	Have lived there (%)
Better living conditions:				
In the country	36	27	23	21
In a small town	27	28	29	23
In a large town	20	25	27	29
In Paris	4	9	12	19
People who have gone to live in Paris:				
were right	41	43	56	59
were wrong	8	11	12	11
Named Paris as having opportunities				
1st choice	8	11	17	31
2nd choice	4	6	7	4
Total	12	17	24	35

Such a reform would have numerous advantages, though its execution would certainly not be a simple matter.

Although a favourable view of this is often expressed, considerable opposition is frequently encountered among the people whom it would affect. 46% of the population as a whole was polled as favouring this proposition, but 29% were opposed to it. In communities of less than 2000 inhabitants, the proportions for and against were about equal. Supporters of the redivision argued for the administrative benefits and increased resources that would result, while those opposed argued for tradition and the local spirit of the existing parishes, and were against the possibility of being geographically distant from the proposed new community centre.

Opposition to the change diminished as the population of the community increased. And if we could assume that Parisians

TABLE 30.

QUESTION: *France is divided into* communes, *which are of varying sizes: 100, 200, or 500 inhabitants up to tens or hundreds of thousands. It has been suggested that the smaller* communes *should be regrouped, combining two or three, and giving them the same municipal council, the same mayor, the same school, taxes, etc. In your opinion, is this a desirable thing? Why? If you think a regrouping should be made, what do you think would be the optimal size for the new townships? (1000, 2000, 3000, etc.?)*

	Total (%)	Population				
		Under 2000 (%)	2000– 5000 (%)	5000– 20,000 (%)	20,000 100,000 (%)	Over 100,000 (%)
Regrouping desirable	46	39	43	51	55	54
Not desirable	29	38	28	20	20	21
No opinion	25	23	29	29	25	25
Total	100	100	100	100	100	100

Comments:	Total
	(%)
Regrouping desirable:	
To improve and facilitate administration	18
To increase community resources	7
For increased economy, diminished expenses	5
For better amenities (doctors, tradesmen)	4
To avoid the disappearance of small townships	4
Other reasons	3
Not desirable:	
Each parish has its own spirit, its own air	9
The town hall and school would be more distant	8
There are rivalries amongst the villages	5
Other reasons	6
No comment, no response	31
	100

would vote in the same manner as inhabitants of cities of over 20,000, the popular vote would be 47–48% in favour of the redivision, and 26–27% opposed to it. To the public as a whole the problem seemed little better than academic: a quarter of the population withheld their opinion on the question. This abstention may hide a negative attitude towards the proposal.

Women were much more hesitant than men to voice an opinion on the redivision (Table 31).

The younger and more educated the subjects the more they seemed to support the redivision. Opposition was strongest

TABLE 31.

	Regrouping of *Communes*		
	Desirable (%)	Not desirable (%)	No opinion (%)
Sex:			
Men	50	30	20
Women	42	28	30
Age:			
20–34 years	50	23	27
35–49 years	45	30	25
50–64 years	46	32	22
65 and over	38	34	28
Profession of head of family:			
Farm owners	33	42	25
Farm workers	32	36	32
Labourers	45	25	30
Artisans, tradesmen	57	23	20
Clerical workers	51	26	23
White-collar workers	53	31	16
Businessmen, professional workers	61	20	19
Educational level:			
Primary	40	31	29
Higher primary	54	29	17
Technical	58	25	17
Secondary	59	22	19
Higher	63	23	14

TABLE 32.

	Total (%)	Population				
		Under 2000 (%)	2000–5000 (%)	5000–20,000 (%)	20,000–100,000 (%)	Over 100,000 (%)
Minimum population of new townships:						
Less than 1000	1	1	1	2	1	1
1000	7	8	7	7	6	5
2000	10	11	8	9	7	10
3000	10	8	9	8	13	13
4000	1	1	2	1	1	2
5000	5	3	6	6	5	7
6000 or more	6	2	7	11	12	5
No reply	6	5	3	7	10	11
Regrouping desirable	46	39	43	51	55	54
Average population	3800	2800	4100	4800	4800	3700

among farmers who employed workers. Artisans and shopkeepers seemed to favour the measure.

Those who were polled as favourable to redivision gave as the optimal size for the new townships villages with a population of not more than 4000. Among rural residents, the optimal size was about 3000 people, while inhabitants of towns named 5000 residents as optimal (Table 32).

Summary and Conclusions

As an extension of the study of immigrants to Paris from the provinces, this study largely confirms and completes our previous observations.

We have examined the degree of mobility of the adult population of France. The sample group can be divided into three sections: those who had never changed residence, those who had moved once, and those who had moved 2 or more times.

Mobility is a phenomenon that affects people of all ages, but the most mobile sector of the population is under 30 years of age. Men are a little less mobile than women, but those men who do move do so a little more frequently than most women. This is because men move in search of better conditions for employment, whereas women are most likely to move on the occasion of their marriage.

The economic motive becomes more active as the size of the community in which the individual resides becomes larger. It is most prevalent among the migrants to Paris. Conversely, family motives (marriage) are more common among the more rural portions of the population. It would be quite accurate to say that geographic mobility is a form of professional mobility, though in the country geographic mobility is particularly related to matrimony.

The pattern of changes of residence was not haphazard; nor were moves made without preparation. More than half the people who had moved had relatives or acquaintances in the new area, often their relatives. One-quarter had thus had help in finding work; one-tenth in finding lodging. Although rural people considered that local conditions were improving much more than did urban people, two-thirds of the rural population still said that young people found it difficult to find work. This is a much higher proportion than was evident among the urban population. Observations such as these permit us to conclude that the rural exodus can be adequately explained by economic circumstances, that it is likely to continue for some time, and that the migrations to date have resulted in a much strengthened network of personal relationships from one area to another throughout France.

The hypothesis that changes of residence are not the result of disagreements or the disintegration of a family, but are rather a regrouping or reconstituting of a family in the new location, set forth in the earlier study of Parisian immigrants, was confirmed to some extent in this study.

Several observations confirmed the theory that Paris exercises an economic, psychological, and human attraction over the whole of France through the network of relationships that migration has created. Only a quarter of the non-Parisian population had never been to Paris, more than half had been there several times or often, and 6% had lived there at some time. Favourable attitudes towards living conditions in Paris were the most common among people who knew the city well. Three-quarters of the population had an acquaintance in Paris, and half had at least one relative there. Almost two-thirds of the population were of the opinion that one would be well-advised to move to Paris; 14% were of the opposite opinion. Forty-eight per cent considered that people had no real choice of destination other than Paris once the decision to move had been taken, while 41% held that people moved there because of a positive attraction.

It is difficult to discern whether the real motive was in fact a negative constraint or a positive attraction. It is a delicate matter to separate these two aspects of any decision, either as actor or observer. If there were the prospect of a better life, this would act to attenuate the constraints already imposed by economic necessity. In any case, the net effect was to reinforce the movement towards Paris.

Finally, we considered where the best living conditions were thought to be, both in terms of better income, and in terms of better possibilities for the future (this is equivalent to a kind of social promotion). Opinions were divided on this point, but they depended to a large extent on the degree to which the individual was satisfied with the position he held at the time of the interview. Thus the distribution of opinions gave a picture of population distribution quite different from what was actually the case.

These results permitted us to conjecture with reasonable certainty that the rural population will continue to diminish, as has already been observed in other studies of opinions on ideal choice of residence. The region around Paris will maintain its relative importance, but towns of the provinces will increase in size.

Paris's attraction is attested by other observations also. The highest proportion of people born in other *départements* is found in the area around the capital. Only the Midi (south) rivals Paris in this respect. In contrast to other cities, for instance Lyon, Marseille, Bordeaux, Toulouse, or Lille, this attraction is felt over the whole of France. Even in the zones where these cities exercise their greatest attraction, the force of Paris is still evident.

These data, when seen as a whole, have many implications. It would be an illusion to imagine that Paris will not retain its attractive force for a long time to come or that it will not continue to grow as a result of the weight of its present momentum. But it seems that, considering the excessive population already within the Parisian area, there should be some way of diverting this trend towards some of the other urban centres of France which have comparable opportunities for employment, and which were in fact judged as more desirable homes with better prospects for the future. Such an undertaking would be in keeping with the aspirations of a large part of the population. In the actual development of French urban centres there is no conflict between the development of the Parisian region and that of the large towns in other areas, which could act as counterweights. Our observations of public psychology and attitude reinforce the recommendations made by a new commission for District Management in the Parisian area. [6]

This orientation is, however, not generally accepted, as urbanization and growing urban concentrations have widespread effects in even the smallest communities, as witnessed by the French Government's division of the country into approximately 38,000 townships, of which almost two-thirds now have less than 500 inhabitants due to emigration from the rural areas. The administrative *communes* no longer correspond to social organization or economic constraint. Nonetheless, hardly half the population considers that the redivision of administrative units into more realistic communities is a desirable thing. Only 30% is in favour of such a move. In rural areas these two opposing viewpoints are equally popular, though the idea of the redivision has not penetrated everywhere. Even a change in the law would not change public opinion on this immediately, as traditional elements are involved. But in the light of the economic and social pressures that are already operating, opinions are beginning to alter, and there is hope that in some cases an official change will eventually merely sanction regroupings that are already in fact realities.

Population concentration with its concomitant urbanization appears to be a certainty in several of the larger outlying cities, especially for those people to whom changing residence is synonymous with finding work, better living conditions, and a better life. Without implying a judgement of the benefits or dangers of cities, it is in cities that the large majority of the public sees the most possibilities for improvement. It is from this fact that most geographic changes of residence arise.

References

1. Mols, R. P., SJ, L'Accroissement de la population de la France selon les regions et l'importance des agglomerations, *Population*, 1963, No. 2.
2. Pourcher, G., Le Peuplement de Paris: origine régionale, composition sociale, attitudes et motivations, from *Travaux et documents de l'INED*, vol. 43, Paris, PUF, 1964; also published in *Population*, 1963, No. 3.

3. CROZE, M., Un instrument d'étude des migrations intérieures: les migrations d'électeurs, *Population*, 1956, No. 2.
4. BASTIDE, H. and GIRARD, A., Niveau de vie, emploi et croissance de la population, *Population*, 1962, No. 4, p. 645–82.
5. GIRARD, A. and BASTIDE, H., Les problèmes démographiques devant l'opinion, *Population*, 1960, No. 2.
6. GENERAL DELEGATION TO THE DISTRICT OF THE REGION OF PARIS, *Preview of the Twelve Year Programme for the Parisian Region*, Paris, Municipal Press, 1963, p. 128.

Italy

Emigrants in the Upper Milanese Area

C. MANNUCCI

THE balance sheets of forty-five local authorities in the Upper Milanese area have been seriously upset by the enormous immigration of recent years. This situation, which was little known outside the province of Milan before last summer, was officially brought to light and discussed at a meeting of mayors held in June in the town of Limbiate, on the initiative of some Socialist and Communist administrators; the subject was immediately taken up in the Lombardy daily press. A few days later the provincial government of Milan appointed a Study Group, which included representatives of all the parties, with the task of examining those aspects of the question that were directly involved. Since then, other mayoral or political controversies on the same issue have followed each other, and now it is one of the issues permanently on the agenda in public life in Lombardy.

The Upper Milanese area is, apart from the metropolis, the most prosperous and advanced part of a province which, as everyone knows, has for some time occupied the first place on the list of the incomes of Italian provinces. In this area there are solid towns like Sesto San Giovanni, Rho, Monza, and Seregno, and smaller centres, having a wide reputation for their production, such as Pero, Cesano, Maderno, Cinisello, and Desio. The industrial economy has grown there without interruption, creating such favourable environmental conditions that in the last decade or so many businesses have transferred their plants there from Milan; thus the area now contains the works of some of the major national industries. It has an excellent road and rail network, and even the small villages have a modern urban character.

All in all, it is one of the most fortunate and dynamic regions, with one of the highest standards of living, in the whole country.

The immigration started when the first industries of some importance had established themselves there, and until the Second World War the inflow of workers from outside was gradual and orderly. For many years the great majority of the workers were technicians and skilled workers attracted by the reasonable wages and the other advantages of a developing area. Some workmen who had been unemployed because of Fascist persecution settled down there quite easily, and many Resistance cadres were drawn later from their number. There was some immigration of labourers from both south and north, but it was then easily absorbed by the industrial labour market.

In the post-war period things changed. From 1945 to 1955 immigration from outside the province alone brought 97,000 people to the forty-five towns; between 1952 and 1956 the net increment to the population of the same towns was more than 100,000. The new influx of immigrants is made up largely of agricultural workers who have left the countryside, of builders' labourers, of small artisans and shop-keepers (often from small rural centres), or of workers of no fixed occupation; all of them are followed, sooner or later, by their families. According to an estimate, more than 40% of the immigrants come from districts in the Po valley, and a large proportion of these are from the Lower Milanese area, an almost exclusively farming area with many severe problems; 30% are from the Veneto and the rest come from Liguria, central Italy, or the southern mainland or islands. The total of the southern immigration is, therefore, far from justifying the complaints of the "southernization" of Lombardy with which certain sections of the press prime their readers almost daily. The current is certainly stronger than in the past, and destined to increase, but it certainly is not the torrential invasion that the rabid "northernists" like to denounce. A comparison of the populations of some of the towns in 1950 and 1956 will perhaps give a more exact idea of the scale of the post-war immigration. At Limbiate, it has risen from 9000 to 14,000 inhabitants, at Senago from 5000 to 8500, at Padreno Dugnano from 14,000 to 19,000, at Cesano Maderno from 16,000 to 21,000, at Sesto from 44,000 to 51,000. As can be seen, in some cases the growth has been striking; at Limbiate 55%, at Senago 54%.

The local authorities, almost all of them left-wing, found themselves facing unprecedented problems. The financial burdens of housing, education, public assistance, services, sanitation, etc., in addition to organizational and technical problems, increased so greatly from one year to the next that even now the budgets no longer seem able to support the institutional tasks. Let us take as an example Cinisello, where Pirelli has recently opened a new factory. The municipality is unable, above all, to deal with the housing problem. In the last 10 years nearly 2000 dwellings have been built, mostly by immigrants. The majority are makeshift dwellings concentrated in townships—the so-called shanty towns —on the fringes of the town. These villages lack everything: sewers, roads, drinking water, doctors' surgeries, asylums. The municipality only succeeds in providing for a minimal part of these elementary needs, which require an expenditure of hundreds of millions. Moreover, almost 200 families are still living in stables and basements and so on. For schools, the situation is no better. The number of children for whom it is necessary to provide education has risen to 2000. "The shortage of classrooms", says the mayor, "is fearful. The authority has 29 classrooms, each one of which needs to hold 70 children. Since it's impossible for a teacher to give a lesson to so many children, they have had to split the classes and reduce the hours. The municipality has taken out a loan of a hundred million lire to build a new school, but each year four new classrooms are needed." The costs of hospital treatment, which in 1946 amounted to a little over a million lire for 36 patients, reached nearly 18 million for 1345 patients in 1956. The town now has 30 million lire worth of outstanding debts for hospital treatment, since legal actions for reimbursement are useless in 70% of the cases, as most of the immigrants are not covered by insurance. Almost all of the new citizens pay no taxes, naturally, since their incomes are below the minimum level, and so they cannot contribute to alleviate the financial strain on the administration.

At the Limbiate meeting the labour market situation was also discussed, and this theme was taken up again and developed further at a meeting of mayors held at Cesano Maderno in August. Several speakers drew attention to the fact that the enormous immigration of these years was not met by a corresponding increase in the number of jobs. New plants have started up, but in some important factories there have regrettably been large-scale redundancies. This means that a large number of immigrants, unable to find work in industry, have no choice but to shift for themselves by setting up as small shopkeepers, or in yet more precarious and irregular trades, or falling back on public assistance. But there are also some, and not a small number, who approach employers without too many scruples who take them on clandestinely, without working papers or insurance; this worries the local workmen.

The resentment felt by part of the population towards the new arrivals is more clearly noticeable in the matter of customs. Too often the immigrants do not try to adapt themselves, in those respects where it is right to adapt oneself, to the habits and attitudes of the district which has received them. To maintain some traditions of special value is logical and human, but almost to flaunt ones different background is counterproductive. In one town in the Upper Milanese, at the time of the Limbiate meeting, the walls of all the houses were covered with posters directed at the "Venetian Colony", asking for mass participation in a religious festival, organized by priests come specially from the Veneto, which was to culminate in a procession in honour of a statue of St. Anthony of Padua, also brought from the Veneto. This resembles the case of certain Italian-Americans who celebrate the feast of San Gennaro each year with rites and displays so alien to most other citizens, even Catholics, that they invariably call down on themselves some very unfavourable comments, and, what is worse, the accusation of obstinate refusal to assimilate to a reasonable extent.

These are unimportant episodes in themselves, but it is precisely little things like this, repeated and multiplied by thousands, which give rise to the intolerance and coolness which are often felt towards the immigrant groups. Sometimes, folklore apart, the irritation is based on facts having a very different impact on the life of the native population. In a town in the Comasco, for instance, quite similar in economic and social structure to those of the Upper Milanese area, Venetian immigrants, when they had established residence qualifications, succeeded in voting out the traditionally Socialist administration and replacing it by Christian Democrats. Similar episodes could happen in the Upper Milanese area too in a few years.

At Limbiate, however, the xenophobia which slipped into some contributions was fortunately not shown in the final reports and resolutions, though some obvious worries tended in that direction, despite good intentions. However, the meeting voted unanimously in support of a document which begins by recognizing that the movement of population is, apart from being constitutionally legitimate, humanly and socially justified, and that the towns of the Upper Milanese area "must consider the new citizens in the same way as it does the native inhabitants, with equal rights and duties". Having made this declaration of principle, the mayors emphasize, nonetheless, that to put it into practice they will need to be able to count on suitable financial aid, and they list various provisions that the Province should consider immediately. Above all, their request is that it should immediately take the responsibility for as much as possible of the redemption payments for the loans they have had or will need to carry out the new public works made necessary by the increase of population. The Province should also take part in setting up ONMI consultancies and medical and obstetric clinics, and ensure greater funds for the ECA, for school camps and for assistance to poor pupils in proportion to the indices of demographic growth. Finally, they ask priority to be given to the requests of the towns with heavy immigration to obtain extensions of the networks of drinking water, street lighting, and sewerage, and for the construction of new roads, gasometers, and methane pipelines, and for the installation of telephones in the new villages which have sprung up on the edge of the main centres.

The mayors also took the opportunity to emphasize the urgent need for action of a more general kind, namely for the following legislative provisions: (i) the rapid setting up of a Regional Council, which would be "a means of realizing the potential resources of the region, and of encouraging individual initiatives aimed at bringing about improvements in depressed areas"; (ii) rapid approval of the Bill on building land, from which would come a new "source of finance to cover the burdens caused by demographic growth"; (iii) reform of the 1931 Consolidation Act for local finance; (iv) the extension to towns with heavy immigration of the legislation on loans to towns in depressed areas; and (v) special provisions for adequate financial assistance for the solution of the problem of immigration in the industrial zones.

Thus the mayors of the Upper Milanese area have taken a step which is praiseworthy from several points of view. Perhaps the most valuable aspect is that they decided to discuss the problem in its natural place, stating it at the municipal level; thus they avoided letting it all get submerged in the opportunistic verbiage of the deputies and officials of the central party bureaucracy. What took place, therefore, was the somewhat unfamiliar spectacle of Communists forced, at least within certain limits, to face up to precise and circumscribed problems in a responsible way; there were also some good Socialist contributions, particularly from trade unionists. Unfortunately, there were also some of the usual universal indictments, clichés, highly-coloured descriptions, and special pleadings—but, on the whole, the proportions were much more reasonable than they are on the ordinary party occasions.

So much for the method. As for the substance, there is a lot to be said. There is no doubt that the recognition of the immigrant's right to parity of treatment is a fact which, because of its source, has a very positive significance, apart from its eventual propaganda value. The reaction of any population which has achieved a certain level of comfort to the prospect of making room for masses of people, generally unskilled, and thus jeopardizing their own standard of living, is very rarely one of benevolence and solidarity. That political forces which represent the majority opinion should in an area like the Upper Milanese area take the position described is an event which, whether or not mental reservations lie behind it, is objectively significant and important.

The picture that emerges from the reports of Limbiate proves for the nth time the absurdity of the Fascist laws against the movement of population into towns: although they are circumvented a thousand times a day in every part of the country they continue to cause as much harm as remains in their power. The immigrant in most cases cannot sign on at the labour exchange, and thus enter the normal labour market, because he does not have a permanent address or a regular dwelling-place; he cannot get a permanent address except by demonstrating that he has a regular job. This vicious circle is at the root of many of the most serious problems reported by mayors and trade unionists. The union activities announced at the following conference at Cesano are therefore welcome; they plan to hold meetings of immigrants to explain to them the trade union rights which they should see are respected, and systematically make known all the employers' illegal practices. It is evident, however, that for as long as the feudal laws against internal migration are not repealed any activity of this kind can only have a limited degree of effectiveness.

There was a particularly lively discussion at the Limbiate meeting between those who held that the immigration was caused by the chronic misery of the depressed areas, and those who attributed it to the desire to improve ones own conditions and enter positively into a more modern and civilized style of life. The final resolution accepted the former explanation, naming as prime cause of the immigration "the economic backwardness and deprivation of some parts of the country, whose origins are ancient and unresolved". There seem to be some grounds for both theories; the divergence between them is basically due to an insufficient awareness of the fact that, even if Italian agriculture was not so backward in many areas and sectors, and the oldest problems were all solved, large numbers of people would still leave the country-side, as has happened and is happening in all the countries moving towards a modern pattern of economic development. Agriculture is in difficulties all over the world, including the United States, because it finds itself in a position of great inferiority to other human activities, especially industry, and will continue to do so for a long time. All over the world there is a great movement of resettlement under way, from the countryside towards the cities and the industrial areas; eventually this will lead to the establish-ment of a new socio-economic equilibrium, and only in that context can a complete agricultural recovery be foreseen. Only in rare cases, in countries where the process of the rural exodus is quite complete, can the phenomenon be given the unfavourable name of depopulation.

All this is going on in Italy now in more dramatic conditions than are met with in other Western countries, owing to certain special circumstances. These circumstances are: population in-creasing at a much faster rate than wealth is increasing; the historic inequality between north and south; the irrationality of the Government's agrarian policies; insufficient economic initiative in various parts of the country, etc. But the process is necessary and cannot be halted. At the beginning of the century, when the industrial sector in Italy was of lesser importance, townsmen and unskilled workers emigrated abroad, mainly to America. Now that the opportunities for foreign emigration are considerably reduced, and the relative social and economic importance of agriculture, industry, and commerce in Italy have changed, peasants turn towards those parts of the country, such as the Upper Milanese area, Turin, and Liguria, where the modern economy is solidly based. There are many difficulties, both for those who go and for those who receive them, but they must be overcome by a certain foresight.

Since this is how things are, to believe that a faster solution to the problems of the south would be enough to bring the immigra-tion completely, or nearly, to a halt is to have an over-simplified picture of the Italian realities, if it is not purely a propaganda formula. The exodus has attacked all the country areas, even the most advanced ones like those around Vercello and Novara. As for the industrialization of the south, even setting aside the mistakes and inadequacies of government policy, this could not have any tangible effects for a number of years, and even then it would not be able to stop the flow of emigrating southern peasants but merely to make it less urgent.

A first impression of some of the proposals made by the Milanese mayors is that, although fully justified, they will meet a severe obstacle in the limited financial resources of the province. The province has to provide for 245 municipalities, many of which (especially in the Lower Milanese area) are much less developed than the 45 represented at the Limbiate meeting, out of a budget of less than 9000 million lire; it already has to spend 1000 million a year on immigrants. It is to be hoped that it will be able to do much more, and that to this end when the Study Group nominated by the provincial government comes to make its proposals they will be given due weight. The request for reforms in the law on local finance is well founded; there is a lot that should be changed. Everyone is in agreement on this, but there is, nonetheless, not the least sign that anyone is preparing to tackle this reform. I doubt whether the towns of the Upper Milanese area can expect any real benefit from this in the short run.

Next, the mayors took up the question of the proposal for a law on building land, which is now almost at the starting point: with good reason, they stressed its urgent nature. The situation is certainly serious, but maybe something could be done about it even without this very necessary law. The technical consultant of Novate reminded the mayors that with the reintroduction of town planning schemes, in which many towns have so far taken no interest, they can influence plot prices, controlling them in the buyers' favour; they can also exercise some control over the buildings, providing against the erection of shanty towns. The development of such districts is thus very often due to the incompetence of local administrators, and insufficient use of existing legal weapons. The same speaker also pointed out that the so-called "plan of construction" lays the responsibility of organizing the water supply, roads, and sewerage in the areas released for building, on the owners of the land, which can very much lighten the burden on the town.

Every contribution to the debate emphasized the necessity of setting up the Regional Council quickly. Frankly, one gets the impression that in this sort of invocation the Regional Council has become an obligatory formula, with all the glitter and the vagueness of a myth. Certainly it ought to be established, but with clear ideas and without attitudes which rely on faith rather than works.

The problem of the financial resources of the region, for instance, is passed over too easily, for it is a key issue; before appealing to the institution of the region in the terms used, this and other fundamental questions should be explored further. Really the institution of the region only makes sense in Italy if it is considered as one of the hinges of a general administrative reform; the problem of the region cannot be separated from that of the province, the municipality and the administration of the state itself. Until one knows precisely what is wanted and what can be done to improve the structure of the country's administration, discussions remain empty academic exercises or propaganda tirades. That is, it is useless to talk in the abstract about the advantages of an institution as if one were in a university seminar; what is wanted is thought and discussion about the details of reforms which would be useful and feasible *hic et nunc*.

In the meeting's final resolution it is stated that the region would follow a policy of "encouraging individual initiatives to bring about improvements in depressed areas". Maybe: One would hope so. But perhaps one should see first whether there is any real sign of the existence of political and economic forces which incline to a regional vision and could unite and co-ordinate their efforts within the ambit of the region. The region would be more solidly based to the extent that it came as the political and juridical expression of what was already in some measure occurring spontaneously in Italian society. Why not, for example, put pressure on the existing unions of provinces to evolve as much as possible, in anticipation of the Regional Council? Then one could already focus on some of the thorniest problems of the region, in a concrete way.

As for the request for the extension to the immigrant towns of the legislation on loans to depressed areas, this, too, seems risky, for little by little other categories of towns would be tempted to ask for it to be extended to them, and in the end the discriminatory legislation would become meaningless.

To conclude, the initiative could give rise to interesting developments: if in the meantime it should broaden out to include other issues of technical and cultural policy, so much the better. Someone maintained that the problem of the Upper Milanese area should be examined in the context of the studies under way for the plan for Lombardy. This, too, is an excellent idea, so long as it does not have the effect of losing the sense of the concrete which is the most comforting aspect now of the steps taken at Limbiate.

Immigrants to Turin

G. FOFI

"IMMIGRANTS" is too generic a name to refer to a situation that differs markedly in accordance with the varying regional origins of the groups. Firstly, it is necessary to see who the immigrants are, how many of them are from the north and how many from the south, how many arrived in the years of the "miracle", and how many before; then it may be seen whether there were or are now differences and varying degrees of integration among this mass of people who have left their own towns to settle in Turin.

If last year's census data were all published, one would know the exact number of people who have migrated from one town to another in these 10 years. Statistical calculations, based on the numbers of people who have changed their residence in each of the last years (excluding all those who have emigrated abroad), suggest that the total is around 10 million, or 20% of the population of Italy. This is probably the largest-scale phenomenon of the kind that has ever occurred in Italy. A large part of the migratory movement has consisted of an exodus from the mountains and the countryside towards provincial and regional capitals, from a depressed region to a developing one, from an area without to one with industries. It was obvious that the road to the big city, to Turin and Milan, was often taken from the south and from the poorer provinces of the centre and north (Tuscany, Emilia, Venezia, and Piedmont).

The majority of immigrants to Turin are Piedmontese; in the 10 years from 1951 to 1960 there were 177,300, followed by 47,400 from Puglia, 35,000 from Venezia, 25,000 from Sicily, 16,000 from Calabria, 13,000 from Emilia, 11,000 from Campania, and so on up to the total of 397,000 from Italy, in addition to

269

which there were 14,000 from abroad. Within these overall figures it may be noted that in the 10 years under consideration immigrants from the south increased, taking 1951 = 100 as a base, to 818, while the index for those from the centre rose to 261 and for those from the north only to 216. Again, while in 1951 immigrants from the South accounted for only 17.1% of the total, against 66.5% from the north, in 1960 the proportions are transformed, and southern immigrants reach 46% to the northern 49.9%; in the following year the southerners outnumbered the northerners.

The problem of integration into the life of Turin has, at least until now, been greatest for the immigrants from the south. Their move has not been facilitated, as it has for the Piedmontese, by the nearness of Turin, by shared dialect and customs, or by the great number of possible reference points; nor has it been helped, as in the case of the Venetians and the other smaller groups of the centre and north, by a tradition of emigration to Turin which has been an accepted part of the city's life for years. I shall deal mainly with them and their problems, although it is clear that these affect everyone to a greater or lesser extent.

There is a fine poem by Scotellaro, dedicated to Turin and I think written in 1953, which expresses the state of mind of those who move from the south to Turin, their expectations, and the myth that led and still leads them on. It says: "Big-hearted Turin, you are a young girl who takes my hand; I set out on my journey, and they sent me far away; here, there are people who dream of you as I do, in the wind of the Fiats." It is known that most of the southerners who came to Turin are from country districts, driven out by unemployment, underemployment, abuses of power by the landlords, and the desire for another kind of life. These areas are those where incomes reach annual figures that tell one everything about the kind of living that it is possible to make in such conditions: 100,000 or 150,000 lire a year per family. These are the areas of the large landed estates in the Sicilian interior, and of the Southern Apennines between Cilento and the Molisan and Puglian watersheds of the Fortore. In these districts, as Rossi-Doria wrote:

the peasant [was] continually searching for land: where and as he found it, he cultivated it, scraping together a number of scattered and varying plots, his own property or that of others, one year this one and the next year another one; part would be around the village in the intensively cultivated belt, part in the valley because the soil is fresher, part on the mountain because that gives a better yield in some seasons, and part elsewhere because that was the only place he had succeeded in finding it.

Peasant towns, too, the dormitory towns of 30,000–50,000 inhabitants where at least two-thirds of the population is engaged in agriculture, send their sons to the north; this is especially so in Puglia, followed by Lucania, Campania, Calabria, and Sicily. These peasants leave in the morning before dawn for their little pockets of land, tiny pieces of a few hundred square metres, scattered at varying distances and in different directions; this is the result of the fragmentation of landholding which is in part the origin of the peasant town, as a centre for the various bits and pieces of land. In the evening, or at night, they return on muleback: when the land does not need attention, which is the greater part of the year, they sit in the square in the evening, and in the morning offer themselves to the big landowners as day-labourers.

Who in the south has not heard of Turin? There is a friend, a fellow-townsman, or a relative who has been there, or—for those who can read—a newspaper, and in recent years, also television. The vision of cars belonging to local professionals or to tourists is a precise and definite summons, whose attraction started in the immediate post-war years. Thus the young man left and still leaves for the city, with a little money set on one side or obtained by running into debt, selling his few household goods or working tools or a little piece of land. The "sunshine express" deposits them at Porta Nuova, where the lucky ones are met by a relative or friend who takes them to his own house for the first few days until they have made other arrangements, or to the inn or boarding house where they will stay. But sometimes there is no one, and they only have an address or vague directions of a fellow townsman to a district, and they set out there with all their uncertainties.

Already from this moment the city shows itself indifferent to the situation of the immigrants. Most of them quickly regroup themselves into nuclei based on the (widely extended) family or village rather than province or region. The circle of acquaintances and friendships, of possible contacts, is very restricted; the strength to face up to the new problems, material and psychological, is sought within this circle. Southern, and I would even dare say Italian, civilization is founded on the family clan and only, secondly, on community or parish solidarity.

After the housing problem has been tackled, if only provisionally, the first thing to do is to look for work; most start on this on the first or second day. Many have work waiting for them, found by a relative or friend from the same town; the rest set off round the builders' yards and co-operatives. Until two or three years ago it was the co-operatives, an illegal group of labour middlemen operating for private undertakings and large and small industries, sometimes brought into existence at the wish of an industry, even Fiat, who found work for these people. The work would sometimes be as labourers for casual jobs like cleaning, modernization of premises or transport, but often it was for work at machines or on the assembly line, alongside workers taken on and paid in the regular way; for the same work, however, the immigrants were paid two-thirds or half the usual amount. The firms saved enormous sums, since they did not have to pay established rates for these new workers, but had them at their disposal when market demand made a temporary increase in production necessary. They also used the co-operatives in order to be able to choose and take on only the better workers, to put a brake on the requests and claims made by the regularly paid workers, to use the immigrants for strike-breaking, and to save paying insurance and allowances. The co-operative was paid a lump sum for the hours worked, and for its services it took from the pay of its so-called partners, a quarter, a third, or half, depending on the season and the type of work and those in charge of the co-operative. Some co-operatives were actually organized under the auspices of a union (which could easily be identified) even inside Fiat.

Those who did not need to rely on a co-operative were luckier.

Thanks to information from friends, they succeeded in finding jobs as labourers or masons in the building trade, or as a labourer inside one of the hundreds of little factories on the fringe of the city or in the surrounding area. Until a few years ago the building trade welcomed the majority of the recently arrived immigrants; a very large number joined it almost as self-employed workers, through the sub-contracting system. The undertaking that had contracted to do the work subcontracted it out to small groups of 5-10 men specializing in the various secondary trades (tiling, finishing, plastering, flooring, etc).; they were paid on a piece-rate, by the metre or square metre according to the job. These small groups, which showed remarkable capacities for independent organization even in a hostile or indifferent environment, formed themselves around some more capable person; he gathered round him relatives or fellow townsmen from the same trade, made the contracts with the firms, and organized and inspected the work. It was a group of "entrepreneurs of their own labour" which, in theory, ought to have been registered with the chamber of commerce. Naturally, in the majority of cases, there was no social insurance, welfare payments, etc.; it was at one's own risk.

Those who found jobs in the small factories found, and still find themselves facing a situation where abuses and the possibility of exploitation were more obvious. There were very complex piece-rates, overtime not paid as such, dangerous working conditions, low wages, and opportunities for the business to hire and fire almost without restriction. The most strongly felt problem, which involved both small and large firms, was the short-term contract; this was a powerful weapon in the hands of the bosses, who could give the sack at the end of three months or renew the contract for another three, in accordance with their own interests and convenience. The way towards the other factories, the medium and and the large Fiat, was long, and for most there was a gradual progress from labouring in the building trade to the small factory where a certain amount of practical training in a skill took place on the job, despite poor education and totally different work habits. (Until a little while ago Fiat was everyone's dream, a mythical earthly paradise seen as the solution to all problems and the highest summit that could possibly be attained.) Then the possibility arose of improving oneself in one of the large factories, which (especially Fiat) have always been accustomed to take on workers who already have some training; this means that the small factories have to keep on training new men. Inside the big factories (and I am not talking now of the situation at Fiat) the immigrant worker did not have great difficulties of adaptation. Despite certain environmental and psychological difficulties, quickly overcome, the great majority succeeded in achieving a high level of participation in the problems of their groups, and had indeed a kind of dignity that has put them in the forefront of workers' struggles in these 3 years. For the immigrant worker at Fiat, however, it was the same as for the Piedmontese worker. The "moulding" and enslaving force, tending to reduce worker behaviour within the firm to a single type, operated on the immigrants as it did on all the others who worked there. Let us not forget that immigrants were taken on after various recommendations, often after signing on with one of the unions in anticipation, or perhaps recommended by Valletta or anyway deferring to him, and with this sense of an entry into the paradise of economic peace and security attained, as peaceful and secure as death. One needs to have seen them at dawn, in front of the Mirafiori, when they go in in their hundreds at the gates kept by braided doorkeepers and guards in uniforms; they go in almost silently, without exchanging a word or a greeting with each other, all with their heads bent, all anonymous and equal in their leather jackets. For me, an immigrant, it was the most disturbing picture in this city. But there, too, fortunately, a lot has changed.

When, a few months after the arrival of the man, his family follows, the most pressing problem is that of accommodation. It is hard to imagine the difficulties southern immigrants have in finding a house in Turin. The commonest solution until a few years ago was to take a garret in the centre, in Porta Palazzo, Via Po, and the neighbouring areas, or else old houses in outlying districts such as Regio Parco, Lucento, and Barriera di Milano.

But the centre is now packed as tight as sardines, the garrets have run out, and so have most of the places to let, and those that are left are damp and unhealthy holes where one freezes in winter and burns in summer. Clever sharks spotted a good thing some years ago, and bought up whole floors of garrets for derisory sums, with which they now make spectacular profits from the immigrants. Men and boys on their own find accommodation in inns and boarding-houses, where they pay around 50,000 lire a month for board and lodging; many live with families who have discovered how to solve their financial problems by putting six or eight camp beds in a spare room, charging 10,000–12,000 lire each. If there are two rooms, you can reach a total of around 150,000 lire a month. New flats cost too much, and in the first stages of adaptation and even afterwards there are prejudices and hostilities: they are not let to anyone with more than two children or who does not work in a factory or is a southerner or does not do this or is not that. A speculative under-the-counter market flourishes; one example among many is the recent development of furnishing agencies linked up with the administrators of new buildings: you can have the house if you buy the "modern" furniture by instalments. (It is now almost impossible to find a house, and because of this many prefer to return to their home towns or to move on to another town and try their luck elsewhere— in Milan or abroad.) Once the house was found, they were in a district full of immigrants. On the one hand, this gave a certain sense of protection, but, on the other hand, there was an element of external imposition, and it ensured that there were few opportunities of meetings or interchange with the natives.

There could be a separate discussion of some aspects of immigration to Turin, and these are the most conspicuous. The boys and young men on their own, who have often set out for Turin on the off-chance without taking serious bearings, settle in the little inns around Porta Palazzo. Many of them, however, are only there temporarily, waiting until they can find a way to bring their families; but some become members of gangs almost involuntarily, given the kind of life they are forced to lead—and let us not forget that many are very young, often under 20. It is they who feed the streams of petty delinquency, and who are often reduced to living from hand to mouth, or by casual labouring at Porta Palazzo in the general markets or in some local business. The figures of juvenile delinquency are not very relevant; many of them do not fall within precisely those age limits. The available figures show, however, that delinquency increases in proportion to the number of inhabitants, even before the influence of immigration is felt.

This situation, where the immigrants must live in certain groups and districts, facilitates the maintenance for a time of habits and customs that are vanishing. Let us mention here that which causes most scandal: the crime of honour. The judges of Turin are, rightly, not very impressed with the idea of honour as a motive "of particular moral and social value".

So far we have briefly outlined the stages in the integration of immigrants into the life of the city. The immigrants organize themselves, find work for themselves, find lodging, friends, and environment for themselves—within the limits set by the nature of the situation. When do the official bodies that should intervene in the various situations intervene, if ever? I have undertaken a long inquiry, without any particular competence in sociology or economics, moved only by the human and political interest of knowing about the situation in which I found myself; it is my conviction, supported by the facts and the results of this inquiry, that there is very little accidental in all this. The Manufacturers' Association has a definite policy which influences life in Turin, particularly that of the immigrants. The Fascist law of 1939 on movement into the towns, which was repealed on a decision of the Constitutional Court only 2 years ago, required travel permits for the protection of the cities; it was never observed in Turin, by agreement between the local authority and the registry office, who devised the formula of "provisional residence" to meet the situation. The demand for labour arising from the development of industry in the Turin area made this solution necessary. The policy of the manufacturers has been consistent and precise:

get as many people as possible to come, spend as little money on it as possible, and do it in such a way that the influx can be checked if need be. It is in the context of this policy that the phenomenon of the co-operatives takes its place, as a means of having labour at ones disposal whenever needed without having to take it into regular employment; it is the same policy which, at the same periods, led to the creation of company unions and to political discrimination in factory recruitment. The co-operatives, fortunately, have almost disappeared in recent years, following intervention by the magistrates; this was requested on information laid by the so-called partners and a few trade unionists, and there were some campaigns by left-wing newspapers. The system of putting work out to various undertakings (even if the exploitation is less than in the co-operatives, and the employees have their papers in order) and of short-term contracts, are other aspects of the same policy; it is no accident that they are used as powerful weapons of blackmail when there are strikes or trade agitation.

It may be true that the greatest increase in labour has been in the small and medium firms, but it is also true that it is the large firms that have had the biggest increase in their revenues, with Fiat in the lead. It is difficult to locate the exact links between Fiat and the other industries, and between Fiat and the local authorities, but it seems to me there can be no doubt of the fact that there are such links. I do not even believe that there can be anyone, especially in Turin, who doubts the influence, or rather power to set conditions, exerted by Fiat over almost everything that takes place in the city: even the groups and bodies whose duty it is to represent the public interest move within the framework of this power.

Let us take a minor but illuminating example. How many immigrants find work through the employment exchange? The hiring of labour is arranged either directly between the entrepreneur and the worker, or through illegal intermediaries; these latter are the co-operatives or, when there is the greatest demand for labour, the bandits who go to the station to meet the "sunshine express", or to the pubs and bars most frequented by immigrants. They may even go to the villages, where they offer contracts which appear excellent by southern standards, but turn out to be starvation wages in Turin. The employment exchange is only used to regularize the position of the new employees. Who observes the employment law? Let us take another example. Every summer there are many serious accidents in the building trade. One has only to visit any little factory or builder's yard to realize that in the great majority of cases the legal requirements for the prevention of accidents are completely ignored. The factory inspectorate has extremely few inspectors, and in the building trade alone in Turin there are about 3000 yards in action simultaneously in the summer.

At a meeting in 1961 on the economic development of the province the Manufacturers' Association presented a report on the demand for labour. This said that every year in Turin 18,000 jobs become vacant, in addition to which 20,000–30,000 new ones are created, the number depending on the growth of production; this makes a total of 38,000–48,000 new jobs a year. Of these, 12,000 are taken up by young people in their first jobs, so 26,000–36,000 must be taken by immigrants. Since only about 40 out of every 100 immigrants enter the labour market, this means that at least 70,000–90,000 immigrants are needed each year, as compared with the actual 47,000 in 1959 and 65,000 in 1960. Immigration is, therefore, fundamental for the development and life of Turin. It follows, according to the industrialists, that it should be favoured and stimulated as much as possible, and that one should try to prevent it going towards other countries. (It seems that some pressure has been exerted to this end at the national level, with definite influence on ministerial policy.) However, still from the point of view of the industrialists, one should try to get the maximum profit from it without any outlay. From this come the low wages in most factories and the various other forms of exploitation described above; and thus, at the level of public administration and the various public bodies over which direct or indirect control is possible, it was decided that not a penny should be spent.

What action has the local authority taken in all this? Let us take a few examples. Schools: in 1960 alone, 16,708 children and adolescents between 6 and 15 immigrated, and this has caused severe problems, both paedagogical and administrative. We all know how they have been met: double shifts, and an average of 40 pupils in a class (which means peaks of 70 to a class). There is a shortage of a thousand classrooms and the need increases every year; at the present rate of growth, 140 new ones are needed every year at the primary level alone. A plan drawn up by the Education Office for 1960–3 anticipated the building of about 500 new classrooms for all types of school, including nursery schools; only recently has discussion of higher numbers started.

The situation is the same in the field of welfare services, where little is done and that badly, delegating the task to the parish churches and Fiat. On the one hand, the Assessor's office acts in a few cases in order to keep up its electoral support by individual charity, and the Public Assistance Board makes some efforts, but has little money and can do little besides managing the hostels and other accommodation for the homeless; on the other hand, there are many donations to clerical groups and bodies. It is Fiat that really does something, spending millions every year to present parcels with the four magic letters of its initials clearly stamped on them to almost anyone who asks for them; this follows the skilful policy of getting as much propaganda as possible with acts of the stalest paternalism. Then there is the society of St. Vincent, which is probably the most active in Italy, and a newly constituted body, the Centre for assistance to immigrants; the latter is again, and not by chance, financed by Fiat. It is run by priests, and declares as its fundamental aim the "rechristianization" of the immigrants by means of a few gift parcels. All these enterprises are paternalistic anachronisms, letting trivial charity fall from on high, and they show the ineptitude of the public authorities. In other fields, such as technical education or popular housing, the clear lines of the industrialists' policy are again revealed; do as little as possible, and make others do as much as possible. Thus there are continual requests for the state, the local government or the Cassa del Mezzogiorno[1] to play a part in technical education; the declared model is that of Holland, where the technical schools are financed by the state but run by the industrialists.

Facing these facts, the administrators in their speeches and reports and budgets say: "If it wasn't for the immigrants . . .", "It's the immigrants' fault . . .", and so on. This is an easy excuse for their incompetence, as is the other one often put forward by the municipality about "the cost of urbanization", the cost of "fixed social investments" for each new inhabitant; this one too ends with a request for extraordinary action by the state or even the Cassa del Mezzogiorno. When thousands of millions are spent in useless ways to satisfy pitiable desires for prestige, when taxes are evaded to totals of thousands of millions of lire, when private schools are maintained at the expense of the public ones, it is absurd to complain and throw the blame on to the weak and the exploited who came because they were wanted, because there is a very great need for them. Since Peyron, the new administration has shown itself a little more active in the projects most wanted by the businessmen, at least in planning. Anyway, it is clear that nothing much has changed.

As an aside, something may be said about the instruments for the formation of public opinion used by the industrialists' policy in the case of the immigrants. In the last few years I think it can be asserted that there has been a definite decline in displays of anti-southern feeling, and the collapse of certain fundamental prejudices which in Turin had taken on an almost racist character. Even if these break out again from time to time, in the judgement of the immigrants themselves there is no longer the same hostility as at first; their presence is now a matter of established fact, and whether they agree with it or not the Turinese have had to accept it. All the same, for the integration of the immigrants what is asked of them is basically that they conform to the model (some-

[1] Cassa del Mezzogiorno: Special fund set up by the Italian Government for development of southern Italy.

times acceptable, but more often to be rejected firmly, in my opinion) of "the ideal good citizen", "the sensible Turinese", like monsù Travet;[2] these models are recommended to them and to Turinese public opinion every day by La Stampa, i.e. by Fiat. That is, "we will accept you if you become like us". Instead of a meeting and an exchange that could be profitable to both parties, what is asked for is an almost complete levelling down of the immigrants to the culture of the stronger party, drawn after old conformist and petty bourgeois patterns which are often shabby and mean.

Unfortunately it cannot be said that there has been continual action on behalf of the immigrants by political organizations or the unions which are not tied to the monopoly, either at municipal or factory level. The Communist party has easily made numerical converts (there is no doubt that it is this party which has collected the broadest electoral support among the new townsmen), but little has been done apart from this except for sporadic attempts with the limited purpose of election organization. Often the unions themselves know nothing, or almost nothing, about most of the small and medium-sized factories with which Turin and its suburbs swarm. There have frequently been campaigns, lock-outs, and strikes inside these factories which they only heard about after the event. Thus a strong impulse, which originated in a consciousness of the dignity of the working man which was easily frustrated in the south, was lost. In the best cases it was absorbed by the stuffy paternalism of the employers, or by the lack of union or political viewpoints and explanations.

The proper response to the dearth or absence of public powers favoured by the businessmen, and to the attempt to say "let's get on nicely on our terms and not on yours", was in the workers' recent industrial action; this is the only response that could be considered appropriate and genuine. Since 1960, the year of recovery, the immigrants have participated intensely, massively and sometimes decisively in all the unrest and struggles that have

[2] An impoverished and insignificant clerk in a comic play, whose name has become proverbial.

taken place—and dozens of factories and different situations could be mentioned; sometimes they started it all. Prejudices current even in the working class of Turin were discredited, and first steps were taken towards a real meeting and exchange as a result of the shared struggle for shared demands. I particularly remember the February strike at Lancia, where the Piedmontese workers started off by saying "We'll never be able to do anything because of the new men, because of the *napuli*."[3] Those young immigrants, newly hired, newly arrived, had tremendous economic problems and no union or political background; yet together they kept up a bitter struggle, and together they won a large part of the demands which the firm had refused them. Day by day they got to know each other, they tightened their belts, they worked together, and prejudices vanished. From this a still uncertain class-consciousness was born which could be the base for an increasingly broad unity of the working class of Turin and which would know how to oppose the industrialists' policy with sounder organization, and with a clarity of direction and perspective in the struggle.

What happened in February at Lancia, and before that in other factories, has now happened at Fiat. The strike of metalworkers employed in private industry has been successfully extended to Turin's largest firm. This has happened after years of union oppression, of silence, and of mistrust by the workers; the myth of the Fiat worker who does not strike has been definitively exploded. This has astonished only those people who did not know, directly and at first hand, the situation inside the factory, the changes made in the organization of work and the workers' grievances. I do not propose to analyse these reasons, which are complex and connected with the whole development of the economy in recent years. (It has been done by others, and some time ago; see, for example, the first number of the Istituto Morandi's *Quaderni Rossi*.) Within the factory this has expressed itself in a process of rationalization of production which cuts down the

[3] Pejorative term for Neapolitans.

worker's autonomy, seeing him increasingly as part of the machine, and raises his productivity markedly; it requires of him an almost perfect control, at the same time as it places him in circumstances where he must react in a more precisely determinate way.

It is my concern, instead, to emphasize how in this case too at the level of the workers prejudices, and divergences between the behaviour of Piedmontese and immigrant workers, have now almost disappeared. They struck together with equal force and conviction. Prejudices are now almost confined to the petty bourgeois office workers and the centre of the city. At the base, in the factories and in the outskirts of the city, a process of integration has taken place which is very different from the kind preached with vulgar colonial paternalist racism in the columns of *La Stampa*. A significant anecdote: in front of one of the gates of Mirafiori a Piedmontese blackleg was insulted by a Puglian fellow worker to the applause of strikers from Piedmont, the south, Venice, and other areas; he called him *marocchino* and *napuli*, the names used in Turin for southerners!

The events of piazza Statuto, which made the orthodox newspapers use up so much type, should be seen in the light of what has been pointed out so far. There was talk of a Communist organization, of a Fascist organization, of anarchist provocateurs, of internationalists, and even for a certain time of the *Quaderni Rossi* group; this group's activities are based on very different principles from those of the anarchic demonstration in the piazza, and this ridiculous rumour was denied first by CISL, which started it, and then by the police. It was more a form of chaotic, improvised protest, whose protagonists were young workers, most of them southern immigrants, employed in the building trade or in small or medium metal-working factories. Explanations based on hooliganism are as absurd (very few of those arrested had previous convictions) as those which suggest Communist organization (very few were Communist party members). The usual professional provacateurs, the Ordine Nuovo and Pace e Liberta fascists, joined the crowd of young men, but they did not start the affair.

These young people, then, mostly have jobs; but their integration into the life of the city is, as we have said, difficult, with no support except from their fellows. Most of them are reached by organizations neither of the right nor the left; they have not joined parties or trade unions because organizational difficulties have prevented the parties and unions concerning themselves with them, and frequently their activities do not respond to the needs and problems of these young people. They are exploited and isolated, they have bitter experiences behind them, and there is no one to give them the perspectives, the social, cultural, and political education that they need. Umberto Segre, the only journalist who has given a valid and reasoned interpretation of these facts (in *Il Giorno* of 13 July), wrote: "Perhaps it is just because they are so isolated that their enemy, in a moment of enthusiasm, becomes huge and generic: they want to destroy everything, to strike at the state through its representatives, to have a direct confrontation with the Police."

There is, then, a hard and patient task, to be faced up to with clear ideas and precise analysis; it will necessarily exclude either dubious alliances with monopoly and its henchmen, or trivial, paternalistic reformism (which sometimes conceals a trace of racism). The problem is not a sectional one; it is a political task which faces the whole working class of Turin without the false categories and divisions between immigrants and natives any more.

Aspects of Internal Migration Related to Other Types of Italian Migration

F. ALBERONI

Introduction

IN THIS short essay it is my intention to attempt to single out the most typical aspects of internal migration in Italy today and relate them to earlier forms of Italian emigration with particular reference to the point of integration.

The work is in two parts: in the first I shall attempt an outline of an abstract typology of Italian migration, and in the second I shall consider the situation in Italy today in which internal migration plays a particularly important part.

I shall not, therefore, proceed along the most usual lines with a study of the structure and socio-economic causes of the various migratory flows followed by an exhaustive analysis of the ones most typical of the currently developing phase of Italian history. Were I to do so, I should lose myself in a sea of facts and figures, for the most part already well known, and run the risk of repeating what others have studied and written about better and more competently than myself. Instead, I must adopt a course peculiar to sociology, attempting to distinguish within the history of Italian migration dividing lines which will enable me to isolate sufficiently differentiated "types" of emigration as they occur— "ideal types" in the sense of Max Weber. It should be borne in mind that these ideal types are not historical in the sense that one precedes the other in a set order or sequence, even though I may describe them as succeeding one another in time. It is not in fact the case that one type of emigration is replaced by another;

rather, the various "ideal types" are realized more fully, but never absolutely, in certain periods and migratory flows whose characteristic form they represent.

Historians may raise their eyebrows at this kind of analysis because it does not respect the chronological sequence of historical types; demographers will find that it contains generalizations which they themselves would not have made, while economists will have the impression that the economic aspects of migration have not received sufficient attention. Indeed, the most formidable objection commonly encountered by the sociologist is that, in studying a phenomenon like migration which is, I should say, patently linked with the search for employment, he does not take as his starting point economic conditions in the countries of origin and destination, or calculate incomes. The fact is that we begin where the economist leaves off, and this is as it should be. From time immemorial people have moved in order to be better off, or at least less badly off. The Italian emigrant setting out for South or North America or for France 60 or 80 years ago would have said, with his modern counterpart travelling from Cetraro to Milan: "Vado a cercare una occupazione conveniente"—"I am going to look for a suitable occupation." We are all where we are because we have moved in search of suitable work; nevertheless, in every case there remains the possibility of a further analysis of the situation, taking as its starting point—simply because they differ—the ideas and hopes involved, and the precise way in which the emigration came about. To take up my former example; in the case of an emigrant from southern Italy going to the United States the expectations, hopes, and motives taken as a whole, the combination of factors which affected him and continued to do so after his departure, are not the same as those which affected me or such of my Italian readers who have emigrated to Rome or Milan. The context as a whole differs in the two cases, as do the social system and the system of reference; hence a qualitative difference in the "type" of emigration. These, then, are the aspects on which I would like to focus my attention; and thus the limits I have imposed are imposed for a specific reason. The real defect of the approach I am about to adopt lies elsewhere: it is impressionistic and hypothetical in character. In this article I cannot put forward a theory of migration and the corresponding integration; at the most I can give a general picture, a rough outline of the main features. It may be that I have given undue emphasis to some features and not accentuated others as I should; worse still, I cannot obtain certain proof that the picture I have given is correct: what I have written has the hypothetical character of topics still at the research stage. In my essay it is my concern to distinguish and differentiate which has been uppermost, rather than the question of proof and documentation, and I would like to make it plain to the reader that although the essay may be of use in guiding him through the tangle of facts, figures, and opinions, he must be cautious of a critical or too rigid acceptance of the results: it is to be regarded as a starting point for thought, rather than a point of arrival.

I. Historical Types

1. Around 1860 the number of Italians abroad, based on an estimate by Correnti, was approximately 200,000; a fairly large number, but nothing like as large as it was to become in the following years. It is after 1880 that the numbers of emigrants really begin to increase. As before, their destination continued to be largely France, Germany, and Switzerland. It is true that overseas emigration was slowly gaining importance, but the flow was still essentially European. The emigrants came above all from regions in northern Italy. Emigrants from the south in the 5 years 1876–80 numbered about 6000; the great boom occurred in the first 15 years of the twentieth century, and then the number was of the order of many hundreds of thousands.

For the most part it was a question of temporary emigration of agricultural workers from Piedmont and Venetia, going to carry out certain agricultural work in France or Germany, and to these were added the masons and builders bound for France, Germany, and Switzerland. The emigrants were predominantly male. The

Venetian and Piedmontese peasants went abroad for a certain period of time, leaving their parents or their wife and children behind in Italy. In general they already knew where they were going, what work they were to do, and also how much they would earn and could expect to save. Sometimes they were away at only certain periods of the year when they would otherwise have been unemployed, returning when there was a demand for labour. Even smallholders sometimes went away at certain seasons, leaving the household and the women to do the small amount of work required. They could not have been said to be "looking for work" —even less "seeking their fortune". There is little or nothing in this type of emigration of the idea of risking one's livelihood: the level of expectations was never exaggeratedly high, and the financial calculations, although rough and ready, always formed the basis of the decision. Thus separation from the family, since it was temporary, did not have the dramatic overtones which we shall see making their appearance in overseas emigration. As regards integration into the host country, it was good in the sphere of work. Frequent journeys to the same place, or a more prolonged stay, gave rise also to partial integration into the local community.

The flow towards the European countries remained almost stationary until the First World War, after which there was an abrupt rise in the number of Italians emigrating to France, and numbers for Germany decreased. In the period following 1933 the flow was dwindling everywhere; then there reappeared a movement towards Germany, which was interrupted by war. From 1926 emigration to Belgium, which later assumed considerable importance in the second post war period, began.

Originally stemming only from the north, the Italian migratory flow into Europe gradually spread, and from 1950 increasingly involved the southern population. In the last few years it has come to be almost exclusively from the south, while the importance of other destinations receiving southern Italian emigrants, including overseas destinations, has dwindled. In spite of these changes in its composition, some characteristics of European emigration remain constant. It involves predominantly men, is temporary, and the emigrant is taking up an offer of employment rather than job-hunting or fortune seeking. In a proportion of cases the emigration has, in fact, become permanent, usually after a prolonged stay. This has almost always occurred in cases where the worker's family came to join him. This is programmed emigration in which financial calculations play an important part; they did so with the masons from the north travelling to Switzerland in 1880, and they do today among the men of Calabria who travel the same road.

2. Around 1887 a new and substantial migratory flow was becoming apparent, directed towards the countries of South America—Argentina and Brazil. This, too, came from the North of Italy, and then increasingly from the south. It differs from the preceding type in that it was more often permanent in nature, and emigrants settled in the rural areas; in other words, it was made up of agricultural tenants, *coloni*, attracted by the prospect of the new lands to be developed. Whole families moved in this way with the intention of settling a sizeable tract of land and building up their own farming business. This is perhaps the only type of Italian emigration actually planned as permanent. Gradually this flow, too, came more and more from the south, and became temporary in part—I am thinking here of the *braccianti*, farm hands from the south who went to South America for seasonal work. The growth of the South American cities and the Italian colonies within them eventually diverted this flow from the rural destination which had characterized it at first.

3. Only towards 1890 did emigration to the United States begin, involving the region of Venetia, but, above all, after 1900 the southern population of Italy. From 1901 to 1905 the number of southern emigrants, which in the period 1876–80 had been less than 6000, soared to 285,000. In the same period the number of people leaving Italy for the United States rose from approximately 10,000 to more than 900,000. As a type, southern Italian emigration to the United States is quite distinct from other forms. It also involved mostly men, and was usually planned as temporary, but in this case the emigrants did not go to take up an offer of employment, or even in search of work. Having accepted their condition

for centuries, the people of the south discovered simultaneously their poverty, the intolerable nature of their condition, and the possibility of escaping it once and for all by making their fortune (*fare fortuna*). At the centre of this emigration lay the idea of making one's fortune, of setting out poor, and finding beyond the Atlantic the lucky chance which would enable the man who was on the look-out for it to make his fortune and then return, rich and important, to his native land.

> These emigrants [writes Pozzani[1]], by contrast to their brothers from the North, offered less resistance to physical fatigue, a lesser degree of specialized training, but had greater powers of adaptation and consequently an attitude better able to resist the first adversities. Any work would do . . . any experience was acceptable . . . they abandoned themselves to seeking their fortune . . . with fatalism. . . .

As we shall see, another characteristic of this type of emigration is the extreme difficulty of integration into the host country.

In the first post-war period, the migratory flow towards the United States tailed off considerably, primarily on account of the restrictive legislation introduced on the American side. Emigration to the countries of South America also dwindled. In the second post-war period the flow towards all three of the destinations we have studied began again, but with diminished vigour and in a different way, with different prospects in view. The development of new lands in South America had long since become an impossibility for those without capital, and the myth of fortune had also vanished. The ones who were leaving now were generally on their way to join friends or relatives, or take up a prearranged job; the family would either leave at the same time or follow on soon after.

Here, too, then, more detailed financial planning was again in evidence. In a short time, however, the thoughts and aspirations of the southern Italians who fed these movements turned towards Europe and towards the industrial cities of Italy, feeding instead the internal migratory movements.

[1] S. Pozzani, *L'Economia italiana. Situazione e problemi*, Comunità, Milan, 1962, p. 148.

4. Internal migration, which has assumed considerable import-ance in the last decade, is a direct consequence of the economic development of Italy made possible by the conversion to industry of the Italian economy. We know that in 1921, 55 out of every 100 of the working population were engaged in agriculture. This went from 49% in 1931 to 41.5% in 1951, and had fallen sharply to 27.5% in 1962. At the same time, the massive number of unemployed, which around 1950 was of the order of a million, fell to some 300,000.

We should also remember that, unlike almost all countries in which the industrial revolution started very early and coincided with rapid expansion of the population, the reduced percentage of agricultural workers was accompanied by an absolute reduction in their numbers. The number of agricultural workers, which was 9,356,000 in 1931 and 8,060,000 in 1951, had in fact fallen by 1962 to 5,624,000. This implied, in effect, an exodus from the country and a change in their type of employment for a large proportion of the population of Italy. The high road of the move from the country to the cities, especially the industrial cities and regional capitals (Rome, for instance), drew first of all upon the neighbouring zones where agricultural labour was particularly abundant (as in Polesine), but then spread evenly over the whole of Italy. Besides the industrial concentration in the north, then, there was also a considerable flow from south to north, to the detriment of migration out of Italy, which was confined to the more culturally isolated zones, where there already existed pre-cedents and migratory traditions to certain countries.[2]

I have recently put forward the hypothesis that the spreading tendency to internal migration has kept pace with (and has therefore been correlated with) a cultural transformation charact-erized by the appearance of new prospects, needs, and require-ments, new hopes and a new intolerance. A chief characteristic of these migratory movements is the predominance of women, a consequence of the ever-increasing part played by women in

[2] See F. Alberoni, Aspetti e caratteristiche delle migrazioni interne in Italia, in *Studi di Sociologia*, 1 (1), (1963) 23–50.

TABLE 1. NUMBER OF EMIGRANTS (in thousands)

Year	Belgium	France	Germany	Switzerland	Argentina	Brazil	United States
1869	—	35.0	2.9	3.7	—	—	—
1870	—	22.7	5.9	3.9	—	—	—
...							
1876	—	34.5	9.6	18.7	3.5	—	1.0 ca.
1877	—	33.3	9.1	13.5	5.7	—	0.8
1878	—	33.5	6.9	10.8	8.6	4.5	1.5
1879	—	39.7	6.7	10.4	13.2	8.0	3.1
1880	—	43.2	4.3	13.1	12.0	6.0	5.7
1881	—	50.7	5.8	10.2	15.9	6.7	11.5
1882	—	53.0	7.7	8.5	23.0	9.0	18.5
1883	—	46.8	12.4	6.3	24.1	7.6	21.3
1884	—	38.5	4.3	5.5	31.9	6.1	10.6
1885	—	33.4	4.5	4.6	37.7	12.3	12.5
1886	—	35.7	3.8	4.3	36.5	11.3	26.9
1887	—	31.2	4.7	5.6	52.4	31.4	37.2
1888	—	27.9	10.1	6.2	64.2	97.7	32.9
1889	—	27.5	17.9	9.1	69.0	17.0	25.4
1890	—	29.3	15.2	10.7	36.7	16.2	47.9
1891	—	31.2	13.9	13.2	24.1	108.4	44.4
1892	—	32.4	15.6	13.7	25.3	36.4	43.0
1893	—	28.7	15.2	9.6	32.5	45.3	49.8
1894	—	23.4	16.6	10.4	32.6	41.6	31.7
1895	—	18.7	14.9	13.9	41.0	98.1	37.8
1896	—	18.0	17.2	18.3	56.4	76.7	53.5
1897	—	19.6	21.1	25.3	36.7	81.0	47.0
1898	—	22.9	26.8	27.6	33.9	38.7	56.4
1899	—	25.0	40.3	29.3	44.2	26.6	63.1
1900	—	39.3	49.2	27.8	40.4	27.4	87.7
1901	—	59.2	46.9	45.8	59.9	82.2	121.1
1902	—	59.8	52.9	50.2	36.8	40.4	193.8
1903	—	49.0	53.6	45.8	43.9	27.7	197.9
1904	—	45.6	55.0	52.3	51.8	19.7	168.8
1905	—	58.0	71.6	75.1	86.2	30.1	316.8
1906	—	62.5	68.3	80.1	107.2	27.8	358.6
1907	—	63.1	75.9	83.0	78.5	21.3	298.1
1908	—	57.7	59.8	76.1	80.7	15.6	131.5
1909	—	56.9	53.4	66.9	84.9	19.3	280.4
1910	—	61.0	53.6	79.8	104.7	19.3	262.6
1911	—	63.4	64.9	88.8	32.7	22.3	191.1
1912	—	74.1	75.5	89.3	72.1	35.6	267.6

TABLE 1—*cont.*

Year	Belgium	France	Germany	Switzerland	Argentina	Brazil	United States
1913	—	83.4	81.9	90.0	111.5	31.9	376.8
1914	—	68.1	55.1	62.4	34.8	14.0	167.5
1915	—	36.3	3.3	27.5	8.8	3.6	51.7
1916	—	44.3	—	17.6	4.0	1.5	66.3
1917	—	22.6	—	7.8	0.7	0.4	11.5
1918	—	16.9	—	5.1	0.7	0.3	2.8
1919	—	98.3	1.3	20.8	12.8	5.6	82.5
1920	—	157.0	2.8	24.3	37.4	10.6	349.0
1921	—	44.8	1.8	8.8	33.3	8.6	67.5
1922	—	99.5	2.1	7.5	63.6	9.3	41.6
1923	—	168.0	0.6	8.8	105.2	13.6	51.7
1924	—	201.7	1.1	12.6	67.4	9.7	35.4
1925	—	145.5	1.7	13.6	53.0	7.4	29.7
1926	3.1	111.3	0.6	14.1	64.2	11.2	34.5
1927	2.6	52.8	0.9	18.1	68.8	9.2	37.9
1928	3.6	49.4	0.8	15.4	25.8	2.6	36.8
1929	9.7	51.0	0.6	17.0	23.2	2.3	31.4
1930	10.8	167.2	1.5	26.0	28.7	1.7	22.1
1931	2.9	74.1	0.8	25.6	19.0	1.5	16.4
1932	0.9	33.6	0.4	11.7	9.3	1.2	11.5
1933	1.1	35.7	0.7	10.7	6.6	1.5	11.5
1934	0.7	20.7	0.6	8.7	5.8	1.3	10.2
1935	0.3	11.7	0.6	7.6	8.4	1.7	13.4
1936	0.3	9.6	0.5	3.9	5.8	1.3	10.2
1937	0.6	14.7	0.7	5.4	8.9	1.3	15.6
1938	0.5	10.6	9.6	5.9	9.9	1.1	12.2
1939	0.1	2.0	2.0	4.4	4.7	1.0	7.5
1940	—	1.1	42.3	1.8	0.6	0.2	2.9
1941	—	—	7.6	0.4	—	—	—
1942	—	—	7.6	0.2	—	—	—
1943	—	—	—	—	—	—	—
1945	—	—	—	—	—	—	—
1946	24.7	28.1	—	48.8	0.7	0.6	5.4
1947	29.8	53.2	—	105.1	27.4	4.1	23.5
1948	46.4	40.2	—	102.2	69.6	4.7	16.7
1949	5.3	52.3	—	29.7	98.3	6.9	11.5
1950	4.2	18.1	—	27.1	72.5	9.0	9.0
1951	33.3	35.1	0.4	66.0	55.6	9.2	10.2
1952	22.4	53.8	0.2	61.6	33.3	17.0	7.5
1953	8.8	36.7	0.2	57.2	21.3	14.3	10.0
1954	3.2	28.3	0.3	65.7	33.9	13.0	26.2
1955	17.1	40.7	1.2	95.0	18.2	8.5	35.1

industry, and in migratory projects and employment planned primarily as permanent. We shall see that, whereas in traditional migration—with the exception of the farmers in South America— the emigrant planned a temporary stay and remained emotionally bound to his community of origin—in this case the relationship is broken off and there are even signs of a rejection of the community.

II. Types of Integration

On the basis of the brief survey contained in the preceding paragraphs I have distinguished four types of Italian migration: that of the tenant farmers or *coloni*, the emigration to the United States from southern Italy, emigration into Europe, and the present-day internal type. Of course, as I have already said, these types are in reality anything but pure, but I have attempted to describe some of the particular characteristics which make it possible to identify them. I shall now go on to examine the ways in which integration takes place. Integration is to a large extent a function of the emigrant's motives, plans, and expectations, and his relationship with the community of origin.[3] For this reason, different types of integration would seem to correspond to different types of emigration.

1. The emigration of the farmers to South America makes up the last category of the rural emigrations on which Oscar Handlin has written in such masterly fashion.[4] The farmers based their decision to emigrate on prospects and expectations which were partially real and partially doomed to frustration. The peasant who saw that he no longer had the prospect of an adequate piece of land in his own village heard that elsewhere land was to be had in enormous quantities. As had already been the case in previous rural migrations, though perhaps less now than before, the

[3] See G. Baglioni, Gli orientamenti degli studi sull'integrazione socio-culturale dell'immigrato: aspetti e questioni di ordine generale, in *Rivista internazionale di Scienze sociali*, 1962, vol. III; also Aspetti e manifestazioni tipiche della integrazione socioculturale dell'immigrato, *ibid.*, 1962, vol. V.

[4] O. Handlin, *Gli sradicati*, Comunità, Milan, 1958.

emigrants had an imprecise idea of what awaited them. Most believed that they would find a geographical and human environment resembling the one they had left, within which they could reconstruct, if it were not already there waiting for them, a village, neighbourhood and trading framework like those they had left behind. Only a few had the hardy spirit of the colonist or the pioneer. In this case, as it turned out, only a part of the emigrants successfully settled on this land where conditions were so different from what they had imagined, while others eventually settled in the trading towns and were largely responsible for the formation of urban nuclei like São Paulo and Buenos Aires. The Latin culture of these places, which had not yet undergone industrial changes, did not as a whole appear strange or incomprehensible to farmers coming from northern Italy, and the language— relatively easy to understand—contributed to their fairly rapid integration, accomplished despite enormous sacrifices. The family set out together, fully conscious of the risks involved, and expectations were never such as to obscure the awareness of reality. The woman shared with the man every stage of the lengthy process and, especially when she began to take an active part in helping it along, her presence hastened rather than delayed integration. In many cases, however, especially when she remained at home in the town for hours on end toiling away at the household chores, she reacted to the frustration by reviving behaviour patterns and values which belonged to the past.

2. Emigration from Italy to the United States in the early twentieth century, predominantly from the south, and dominated by the theme of fortune, presents quite a different picture. The exodus, first episode in the history of any adventurer, gradually becomes the collective solution to a problem which is aggravated by the act of emigration itself—the problem of *status*. In a society which had stood still for centuries, and in which the number of wage-earners in recent years had steadily increased, the dominant feeling had become resignation to one's condition which had been construed by learned men such as Wagner as constitutional apathy. In reality, within this poor and stationary social system

there still flourished secretly the hope of a radical change for the better, envisaged not in collective terms or in terms of class or conquest, but in individual terms. The success of the few fired the imagination of the many, and little by little social life grew to be dominated by this new "possibility". As I have said, betterment was still thought of as a radical change in personal and family status, a change which might be brought about not by following a definite plan or by carrying out a series of rational actions directed towards an end in such a way that the steps towards it were clearly envisaged beforehand, but by making a single decision, a single tragic and courageous gesture—to go to America. It meant risking everything on an adventure which might prove fatal, but in which success depended far less on ability than on the unpredictable agency of chance which dispensed its favours more liberally over there than at home. Once this possibility had revealed itself, it was impossible to accept passively a place in society which increasingly seemed humiliating and undignified. In a society concerned less with income and consumption than with inheritance and property, the value and respect accorded an individual by others had been and were increasingly a function of his ownership status. Everything, indeed, depended on property and possessions: the possibility of survival, of treading but not being trodden underfoot, the possibility of marriage with the girl one loved, as well as finding a suitable husband for one's sister or daughters. Women, who had rarely played any active part in these migrations, were, in fact, the mute protagonists of the whole process. In a system of stratification based on professional status, the value of women is a function of status, while their possessions derive from duties and privileges of status.

The sociologist or historian studying migration from the south in depth should make a careful examination of the role played in it by matrimonial and family structure within the framework of patrimonial stratification. For very many years the system of marriage based on heritage had remained stable. Each man knew his own status and that of the others in his village; a set of predetermined patterns for behaviour and expectations governed people's choices, making them want the things which they could and ought to have, and not wish, on the contrary, for the other things which in any case they could not and should not have had. No mechanism was provided for the contingency of a massive increase or prospective increase in upward social mobility. This is proved by the fact that many years later the rise in status, the improvement, is still seen as individual, and still follows to a large extent the logic of competitions within a stationary context, whereby if one man acquires something, it means a corresponding loss for someone else. Emigration increased upward mobility and the prospect of it. The system yielded to this first shock rather than re-form itself into new moulds (free choice of husband or wife, status based on income, and so on). Thus it was the old system which channelled the hopes and prospects of those who went and those who remained behind. The former resolved to make their fortune, then return and settle their families and themselves in positions of higher status, and enjoy the attendant honours and privileges. Those who remained behind, on the other hand, were waiting fairly confidently for the day when their status would change for the better. But the very fact that a member of a family had left home made its status problematical. As the migratory urge gathered momentum, status itself changed, becoming somewhat more detached from heritage. At this time, to leave home became for many a duty, a sacrifice which redeemed or would redeem their own people. If emigration from the south had continued unchecked after 1915, the whole social order would probably have entered a state of crisis. However, as we know, the flow was checked. As a consequence, conservative forces prevailed, and the features of this type of emigration remained within the terms already given. The emigrant's objective was to improve his own family status within the undisputed and legitimate social structure of his community of origin. The basic system of reference, the *locus hominis*, the society of men in which the hoped-for fortune and the sacrifices necessary to obtain it required significance, continued to be the village (paese) of origin. The man departed amid the tears and lamentations of women and relatives, and heart-rending scenes—a combination of adventurer and sacrificial victim. A deep-seated emotional ambivalence has always characterized these departures, because those who remained unconsciously felt themselves to be responsible for the sacrifice, and those who departed unconsciously felt themselves to be victims. The separation thus came to be felt by the former as a punishment for their own guilt, and by the latter as aggression in the others' attitude (of a melancholy type), which in its turn generated guilt feelings.

This ambivalent and conflicting emotional bond became an umbilical cord joining the emigrant to his people at home, and reinforcing factors like language difficulty and local prejudice contributed to estrange him from the host country. His state of unpreparedness, his spirit of adaptation, his capacity to adapt to the most humiliating situations, his patience, as well as his difficulty in methodical work and in acceptance of "rationality" or logic in the institutions which he came into contact with—these to a large extent were all due to his relationship of emotional and mental detachment from the host society. Thus his capacity for adaptation was not accompanied by a corresponding capacity to integrate. Pozzani writes:[5]

> Meanwhile, in this country with its rapid capitalistic and technological development, emigrants of other nationalities (and also Italians from the north) were adapting to the discipline of mass production: they were entering the factories and mines, making their way, though somewhat hampered by their language difficulties, into the local affairs of their adoptive country, embracing its customs and ways of life, and realizing its progress as citizens of a developing country in contrast to their former situation. On the other hand, the southern Italians remained faithful for the most part to their own noisy and emotional individualism, settling in separate neighbourhoods, forming "little Italies" with the appearance and customs of the old rural areas and towns, abandoned but still mourned.

What had been planned as a temporary stay would, in fact, become permanent, either because the emigrant had made his fortune or because, not having made it, he hoped to do so, and was ashamed to go back. Very often he was later joined by his

[5] S. Pozzani, *op. cit.*, p. 148.

wife, and once there was a family, things became more difficult still. The woman was, if anything, even less prepared for her new environment than her husband, and the extent of her role, active or passive, in the construction of the "little Italies" would bear investigation. It is certain that the woman brought with her the initial values of emigration which placed her in the position of creditor. Deprived of the human and social environment in which she lived, frustrated and threatened, it was impossible for her not to make every effort to reconstruct and to safeguard jealously the *mores*, the customs, and type of relationship upon which her "value" was founded.

For the man, the presence of his wife and children healed an open emotional wound and alleviated tension by counteracting the effects of failure, but it required in return the acceptance of the corresponding values and the prolongation of his own role, now completely unrelated to reality. Hence the reconstructing of a society similar to the old one, a society where a largely stationary existence did not dispel the illusion that the great leap had carried them only a short distance; an outpost for people who had for the most part stopped persevering; an existence which, for the women, continued to be exile in a hostile land, accepted as a duty and a necessity, and for the man a halting place where he knew, however, that he would remain for ever, caught in a trap. Neither the man nor the woman had the strength or ability to break with the forces of tradition on which their "value" was based. Each remained, in the eyes of the other, a witness to the duties and meanings which had their root in the far-distant village, and which the emigrants nourished in this caricature of a village, so that they would not have to change.

3. In the migration of southern Italians to Europe similar traits reappear, as also in the internal migration now taking place, but not so strongly marked as to be characteristic of the type.

As we have seen, the emigrant to Europe sets out with a more definite plan, more modest expectations, and a greater sense of reality. He does not seek his fortune, but rather a certain type of work, and the possibility, calculated beforehand, of saving a certain amount. Even for emigrants coming from the south of Italy, the shorter distance, the fact that it is easier to return home and to make another attempt, the absence of any idea of fortune, and hence the absence of a dream of radical and largely "magical" betterment of their condition, are factors which relegate the elements of risk and sacrifice to a position of secondary importance. The beginnings of genuine socialization of a rudimentary kind are often observed, especially in emigrants from the north, although controlled by very definite mechanisms of isolation from the host society. In fact the basic system of reference for these northern emigrants also tends to be that of the village of origin; it is here that they plan to fulfil themselves within the previously existing and accepted social structure of values. But there is some connection between actions rationally directed towards an end, and the end itself, a connection by virtue of which success appears to a greater extent as the result of an appropriate and perfectible course of action, set apart from chance and from regressive ideas of merit–reward connections. This involves a certain restructuring of values, and hence experiments with unrewarded virtue and non-virtuous but effective procedures which can, in certain instances, lead to anomic situations. However, they usually result in the initiation of a new, integrated, constructive, and modern scheme of virtue and reward.

The role of the woman is different too. She does not expect a miraculous change of circumstances nor remain in a state of perplexed inertia nor limit herself to fostering the things which, amid an overwhelmingly new and incomprehensible environment, give a sense—in the old terms—to her being there. When she goes to join her husband—with or without the children—it is because he has found decent accommodation from which he can plan a life, although temporary, in the host country, man and wife working together to bring the endeavour to a successful conclusion. Guaranteed employment, the possibility of a modest but continuous improvement following a rational *iter* responsibly planned and shared, without hankering after the impossible, with no, or far fewer, sacrifices obsessively assumed under the impulse of a conscious or unconscious sense of guilt: all these factors combine to make the woman in this case a companion, favouring the development of family life towards an understanding of the surrounding environment and, in spite of the stay being planned as temporary, also favouring the acceptance of modern, rational elements, and hence integration. This comes out in attitudes to the children's education, which readily centre upon the schools giving the best prospect for advantageous employment later. This changed picture is also a consequence of the differences of European culture from North American culture. In the latter the hierarchy of social values was substantially more homogeneous and centred entirely on the basic value of economic success. For the poor wretches arriving there, this meant a rise in the level of their expectations and a dream of upward mobility which spread like wildfire and was bound to produce terrible frustrations. In France, and more recently in Belgium, this has hardly happened at all. Society does not extend golden promises of riches, nor does it link the acquisition of wealth to self-respect, but at the same time it does offer many small, attainable targets which can be achieved by rational behaviour. It is to these that the immigrant turns his attention, so that he now has less need of anticipatory symbols of status and success, less need of social and individual isolating mechanisms to shield him from frustration. In addition, the language of these two countries is easier for him. The outcome is that the necessity of Italian immigrants living grouped together—and this goes for southern Italians too—in the same district, as happens for instance in Belgium with the miners, does not result in the creation of "little Italies", and the families, on the contrary, form new relationships with neighbours.

In the majority of cases the presence of the family promotes rather than hampers the chances of integration. While the figures for unmarried men returning to Italy are very high, with married men emigration fairly frequently becomes permanent. Nevertheless, it is not so much the shame of returning home poor which influences the decision to remain (for as a rule the savings set aside would often permit a dignified return) so much as slow and gradual acceptance of the new country and the possibilities it holds for the man himself and above all for his children.

4. If we now go on to examine present-day internal migration in Italy, we shall find something very different from what we have seen so far. As I have said, this migration is the expression of a considerable economic development leading to a transformation in the occupational structure of the population and a redistribution of the population over the face of Italy. These migrations are largely conditioned by a considerable portion of the active population switching from farming to other activities, and by an almost total disappearance of unemployment; by an increase in the overall national income, as well as the income *per capita* and that of the greater part of the population; by a reinforcing of the contractual strength of the workers; and by the spread and improvement of social security. These migratory movements, then, are taking place within a framework of objective economic improvements, and not a relative worsening of conditions as happened, for instance, in the industrial revolution in England. The social system within which this is happening has undergone a profound process of integration: the isolated communities which once characterized Italian society have lost their resistance: their boundaries have dissolved; mass communications exchanges and the spread of distribution networks and formal education, with a considerable increase in the number of schools, have all helped to broaden the horizons of individual communities and create a national community outlook.

This emigration therefore began at a point when prospects of radical improvements for a large proportion of the population were maturing, multiplying, and coming into effect. This could not happen without affecting the nature of the emigration; in fact—and this is the thesis I have put forward and attempted to demonstrate elsewhere[6]—it acquired a particularly optimistic character of peaceful revolution. Within this frame of reference, dimly perceived and imperfectly understood, but grasped in its

[6] F. Alberoni, Caratteristiche e tendenze delle migrazioni interne in Italia, in *Stradi di Sociologia*, **1** (1) (1963), 23–50.

general outline, the motives and hopes of the individual have taken on a new quality, opening up to new perspectives. Totalled together, these prospects, aims, and aspirations have given rise to a collective movement towards the new (represented by industrial society), a movement which has been satisfactorily absorbed, and has, indeed, promoted the economic development of the nation. What has occurred does not therefore present a parallel with what is now happening in many African countries, where eagerness for the new and ambition to achieve a different way of life result in shifts of the population which newly formed industries cannot absorb, in the spread of expectations doomed to frustration, and in a massive and chaotic urbanization which only a restructuring of the State will hold in check and reduce to order.

The internal migration in Italy, then, does not consist of an unobtrusive series of isolated departures of people who have arrived at their individual decisions under increasing pressure from individual difficulties; it arises out of the spreading of new ambitions and a new vision of one's present state in relation to what one could be in another society developing along different lines; it is the upsurge, gradual at first but growing stronger, of a new social perspective, a new prospect of livelihood which eventually leads to the individual feeling estranged from his own community while he belongs in spirit to another which, although still in the process of development, already has a structure and a definite identity. It is above all young people who are involved, but older age groups are not excluded; not only men but women are concerned; the process is set in motion at first by concrete possibilities and information about what is happening near at hand, but it gathers momentum and becomes a large-scale social movement through the formulation of a vision, a hope, a collective concept of the world. Well-being, adequate means, a steady job, a comfortable house, the possibility of social advancement for oneself, one's household, and one's own children had at one time been envisaged as individual opportunities or the privilege of the *élite*. During the period of the great migrations overseas, hopes were high, indeed illusory, but they still took the shape of individual success repeated innumerable times; it was a question of privilege, the idea being to move higher up the ladder, leaving poverty and the other wretches behind. Although embarked upon by millions, emigration presupposed a society naturally avaricious and unequal, within which only the individual could seek to raise himself from his condition or, if a multitude did so, it was only by living parasitically off an already wealthy society like the United States. The new prospect is quite different: what emerges increasingly clearly as economic development continues, is the opportunity for everyone to achieve well being, and a different kind of life. One endeavours not to be left out or to arrive too late in the process. More and more as this prospect spreads, it is the idea of privilege which is questioned. What once appeared as an individual goal, to be reached only with a struggle and with the aid of "fortune", gradually comes to be experienced as a human right, a collective state.

The rigid social stratification with the privileged at its apex and the non-privileged at the base, a stratification often accepted, less frequently the object of blind aggression, now appears as something which is not legitimate and as an anachronism to be wiped out. The class barriers are crumbling, and in their place the idea of the new class is making slow progress. For many, it appears in Marxist terms as a struggling proletariat; many others see it as a new middle class in which the existing differences in income and type of work lose their importance when confronted with a substantial levelling out and a sense of common membership, ideas actively propagated in the community by mass media and their protagonists. It is possible to achieve this state of affairs only when three conditions are present together which could not come together in the past: (a) The concrete example of a society in which (e.g. the United States today, England, Scandinavia, Switzerland, and to a certain extent the industrial cities of northern Italy) it has already been accomplished. For the peasants, the unemployed, and the farmhands of the south, the life of the work-men and employees in the great cities represents a life of this kind. (b) The fact that the society is developing not in a distant country but within the nation itself, in towns which are relatively close, sometimes very close indeed; the fact that it is in part starting to develop directly in the village itself, in the houses of neighbours, friends, and relatives, through the agency of mass media and mass consumption. (c) The fact that politicians, political parties, and trade unions maintain that this state is not only attainable but must and will be attained (after some struggles and after over-coming certain forces which are holding it back), in an interval of time which must be made as short as possible.

It is the community of origin which, in this process, loses its prominence and, as a basic system of reference, gradually dis-appears.

In traditional emigration the community, even when deprived of its men, lived on virtually unchanged in those who remained and in the emigrants themselves, who continued to accept its structure and values. It was, indeed, the community itself which required its members to set out in search of improved status, thus fulfilling their obligation to the community and their family. For the distant emigrant his *locus hominis* remained back home with his family, and when he had his wife and family with him it still remained with his relatives and friends in the land where the normative values he recognized and was subject to still applied.

In the regions from which young men and equally young women set out for various destinations, no one today would require them to leave. The urge to leave stems not so much from a rejection of one's own place in the community as from a rejection of the com-munity and its structure. Those who depart do not go in search of work which will allow them to save some day, nor are they seeking their fortunes in order to return later and take up a more advan-tageous position in the community. Those who leave go in search of a different way of life, another society in which they can fulfil themselves more completely, with reference to new values with which they must, therefore, have been in sympathy before their departure. They are not going to colonize, nor into exile, nor to the adventure-sacrifice, but in search of a new land where they can find a dignity and freedom which it is impossible to achieve within the structure of the old community.

On the psychological plane we find that it is a growing awareness of the increased differential between short- and long-term prospects in one place compared to the other which triggers off the emigration mechanism. The people who go away plan, or hope, to stay away; they have already renounced the kind of life they are leaving behind, and the society they are moving to seems to them not only to offer work which the first was unable to give, but appears superior to it in other respects. To the older peasant it means that his children will have a modern house and the opportunity of going to school. For young men it means the opportunity to improve their position over the years by work-study courses; being able to put on a clean suit and go out in the evening without people thinking of him as a poor devil; the possibility of holidays by the sea or in the mountains in a few years' time if not now. For the girl it means marriage with the man of her choice, living in a modern house with domestic electrical appliances and a floor which stays clean, being able to take good care of her children, and so on.

All this the little village is unable to offer today, not only because there is no drinking water or electric light, but above all because of its particular socio-economic structure. Because the young man in the evening is still an object of pity, and the "padrone"—although he no longer has his former power—continues to be a person of consequence because the community criticizes and condemns those who try to improve their status, and so on. All these traits cannot be suddenly erased; they do not disappear with the coming of electric light or gas or water. The process of social decomposition by which the old structures crumble away has to be followed through to the end. In other words, the rural world must be urbanized if it is to become hospitable once more.

The Situation Today

At the beginning of my essay I stated that I would treat the question in a particular way, not concerning myself in the first section so much with the reconstruction of historical types or a description of the present as with the formulation of ideal types. Now I must turn my attention to the present, and describe— basing myself on the concepts discussed so far—what is actually happening in Italy today. We find internal migration going on, and we know that it has essential characteristics which differentiate it from other migratory types; however, this does not mean either that there are no other migratory movements going on, or that all internal migration possesses the characteristics ascribed to the ideal type. Reality is always complex, composite, and contradictory: our theorizing provides us with an aid to investigating and understanding reality, but not with a faithful portrait of it. Indeed, we can very easily demonstrate that all four migratory types I have described are present in Italy today, each with several variants. But the relative predominance of the different types is not the same, and if there is one in particular which characterizes our time, it is, on the whole, the last I have described. For example, the "tenant farmer" or *colono* type is represented by the peasants of Venetia and the south who go to live in abandoned farms on the Apennines and in other regions. Whole families move, and this, according to Barberis,[7] may lead to the introduction of southern elements into farming. In reality, the numbers involved are not very great, and doubts could be expressed as to its future, at any rate in the present family form.

As for the European and overseas types of emigration, let us remember that in 1961 the Italian working force abroad totalled 576,000: 474,000 men and 102,000 women. In the years immediately before that, the figures were as follows:

Year	Men	Women	Total
1958	433,000	119,000	552,000
1959	381,000	107,000	488,000
1960	381,000	99,000	480,000

[7] C. Barberis, *Le Migrazioni rurali in Italia*, Feltrini, Milan, 1960

The totals, then, remained roughly stationary; the same goes for departures from and returns into Italy, seen below:

Year	Leaving	Returning
1956	344,802	155,293
1957	341,733	163,277
1958	255,459	139,038
1959	268,490	156,121
1960	383,908	192,235

It is interesting to note that in the last few years there has been a drop in the number of emigrants less than 14 years old, which has gone down from 39,000 in 1958 to 23,000 in 1959, to 16,000 in 1960, and 13,000 in 1961.

Another change worth mentioning is the drop in the number of household dependants among the emigrants. In 1958 the working emigrants were 66.4% and the dependants 33.6%, while in 1960 the working emigrants were 83.4% and the dependants 16.8%.

Let us compare the data for overseas emigration and European emigration which give the official motive for emigrating (Table 2).

TABLE 2.

	1958	1959	1960
Overseas			
Work	29.1	29.3	35.5
Family	70.4	69.4	63.9
Other reasons	0.5	0.8	0.6
Europe			
Work	89.4	91.6	94.6
Family	10.2	8.2	5.3
Other reasons	0.4	0.2	0.1
Total			
Work	66.4	74.1	83.2
Family	33.6	25.9	16.8

The relative proportions changed essentially because of the conversion of southern Italian emigration from overseas to European. Although overseas migration was largely a family affair, European migration is predominantly undertaken by the individual for reasons of work; in fact the proportion of dependent emigrants and extra-European emigrants from southern Italy varied in this way (Table 3).

TABLE 3.

	% dependents abroad			% working in non-European countries		
	1958	1959	1960	1959	1960	1961
Sicily	56.8	50.2	33.7	47	30	20
Calabria	57.7	51.0	33.1			
Basilicata	26.5	19.1	10.1	40	30	15
Puglie	20.5	15.9	8.9			
Abruzzi	44.0	36.1	20.3	55	45	35
Campania	38.7	27.8	17.0	46	42	30

The length of stay in European countries has also decreased. For example, in 1958 53% of the emigrants were staying less than a year; this rose to 60% in 1961. Thus there is a considerable amount of emigration into Europe going on and a continuance of overseas emigration which, nevertheless, no longer retains any vestige of the "fortune" element, but is rather an emigration of families. The points of departure for this overseas emigration, when it still takes place, are the most depressed regions of Italy, in which it was firmly established in the past, notably Sicily, Calabria, and Abruzzi. It appears, however, as a survival from an earlier age, an outmoded form of emigration belonging to regions which have not yet discovered the new prospects in Europe and above all in Italy itself, and go on along the lines laid down by tradition. Beside this relic of former times we find, more fully developed and still expanding, European emigration, which has now been discovered by the regions lagging behind in relation to

the places where it first started—those same places where subsequently more intensive economic development occurred,
making them what they are today—centres of attraction—not
points of departure. The southern Italian emigrating to Europe
usually plans a temporary stay and goes alone; he is, as a rule,
capable of financial calculations, and he makes his plans before
leaving. He hardly ever risks his livelihood, and he knows in
addition how much he can save. The relationship of the man with
his community of origin influences the use his savings are put to
in one of two ways. Some of the emigrants plan to acquire a
piece of land and a house in the community they left and enjoy
there a more elevated patrimonial status—but this archaic procedure is falling away under the influence of farming difficulties
and the change in the system of social stratification (by economic
status), in which income is increasingly gaining ground over
property, and the "guaranteed standard of living" over wealth.
The others, who are little by little becoming a majority, are uncertain, and renew their working contracts abroad, concentrating
on increasing their earnings and putting off the decision. Probably
a fair proportion of them will end up by not returning to their
community of origin, and will either remain abroad or more
probably find work in one of the industrial towns of Italy.

Even in the more isolated, depressed regions traditionally
oriented towards emigration abroad, an impression is being made
increasingly by the attraction to the urban way of life and the
rejection of the community of origin which, according to the
theories I have advanced, is the cornerstone of internal migration
and which is observable in its most strongly marked form above
all in the country regions of north Italy and around the great
cities—Rome, Milan, Turin.

However, in this case, too, there are many variants. Anticipatory socialization and plans for permanent emigration vary
from case to case, only becoming the rule as one approaches the
centre of attraction. A substantial proportion of emigration from
south to north has many similarities to emigration abroad, and
to a certain extent elements of "fortune" are still present, whereby

the emigrant risks everything, making no preparations, but hoping that through the help and recommendations of friends and relatives the lucky chance will come his way. Indeed, this type is more frequent perhaps in internal than in European migration, where the difficulties are greater and the controls more stringent. In such cases the emigrant is restless, very inconsistent, easily led to expect miracles, undecided whether to stay or return home, according to the frustrations he is exposed to. In the majority of cases, however, the elements of acceptance prevail over the pull of the old society, and although emigrants frequently encounter hardship and conflicts arising out of the lingering models of socialization belonging to the society of origin which is stationary, circumscribed, rural, and archaic,[8] they eventually discover and accept the "logic" (otherwise expressed as models of correspondence between gratification and moral values) of the new system.

The position of the woman deserves to be mentioned separately. It, too, can be interpreted in terms of an ideal type for internal migrations in Italy, and a new element can easily be distinguished, characteristic above all of the north and the centre, but also spreading to Venetia and the south. The preceding pages have already given some idea of it. The young woman no longer wishes to live in her community of origin, doing the work she has always done. This leads to an ambition to marry a man who will go and work in industry in the city, and a rejection of those who are content to remain as peasants; or to the desire to find employment herself in industry or in service. These are two faces of the same coin, the first more old-fashioned because it still entrusts to the man the task of redemption, the second more modern in that it implies the acceptance of a new role. The first is found mostly in rural zones at a distance from the great industrial centres, the second increasingly as one goes towards them. Female pressure on men, statistically invisible but nonetheless a very real influence, gradually becomes, as one proceeds along this theoretical axis of nearness to the cities, an increase in the number

[8] I have discussed this problem in my book *Contributo allo studio dell'integrazione sociale dell'immigrato*, Vita e Pensiero, Milan, 1960.

of working women. The first induces internal male emigration, the second is translated directly in terms of female emigration.

Let us take, for example, emigration into Milan from 1932 to 1959. In this case we shall see that the percentage of women is fairly high, especially young unmarried women. In the category from 15 to 24 years old, women from the northern regions actually outnumber the men. Emigrants from the south in this age group number more men than women. On the other hand, the percentage of older women from the central southern region exceeds the percentage of men. Thus young women pass in a steady stream from the northern regions to Milan, while the women who leave the central southern region are for the most part wives going to join their husbands, or elderly women going to join their husbands and sons.

> In the city of Turin, [observes Anfossi[9]] while immigration from the northern regions is characterized by a predominance of women, immigration from the south shows a clear masculine majority . . . concerning immigrants from the south [we observe that]: as the young immigrants get satisfactorily settled in the towns, they tend to summon their elderly parents, and in particular their mothers; as a consequence the elderly categories, and especially women, are on the increase during the years under consideration.

In farming, in many places, the women have replaced the men, who have gone on to other activities, but the number of women employed in industry has gone up considerably, the number in service even more. The young women of whom I was speaking just now leave zones which are predominantly rural to find a job in industry or in service, which they retain as a rule until their marriage, and in some cases at any rate, even after marriage.

Thus the main new aspect of female emigration is the working migration in which the woman leaves home to do a job. In this context we should remember that the separation of home and work is one of the primary constituents of the industrial system. The separation can be geographically large or small, but in either

[9] A. Anfossi, L'Immigrazione meridionale a Torino, in *Immigrazione e industria*, Comunità, Milan, 1962.

case it entails a differentiated set of rules for behaviour, and distinct rights and duties, for the two contexts the individual simultaneously belongs to, although these may be more or less integrated. It means, too, a diminishing of the social control exercised by the family over a section of social behaviour, and this is a prelude to a split in the modes of evaluation that the members of the family will use with regard to the extra-familiar behaviour of the other members.

This type of separation has been on the increase, one could say, from the early eighteenth century until today, corresponding with the progressive reduction in agriculture, crafts, and domestic work relative to others. In the early 1700's in fact something like 80% of the population probably made a living from agriculture. The peasants, whether tenant farmers (*coloni*), métayers (*mezzadri*), or farmers working their own land (*coltivatori diretti*) for the most part worked where they lived. The same was true of the majority of craftsmen belonging to the guilds, and for the large numbers of workers, often members of farming households, who worked for contractors in the so-called Verlag-system. The servants, too, lived in their master's house with their families.

Gradually but steadily there grew up a broad category of people going to work for a third party somewhere outside their domicile. This included factory workers, hired farm hands, and domestic servants in town houses and aristocratic households. In Italy, where there was no early industrial revolution, this process did not take place so suddenly, and did not cause a radical upheaval of the occupational structure of the country and of the masculine and feminine roles, as happened, for instance, in England. We know that in England many women and children were recruited, while the men often stayed at home, out of work. In Italy, however, as I have said, the industrial revolution began very late and, generally speaking, it was the man rather than the woman who went to work outside the home. There were many exceptions to this rule, and individual instances, especially in the industrial zones of the north, but taking the country as a whole the separation of the family from place of work concerned men rather than women.

This is not to say that the women stayed at home tending her hearth and children—far from it: women usually worked— worked very hard—on the same footing as the men, but this work was generally done in the home or within the family business— farming, craft, or a mixture of the two (through the persistence of the Verlag-system),[10] assisting the men. Although this is no longer a part of the *mores* of many Italian communities, the woman, especially the young woman, who goes to work outside, especially far from home, is still sometimes considered little better than a lost woman. Only women who migrated seasonally were excepted from such criticism, women who worked in the rice fields and elsewhere, but these were situations which did not occur regularly. The migratory flows which I have discussed preserve this pattern: they consist either of men leaving their families behind and going abroad temporarily in search of work or to seek their fortunes or else of whole families leaving together. The woman never goes alone to look for work. The separation between home and work does not befit a woman, it does not enter into her role. With the development of industry, the employment of women has grown but never to the extent of altering this pattern. The existence of very widespread chronic unemployment undoubtedly played a part in this, since it led those responsible for the welfare of the State to favour the employment of the male head of the family. The overall situation soon after the Second World War shows fairly restricted employment of women, while the working rate of women, actually still extremely high, is not reflected in the statistics for the working population, or else appears officially as assistance. In most cases, the rule is still respected whereby the man's employment is situated away from his home, while for the woman home and place of work tend much more to coincide. During the last 10 years, however, the rule has been less in force; employment of women is on the upgrade, above all in agriculture, where the women replace the men who go into other kinds of work, with an increase also in industry and the other categories. In the case of agriculture, the appearance of women

[10] See L. Dal Pane, *Storia del lavoro in Italia*, Giuffrè, Milan, 1958.

among the working population does not imply for the most part a real change of role: the woman continues to work as before on the family farm, with a different juridical status, but her contribution remains the same, and is now, as it was then, statistically invisible for the most part. The situation is quite different in industry, and the other main branches in which the woman goes out to work is answerable to another authority, and has cash earnings of her own which she can put towards the housekeeping or keep partially or *in toto* for herself.

A final postscript about the journey in commuting. As a rule the journey is thought of only as time subtracted from work or community life, rarely as an occasion for encounter. If the place of work is near by, the encounters are only within the business, but with a place of work which is a long way from the inhabited district, or if people from various localities come together to it, the journey is almost always made as a group. When the distances are great, the group forms on trains and other means of transport. People from the same area or from different areas meet together, forming a new group which is not the working group or the group of friends in the village. The journey thus becomes an occasion of encounter, and for young people especially the experience is not at all unwelcome, and not infrequently constitutes a factor of attraction. Those who have observed or studied the phenomenon at first hand have been unfavourably impressed by the promiscuity of the sexes, by the low level of interests (sport, gossip, and jokes) of these people, or by their vulgarity. There is no doubt that the reduction of social control exercised by the community leads to more uninhibited expression of instinctive behaviour, especially sexual behaviour; I do not think, however, that the attraction of the journey derives only from this. It also has another meaning: in the group the desires, aspirations, and anxieties of the individuals find a collective solution, and are amalgamated into a collective vision of reality and of the actions of all the members; a new sense of solidarity and participation emerges, as well as a new set of norms. For example, it is probable that the group exercises an important function of vocational orientation. The separation of home from work, with segregated roles, is as if institutionalized in these itinerant communities which act as a melting-pot of experiences and possible action; moulds, therefore, of a different way of community life.

Spain

Problems of Adjustment in the Case of Internal Migration:

An Example in Spain

R. Duocastella

Object of the Survey

The ability of immigrants to adapt themselves in a new country has been the subject of considerable study. Much less is known about movement within a country, partly because it is much harder to estimate, but principally because to those doing research in these matters it does not appear to present such severe problems, although it in fact concerns a greater number of people.

This article is an excursion into a relatively unexplored field and is centred on a particular case in Spain, an industrial town called Mataro, in Catalonia. It has 36,000 inhabitants and is situated on the coast, about 18 miles north of Barcelona. The growth of this town is due, to a large extent, to the arrival of immigrants from rural districts of Catalonia, but also from all parts of Spain. It is from this point of view that we have examined several aspects of adaptation to the new life by "migrants" coming from the same country but from provinces with very different characteristics.

The Catalan way of Life

Catalonia is an interesting case; the language spoken there is, in fact, very different from Spanish, and the linguistic difficulty adds to the problems of moving from the country to the town, and from agricultural to industrial work, together with living in different and unfamiliar surroundings. Besides, the social and cultural atmosphere of Catalonia is dictated by ancient democratic traditions. Since the eleventh century, the "Customs" laid down by Ramon Berenguer the Ancient provided a written working constitution which defined the powers of the sovereign, and the Cortes, or senators, had a legislative and almost executive authority. From the thirteenth century, Ramon Llull formulated the principle of the sovereignty of the people, thus enabling them to depose kings who were found to be opposed to the laws, and to choose others.

Finally, Catalonia enjoys a very mild Mediterranean climate, and its soil is much more fertile than in other parts of Spain. The population in rural areas has always been very stable, as a great number of people are small landowners: at present the population is still made up of 66% landowners, 15% farmers, and as many rent their land (plus 4% of varied or undetermined employment).

Catalonia was one of the first areas in Spain to be industrialized and developed very rapidly, which is another explanation for the growth in population. Whereas the increase in population from 1900 to 1950 was 50% in the country as a whole, the increase in Catalonia was 64%, which was the highest except for New Castile, as it included Madrid.

Mataro

Mataro, an industrial town important for textiles, cotton, and nylon, is an important supplier of underwear, socks, and stockings for the whole of Spain.

Agriculture is also quite important in certain parts, and recently the cultivation of flowers, in particular carnations, has become significant, and are sent to the large towns and cities of Spain.

Population Increase in the Province of Barcelona and in Mataro

From 1900 to 1950 (Table 1) the population of the province has more than doubled and that of Barcelona has increased $2\frac{1}{2}$ times.

TABLE 1. LEGAL POPULATION FROM 1900 TO 1950

Years	Province of Barcelona		City of Barcelona		Mataro	
	Numbers (thousands)	Indices	Numbers (thousands)	Indices	Numbers	Indices
1900	1055	100	535	100	19,704	100
1910	1142	108	587	110	19,918	101
1920	1349	128	710	133	24,125	122
1930	1801	171	1006	189	28,034	142
1940	1932	183	1081	203	29,920	152
1950	2232	212	1280	240	31,642	161

TABLE 2. WORKING POPULATION OF MATARO IN 1950

	Total population	Total active population	Working population			Employers	Salaried workers	Others
			In agri-culture	In industry	Others			
Total	31,642	18,201	1815	10,990	5396	1426	16,010	765
Men	14,672	11,034	1687	5,659	3688	1219	9,277	538
Women	16,970	7,167	128	5,331	1708	207	6,733	227

The population of Mataro has increased from 19,700 in 1900 to 31,600 in 1950, and this rate of increase has recently become much higher: according to the census taken in 1955 the population was 34,767 or an index of 176 compared to 100 in 1900.

In 1950 the working population of Mataro represented 58% of the total, occupied mainly in industry, but also in agriculture (Table 2). The number of women employed in industry is as great as the number of men. Nine-tenths of them are salaried workers.

Geographical Origin of Immigrants

The increase in population in the province is chiefly the result of the influx of immigrants from Catalonia and other areas of Spain. The census gives for each province the number of inhabitants born in the province and born in other provinces giving, where necessary, the place of origin. In addition, inhabitants of important towns are classified further into those born in the city, those born in other parts of the same province, and those born in other provinces, the province of origin being given. According to the calculations of Jesus Villar Salinas,[1] the extent of immigration in the province of Barcelona, between 1940 and 1950, reached 27%, which was surpassed only in relative numbers by the province of Madrid; in absolute numbers, however, the total number of immigrants was 232,000, compared with 226,000 in the province of Madrid.

Table 3 shows, for the census taken in 1950, in total numbers and percentages, the number of Spanish immigrants for the whole of the province, for Barcelona, and for Mataro, which are 38%, 44%, and 29%, most of these being women, which is typical of the rural areas.

The various regions of Spain have been divided into four large groups (see the map).

[1] See Jesus Villar Salinas, Mobilité geographique contemporaine de la population espagnole, from *Études européennes de population*, Paris, INED. 1954, pp. 215–32.

TABLE 3. IMMIGRANTS COMING FROM PROVINCES OTHER THAN BARCELONA
(1950)

	Province of Barcelona		City of Barcelona		Mataro	
	Numbers	% of the total population	Numbers	% of the total population	Numbers	% of the total population
Total	845,543	37.9	567,112	44.3	9007	28.5
Men	363,298	35.3	235,372	40.8	4288	29.2
Women	482,245	40.1	331,740	47.1	4719	27.8

A. Neighbouring regions of Catalonia (Aragon, Valencia, the Balearic Islands, and Murcia) which at one time comprised the Catalano–Aragon Confederation. Catalan dialects predominate, and the way of thinking is quite similar to that of Catalonians.

B. Andalusia, a very poor region where a Castilian dialect is spoken.

C. Central plateau of Spain (Castile, Leon, and Extremadura), where the population differs most from the Catalans. The home of the Celtiberes, a very reserved race who take easily to hard work: a tough race of conquerors, providing most of the soldiers and heros of the American Conquest. Immigrants from these parts work generally in administration, the police force, and the army.

D. Other regions of northern Spain: Galicia, noted for its rain, although the soil is very dusty; their dialect is similar to Portuguese; the mining regions of Asturia; and, finally, the Basque country and Navarre, who have their own cultural and linguistic peculiarities.

Table 4 shows the trends in various regions of Barcelona. Migration from neighbouring regions has decreased in favour of the more remote areas.

TABLE 4. GEOGRAPHICAL ORIGINS OF NON-CATALAN IMMIGRANTS TO BARCELONA

Regions of origin	1920 (%)	1930 (%)	1940 (%)	1950 (%)
A. Neighbouring regions	21.25	22.19	17.29	16.69
B. Central Spain	2.88	4.31	4.45	7.14
C. Southern Spain	4.08	5.00	5.26	7.00
D. Northern Spain	2.30	2.79	3.27	4.44
	30.51	34.29	30.27	35.27[a]

[a] Not including immigrants from Catalonia.

As far as Mataro is concerned, for want of an official source, our 1955 survey concerned 30% of the immigrants, being 3270 of which 1104 were non-Catalan, who were at Mass on 9 October 1955 and who enabled us to make certain assumptions as shown in Table 5. Immigration of non-Catalan people started later than immigration of Catalans to Barcelona. Up to 1940 it was only on a very small scale; between 1940 and 1945 it reached an almost equal ratio of 143 non-Catalans to 166 Catalans, then the increase was more rapid, from 1945 to 1950 (177 to 227) and during the last 5 years has represented 60% of all immigrants (548 to 228).

The important factor is the increase of movement from one place to another—as many new people arrived in 5 years as during the preceding 25 years.

On the other hand, total distribution of non-Catalan immigrants shows that most come from the southern part of Spain, 31.6% greater than in the neighbouring regions, which only represent one-fifth of the total.

Urban censuses taken between 1925 and 1949 confirm and enlarge upon these facts. The increase between 1928 and 1931 was possibly due to the demand for labour for the International Exhibition in Barcelona; the ensuing decline caused by the civil war (1936–9) followed by a considerable increase from 1940 onwards; another decline occurred between 1944–6 after the end of the war in Europe. Since 1950 the rate of immigration has gathered momentum, doubling itself in the northern regions, five times as great in the south, where the low standard of living and over-population are the most acute. Similar tendencies in other areas have been observed, except for a drop during 1945–50, in central Spain. However, people coming from these regions are always found, in Catalonia, mainly in administrative posts, the police force, and the army, and arrived in the greatest numbers after the war.

Settlement in the Town of Mataro

Although the great shortage of housing does not allow new-comers to settle wherever they please, they do in fact keep to

TABLE 5. GEOGRAPHICAL ORIGINS OF NON-CATALAN IMMIGRANTS TO MATARO

Period	Neighbouring regions		Southern regions		Central regions		Northern regions		Miscellaneous		Total
	M	F	M	F	M	F	M	F	M	F	
1950–55	22 +	65	67 +	169	52 +	89	24 +	40	3 +	17	548
1945–50	10 +	19	19 +	32	15 +	42	7 +	18	10 +	5	177
1940–45	11 +	24	4 +	13	12 +	48	4 +	14	7 +	6	143
1930–40	5 +	14	2 +	8	2 +	9	3 +	9	5 +	13	70
…–1930	12 +	34	11 +	24	12 +	…	11 +	28	10 +	24	166
Total	60 +	156	103 +	246	93 +	188	49 +	109	35 +	65	1104
Numbers	216		349		281		158		100		100.0
%	19.6		31.6		25.4		14.3		9.1		

certain areas, and where they settle depends on which part of Spain they have come from.

Three surveys have given indications of this.

1. SETTLEMENT IN CERTAIN DISTRICTS

The town is divided into twenty-four districts. In absolute numbers, immigrants live in districts with the highest population density: 2, 3, 10, 11, and 12, which are also the oldest parts of the town and particularly overcrowded; but in relative numbers, certain districts seem to attract the immigrants particularly: districts 5 with 40% of immigrants, 15 with 41%, 7 with 31%, 24 with 30%, 22 with 27%, 23 with 24%, and so on.

These facts are very significant: in fact, they have caused considerable upset in the town, since the tendency of immigrants to congregate in certain districts has caused some inhabitants of Mataro to sell their houses and move elsewhere.

Those coming from the south of Spain have gathered mainly in the outer suburbs of district 15: 53% of all the immigrants live there. The Castilians are concentrated in districts 19 (55% of the total) and 3 (42%). Those coming from around Aragon and Valencia, the first to move to Mataro and consequently the most accustomed to local life, are found mainly in district 17 (39% immigrants).

2. SETTLEMENT IN PARTICULAR STREETS

Within a district the immigrants select particular streets to inhabit, according to their geographical origin.

In district 15, out of a total population of 2020, all the immigrants living in Gaudi Street originate from the Catalan region, as well as those in the de la Creu Road (11 out of 13) and Mayor Street (15 out of 17).

Immigrants from the south have settled in "San Desiderio" Street, where 10 out of 15 come from the province of Murcia and Almeira; those in Roca Street come entirely from these two regions. "Norte" Street is occupied by people from Almeira and "Nuria" Street by people from Murcia, and "Esperanza" Street by Andalusians.

Thus the reason why certain immigrants keep together is not only governed by which region they come from, but also by the particular district within the region.

3. SETTLEMENT IN PARTICULAR HOUSES

A third survey taken of certain streets of district 15 showed that groups of similar origin tended to live in the same houses. In the 15 houses included in the survey, 25 out of 30 groups of families living in one house came from the same region.

Housing

The manner in which immigrants tackle the problem of housing reveals one aspect of their adjustment. We must remember that housing facilities are of a very low standard in the south of Spain, where most activities take place outside the home and where slums are a common sight in the suburbs of large towns. One can even see "houses" hollowed out of the rocks on hillsides in Andalusia. The situation is little better in the suburbs of Barcelona and in some cases to have running water and electricity is absolute luxury. To have a water-closet is even more uncommon.

In Mataro one would only find about 40 or 50 shanties, in a quarter called El Gallao by the edge of the sea, but nowhere else, which is somewhat exceptional in this region.

If the situation is better in Mataro, it is no doubt due to the action taken by the authorities to avoid slums being created, but probably also due to psychological reaction. Mataro is said to be a very middle-class town, and what counts most is to have a great many possessions, even if one only gives an impression of being well off. Working hours are very long, about 12–13 hours a day.

The immigrants make a great effort to follow this rhythm of activity, and one could draw a slightly exaggerated, but typical, picture of the new immigrant; if he is single he takes a room somewhere, eats in cheap restaurants for a very meagre sum, and saves the rest of his salary, 35–40 pesetas out of a total of 50. As soon as he has saved up enough money, or even borrowed some through the widespread system of buying on credit, he buys new clothes, goes to a photographer, and writes to his family and friends, telling them all the advantages of his new situation, thus explaining to some degree the migratory movement from the southern areas where some towns have seen a considerable decrease in their population in the course of a few years.

Whether or not that is true, we have studied three groups, each made up of sixty-two families, some from Mataro, others from Catalonia, and some from Andalusia. These families were chosen at random after a census taken by the mayor of district 15 during the summer of 1955 (Table 6).

Twenty-three out of the 62 Andalusian immigrants, compared with 30 and 31 in the other groups, already have their own land, although they arrived less than 5 years ago. Almost as many own their houses. More Andalusians, who are reputedly lazy, have built their houses themselves. A greater number possess water and electricity, which mean large installation costs and bills.

To sum up, the immigrants from the south have become acclimatized more quickly than others, at great personal sacrifice, which leaves one wondering what produces this dynamism among the lower-class members of the population.

The Language

Linguistic adjustment in Mataro is indicated in a very strange manner. The new arrivals find themselves in a situation completely opposed to the usual one. They have to get used to a regional language, Catalan, which geographically and culturally is much less well known than Spanish. The result of this is that some immigrants, particularly those in official posts, express a certain contempt for a region upholding the principle of linguistic separatism, which has often been the cause of civil disturbances during the last 50 years. They often maintain an attitude of suspicion and even hostility. According to the police, most of the disturbances and consequent arrests have been caused by misunderstandings and arguments due to the use of expressions of mutual contempt between immigrants and natives.

However, adjustment to the Catalan language is taking place in spite of everything, apparently for economic reasons. The

TABLE 6. HOUSING CONDITIONS IN THE THREE DIFFERENT GROUPS

	Natives of Mataro	Catalan immigrants	Andalusian immigrants
Total number	62	62	62
Owners of land	30	31	23
Owners of their own house	35	36	33
Those having built their house themselves[a]	11	13	25
Those having completed the construction of their houses	52	48	45
Those having water and electricity	57	53	58

[a] 40, 47, and 52 respectively have moved to district 15 from the centre of the city.

natives have a higher social standing than the immigrants, who feel inferior and dependent upon the inhabitants.

One question asked during the survey conducted among the immigrants was "Do you understand Catalan?" Of the 1611 non-Catalans who were asked, 65 did not reply at all and 1159 (that is 75%) of those who did reply stated that they were able to understand Catalan.

(a) GEOGRAPHICAL ORIGINS AND LENGTH OF STAY

According to the region, replies in the affirmative were made up as follows:

Region A (neighbouring regions)   197 out of 255 (77%)
Region B (the south)   259 out of 397 (65%)
Region C (central Spain)   183 out of 321 (57%)
Region D (the north)   130 out of 186 (70%)
                                      ‾‾‾‾   ‾‾‾‾‾
                                      769   1159

The regions most unwilling to learn the language appeared to be the various parts of central Spain, whereas people from the north and south were much more accommodating. Table 7 gives

TABLE 7. ADAPTATION TO THE LANGUAGE ACCORDING TO ORIGIN AND DATE OF ARRIVAL IN MATARO

Date of arrival	Region A (neighbouring)	Region B (south)	Region C (central Spain)	Region D (north)	Total
1950–5					
Total	87	236	141	64	528
Able to understand					
Catalan	48	134	67	45	294
%	55	56	47	70	55
1945–50					
Total	29	51	57	25	162
Able to understand					
Catalan	26	40	40	21	127
%	82	78	70	84	78
1940–5					
Total	35	17	60	18	130
Able to understand					
Catalan	30	14	39	15	98
%	85	82	65	83	75
1930–40					
Total	19	10	11	12	52
Able to understand					
Catalan	18	8	9	10	45
%	94	80	88	83	86
. . . –30					
Total	46	35	12	39	132
Able to understand					
Catalan	43	32	10	36	121
%	93	91	83	92	91

the breakdown of those said to be able to understand Catalan according to their origin and when they arrived in Mataro.

It can thus be estimated that all types of immigrants are able to understand Catalan a little. The adjustment takes place most rapidly during the first 5 years and is still noticeable after another 5 years and then becomes gradually slower.

The progress of adaptation varies according to geographical origin. Amongst immigrants from neighbouring regions, where Catalan is reasonably well known, progress is immediate and rapid, amounting in all to 93%.

Those coming from the south also adjust very quickly, which can be attributed to the lively and intelligent mind of the Andalusians, who will be seen to settle down most quickly in strange places. The particularly unfavourable conditions at home perhaps encourage them to make greater efforts.

Immigrants from Cantabrica, in spite of a considerable difference in character, adapt just as quickly as the Andalusians for the most part, but mainly during the first 5 years.

The Castilians are the slowest to adapt to the language. The explanation already suggested is shown to be true here, and the preponderance of negative replies, given by people who arrived between 1940 and 1945, after the Spanish Civil War, is explained by the fact that most of them are civil servants and are employed in the police force and the army: in fact they regard themselves as conquerors and refuse to speak the language of a conquered people. This applies to 32 out of 66 immigrant civil servants.

Table 7 precludes children already able to speak Catalan—although non-Catalan by birth—and miscellaneous persons.

(b) Sex

Table 8 appears to show that more women learn Catalan than men: 69% compared with 65%. The fact that women lead in this respect, which is especially noticeable in people from the north, is surprising, since it chiefly concerns women who do not work and those who are married. They have fewer children than natives of the region and have very little contact with the outside world.

TABLE 8. ADAPTATION TO THE LANGUAGE, ACCORDING TO THE REGION OF ORIGIN AND THE SEX

Regions		Men	%	Women	%
A	(neighbouring regions)	65 out of 79	82	132 out of 176	75
B	(the south)	82 out of 122	67.2	177 out of 275	64
C	(central Spain)	60 out of 117	51	123 out of 204	60
D	(the north)	41 out of 65	63	99 out of 121	81
Total		248 383	64.7	531 776	69.7

(c) AGE

Obviously children settle down more quickly than their parents, but according to a survey done in one of the immigrant quarters it was found that far fewer children of school age, that is 7–14 years old, understand Catalan than those who are between 15 and 20 years old and go out to work. Children at school are taught in Castilian Spanish, whereas those who work are in much closer contact with people speaking Catalan.

Number of Children

This varies considerably in different parts of Spain. The following is the result of the 1950 census, giving the number of children per family on average:

Whole of Spain	3.3 children
Catalonia	2.3 children
Province of Barcelona	2.2 children

In Mataro the average is only 1.8 children per family. The rate is higher amongst the immigrants than the population as a whole, at 2.42 (976 children in 403 families). Noticeable differences appear between the different regions of origin in spite of the fact that the survey was only carried out on a small section of the population.

Neighbouring regions: the lowest average, and that approaching most nearly that of the total population, 1.79; this applies to the immigrants who have been in Mataro for the longest period and also to those coming from regions similar to Catalonia, where even so the average rate is higher—2.23.

The south: the highest average, 3.18, higher than in the region of origin, which is 2.84. This is because the families concerned have left their homes as they found it very hard to bring up a large number of children.

Central regions: the same tendencies are observed as with the unwillingness to learn the language. The rate of 3.16 is almost the same as that of the place of origin, 3.21.

Finally, the rate amongst immigrants from the north quickly becomes similar to that of Mataro at 1.83, compared with 2.94 in the place of origin, which is a very pronounced difference.

An analysis of the number of children born in district 15, a quarter which is completely isolated, half a mile away from the nearest suburb and containing 90% immigrants, confirms this variation in the number of children per family among people from different regions of Spain. The average rate is 1.88, made up as follows:

Group A	(neighbouring regions)	1.4
Group B	(the south)	2.23
Group C	(central Spain)	1.9
Group D	(the north)	1.4

In this quarter the number of children born of immigrant parents who have kept up their religion is 2.2, which is higher than the rest:

Group A	(neighbouring regions)	2.23
Group B	(the south)	2.84
Group C	(central Spain)	3.2

and for the whole of Mataro the rate is 2.03 against 1.8.

Religious Behaviour

While awaiting the results of a survey conducted on 19 October 1955 by sending out written questionnaires on weekly attendance at mass, a very limited investigation has already been made in four different fields to discover if immigration has any effect on the religious behaviour of immigrants. Naturally, it was only concerned with external behaviour, without trying to estimate the depth of one's religious sentiments.

First, attendance at mass was considered: the number of the most devout who went more than once a week has dropped from 6 to 5; of those going every Sunday from 20 to 18. As for irregular attendance there are 6 at the most instead of 13, whereas 11 said they no longer went at all. The difference in behaviour was more noticeable amongst irregular churchgoers, because all of them are immigrants from the south of Spain where attendance at mass is much lower and they have often given excuses for their absence such as "work" or "the distance from the church".

A much greater change is shown in the number taking part in processions; whereas 35 would participate in their own villages, only 14 were said to continue the practice in Mataro. They justified their action not by criticizing the processions in themselves, but because they are done "in a very different way at home", as the Andalusians say, or else because they are followed "by people of a different social class ' as other immigrants say. They therefore attach a more or less social significance to this religious act and they stay away from them as they cannot recall the atmosphere of former traditions because the outside influence has dispelled it.

Thirty-nine out of 40 immigrants still possess sacred statues of the Saints, the Virgin or Christ in their houses, just as they would in their home towns.

Lastly, going into a more intimate sphere—individual prayer—little change is observed: 14 instead of 15 pray regularly, that is almost every day, whereas 11 instead of 7 are said to pray at certain times, such as at mass, during the night, or when in danger. On the other hand, the number who pray more regularly than this has fallen from 11 to 7, so that the number of people who never pray at all has increased from 6 to 8.

In other words, the changes have taken place in outward behaviour and are of a social nature, rather than in the more intimate and personal forms of religious life, where the influence of one's surroundings has the least effect. Under the surface the individual does not appear to be seriously disturbed by the uprooting process, but rather the external behaviour is affected. Similar comments have been made in France and Belgium about immigrants from Italy and Poland.[2]

Likewise in France, noticeable differences have been registered when considering the number of children born to various groups of immigrants of different social standing, which are not without similarity to the variations observed in Mataro; particularly the Italian landowners who have settled in the south-west, whose social standing has changed the least or has risen slightly, have maintained their former customs of large families, whereas the rate falls in other groups whose social standing is lower.

Thus the behaviour of newcomers in mixed surroundings would be explained much less by an unconscious influence and a desire to "be the same", than by the nature of the social relations which are established between them and the natives.

The General Impression

This collection of facts, although fragmentary and limited in scope, gives certain indications about general tendencies.

The immigrants who have come to Mataro appear to react in a different manner according to the regions from which they have come. To be sure, among those who have stayed, all have become accustomed, to a very large extent, to the life, but the rhythm and extent of adaptation vary considerably.

The difficulties to surmount for immigrants from the neighbouring regions of Aragon and Valencia are not great, and this is

[2] See A. Girard and J. Stoetzel, *Francais et Immigrés*, Paris, INED, Vol. 2, 1953 and 1954. R. Clemens, G. Vosse-Smal, and P. Minon, *L'Assimilation culturelle des immigrants en Belgique*, Liège, 1953.

clearly shown. But differences between groups coming from central Spain and those from the south are very marked. The former are the most unwilling, the latter the most dynamic. The explanation seems to depend on whether they are the dominating or the dominated, or, inversely, whether or not they feel at home with the natives.

From all the factors likely to favour or oppose the process of adjustment, economic values seem to play a very important part with groups from less developed areas: their feeling of economic dependence, the social gap which separates them from the natives, fires their energy, and the degree of adjustment seems to be in inverse proportion to the degree of dependence; the more rapid the adjustment, the lower the standard of living in the areas they have left.

The linguistic adaptation, similarity in numbers of children born with that of the surrounding area, the determined search for material comfort, external manifestations of religious sentiments, seem to indicate in different ways the place of origin, the desire to lessen the social gap between themselves and the society around them, or, on the other hand, to widen the gap, as the Castilians do. The process of adjustment is in itself like a process of elevation. The surroundings would act less, it appears, by a kind of physical influence than by a desire by those who have found themselves isolated to jump the barriers which separate them from the rest of society.

Thus observations on the adaptation at the time of internal migration would link up to a certain extent with those made on migration from country to country.

It would be of prime importance in any case to conduct them on a larger scale in other countries and in different social groups, and at the same time to do them in a much more detailed manner in order to understand the reasons which drive people away from their homes or else to help us prevent them doing this. If they do, however, we could at least ensure that the need for psychological equality among individuals and groups would favour peace between men instead of putting it in jeopardy.

Sweden

Internal Migration in Sweden and Intervening Opportunities

E. C. ISBELL

THE present attempt to test Stouffer's theory of intervening opportunities as a generalized expression of the relationship between migration and distance[1] was prompted by the belief that the potential utility of the theory justifies repeated efforts to determine its adequacy and by the availability of Swedish census data which could be employed for the purpose. The results of the current test, like those of the earlier ones by Stouffer and by Bright and Thomas,[2] tend to substantiate the theory despite the crudeness of measurements and the doubtful suitability of the data used as criteria of opportunities.

In Stouffer's words, his theory "assumes that there is no necessary relationship between mobility and distance. . . . It proposes that *the number of persons going a given distance is directly proportional to the number of opportunities at that distance and inversely proportional to the number of intervening opportunities. . . .* The relation between mobility and distance may be said to depend on an auxiliary relationship, which expresses the cumulated (intervening) opportunities as a function of distance."[3] The results of both Stouffer's application of this theory to data on residential mobility in Cleveland and Bright and Thomas's experiment with

[1] S. A. Stouffer, Intervening opportunities: a theory relating mobility and distance, *American Sociological Review*, **5** (1940), 845–67.

[2] M. L. Bright and D. S. Thomas, Interstate migration and intervening opportunities, *American Sociological Review*, **6** (1941), 773–83.

[3] Stouffer, *op. cit.*, pp. 846–7. The basic formula is $\dfrac{\Delta y}{\Delta s} = \dfrac{a}{x} \times \dfrac{\Delta}{\Delta s}, \Delta y$ equalling the number of persons migrating from an origin to a circular band of width Δs; x the number of intervening opportunities; Δx the number of opportunities within the band of width Δs.

net interstate migration data for the United States as of 1930 were "encouraging" in showing conformity between *patterns* of expectation and observation; but Stouffer recognized that many discrepancies were too large to attribute to chance, while Bright and Thomas's application of the chi-square test to Stouffer's and their own results indicated that "a real discrepancy" was involved in both cases. They suggest, however, that the chi-square test may be too sensitive to be applicable.

Bright and Thomas found discrepancies of two sorts, one of which they were able to reduce markedly by increasing the qualitative similarity of "opportunities" (i.e. by eliminating migration to California in their computations) and by holding constant the factor of direction. The other discrepancy, namely, an excess of expected over observed net migrants in the two smallest distance intervals, was attributed (1) to necessary crudeness of measurements which meant that these intervals represented "nearest migration" or "'opportunities' without 'intervening opportunities'"; and (2) to the fact that Stouffer's formula, "although the theory on which it is based postulates no necessary relationship of migration and distance, . . . does overweight appreciably *absence of distance* in the first interval merely because intervening opportunities are necessarily measured in terms of distance bands."[4]

For further investigation of these possible sources of discrepancy, Swedish census data on intercommunity migration seemed especially suitable. The census of 1930 tabulates all persons migrating from one community to another in Sweden between 1921 and 1930 by county of origin and county of destination of *last migration*, by sex,[5] and for intra-county migrants the tabulation is further broken down into districts (*bygden*) of origin and destination.[6] Applying Stouffer's terminology to the data for males the "opportunities" in each county can be defined as the total number of males settling in the county, including

[4] Bright and Thomas, *op. cit.*, p. 779.

[5] *Sveriges Officiella Statistik, Folkräkningen den 31 Dec. 1930*, II, 178–185 (table 21).   [6] *Ibid.*, pp. 206–27 (table 24).

those migrating from one community to another within the county as well as in-migrants from all other counties, between 1921 and 1930. Obviously, some short-term "opportunities" superseded by subsequent migrations are not included, but the picture is far more nearly complete than that which would be shown by net intercounty migration. A more serious limitation of the data, for our purposes, is the heterogeneity of the opportunities represented by male migrants of all ages. The migrations of young and middle-aged men doubtless do represent opportunities of an economic nature, but the incidental migrations of children as members of family groups and the moves made by older men who have retired reflect very different sorts of opportunities from those which primarily involve employment. Only if the ratio of young and old to middle-aged migrants were relatively constant for all distances would the effect of this heterogeneity be minimized. A further limitation of the Swedish data derives from the fact that, although they do not include intracommunity or purely residential moves, some of the short-distance moves between adjoining communities and counties, particularly between cities and their suburbs, in all probability do represent merely residential moves; and this introduces another element of dissimilarity in "opportunities" which will be seen to be a disturbing factor.

With the above definition of opportunities, "intervening opportunities" were, of course, the cumulated number of male migrants settling in all counties between the county of origin and the county of destination. Expected migrants or settlers at given distances were calculated for each county of origin by applying Stouffer's formula to these opportunities, intervening opportunities, and the number of male migrants originating in the county. Only crude approximation of migration distances was possible. The distances between the population centers of each pair of counties as computed in the census of 1920[7] were available;[8] and

[7] *Ibid.*, p. 92.

[8] Stockholm University, Institute for Social Sciences, *Population Movements and Industrialization, Swedish Counties, 1895–1930*, Stockholm Economic Studies No. 10, London, P. S. King & Son, 1941, pp. 72–73.

100 kilometer intervals were used for computing expected inter-county migrants, preceded by two intervals for intracounty migrants, in general representing less distant moves than those to the nearest counties: (1) intracounty migrants moving within the same district (*bygd*), i.e., on the whole the shortest moves; and (2) migrants between districts in the county.[9] In other respects the computation procedure was identical with that described by Bright and Thomas,[10] except that counties were substituted for states and total migrants over a period, for net migrants as of a particular date.

When the resultant distributions of expected migrants by distance were compared with those of observed migrants from the respective counties (24 counties and the separate administrative area of Stockholm City) and combined to afford comparison for the nation as a whole and for geographic divisions,[11] the correspondence between the patterns of distribution of observed and expected migrants was again close enough to be termed "encourag-

[9] Use of these two nearest classes instead of including all intracounty migrants in the 0–100 kilometer distance group or arbitrarily in a single "nearest" group seemed to improve the agreement of expected and observed migration enough to warrant a preliminary application of Stouffer's formula on the basis of the smaller geographical unit, the district or *bygd*, so as to estimate "opportunities" for intradistrict movement in each county and avoid the assumption that their number was identical with the actual number of migrants in this category (the only one in which the definition of opportunities is affected by origin of migrants). The procedure was based on the assumption that on a county basis opportunities for intradistrict movement could not be separated from other opportunities in the county, and that opportunities in any district were represented by all moves into the district. Hence preliminary computations of expected migrants from each district to itself, to the rest of the county, and to all other counties at 100 kilometer distance intervals were made, and the expected intradistrict movement summed for the districts in each county to approximate the opportunities which would be taken up by intradistrict moves in the county. Subtracting this sum from the total in-migrants to the county gave an estimate of the remaining opportunities in the county.

[10] Bright and Thomas, *op. cit.*, p. 777.

[11] The divisions used are combinations of those delineated in D. S. Thomas, *Social and Economic Aspects of Swedish Population Movements 1750–1933*, New York, Macmillan, 1941, pp. 203–4. Divisions I, II, and III are combined as southern Sweden; IV, V, and VIII, as central Sweden; and VI and VII as northern Sweden.

ing". (See Figs. 1 and 2 and Table 1.) Major discrepancies were again found in the first two intervals (representing intracounty or nearest migration), but in contrast with Bright and Thomas's results, the observed migrants were greatly in excess of the expected. In the four counties of Malmöhus, Gothenburg and Bohus, Östergotland, and Stockholm, which are the sites of Sweden's four largest cities, this discrepancy was much reduced or reversed in the first interval and very much exaggerated in the second,

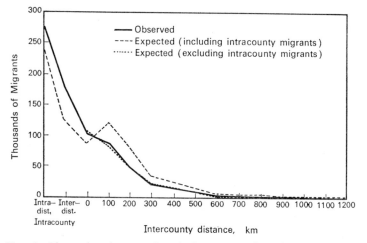

FIG. 1. Observed and expected male intercommunity migrants, Sweden, 1921–30, by distance of last migration.

containing the large cities. (See Table 2. For Stockholm County the latter characteristic appears in the 0–100 km. interval containing Stockholm City.) Several factors may account for this divergence of the pattern of correspondence: first, the data for these counties are not strictly comparable with those for other counties. In the first three, intradistrict migrants are relatively few because the cities of Gothenburg, Malmö, and Norrköping constitute separate districts for which intradistrict migrants are identical with intracommunity migrants who are not included in the census tabulations; and for Stockholm County intradistrict migration is relatively infrequent compared with the great number of migrants crossing the boundary into Stockholm City. At the same time, as Bright and Thomas point out, because of the "absence of distance" in the first interval the opportunities in it are relatively

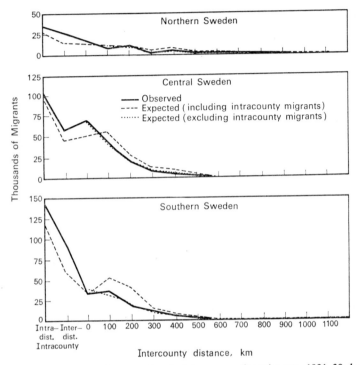

FIG. 2. Observed and expected male intercommunity migrants, 1921–30, by region of origin and distance of last migration.

overweighted compared with those in the second and higher intervals. Also, the great excess of observed migrants in the intervals containing great cities strongly suggests a qualitative difference in the opportunities in such cities not adequately allowed for in an application of Stouffer's formula to total migration data.

TABLE 1. MALE INTERCOMMUNTY MIGRANTS IN SWEDEN, 1912–30, BY REGION OF ORIGIN AND DISTANCE OF LAST MIGRATION, COMPARED WITH NUMBERS EXPECTED ACCORDING TO STOUFFER'S THEORY

Thousands of Migrants

Distance (kilometers)	Total Sweden		Northern Sweden (5 counties)		Central Sweden (9 counties)		Southern Sweden (11 counties)	
	Observed	Expected	Observed	Expected	Observed	Expected	Observed	Expected
Intracounty								
Intradistrict	282.6	248.0	34.4	28.8	105.1	99.6	143.1	119.5
Interdistrict	178.9	123.6	26.0	15.4	58.7	46.5	94.1	61.7
Intercounty								
0–	102.6	85.9	—	—	70.1	52.3	32.5	33.6
100–	86.5	120.4	7.9	10.9	42.6	56.2	36.0	53.3
200–	49.0	80.9	11.5	11.5	19.1	28.3	18.4	41.1
300–	20.4	34.4	1.4	5.3	7.3	13.3	11.7	15.8
400–	14.0	26.1	5.6	7.4	4.3	9.1	4.1	9.6
500–	8.4	13.9	1.4	3.6	2.9	4.8	4.1	5.6
600–	2.9	6.6	1.7	3.9	.4	.4	.8	2.2
700–	2.5	3.9	1.5	2.6	.8	.8	.2	.6
800–	1.7	4.1	.9	2.1	.4	.3	.5	1.7
900–	.6	1.1	.3	.6	.1	.2	.2	.3
1000–	.9	1.7	.5	.8	—	—	.4	.8
1100–	.2	.3	.1	.2	—	—	.1	.2
1200–	.4	.7	.2	.3	—	—	.2	.4
Total	751.6	751.6	93.4	93.4	311.7	311.7	346.4	346.4

TABLE 2. MALE INTERCOMMUNITY MIGRANTS FROM SWEDISH COUNTIES CONTAINING LARGE CITIES AND REMAINING COUNTIES OF CENTRAL AND SOUTHERN SWEDEN, 1921–30, BY DISTANCE OF LAST MIGRATION, COMPARED WITH NUMBERS EXPECTED ACCORDING TO STOUFFER'S THEORY

Thousands of Migrants

Distance (kilometers)	Central Sweden							
	Stockholm City		Stockholm Co.		Östergötland Co.		6 remaining counties	
	Observed	Expected	Observed	Expected	Observed	Expected	Observed	Expected
Intracounty:								
Intradistrict	—	—	15.8	22.5	19.9	19.2	69.5	57.9
Interdistrict	—	—	9.1	10.0	16.7	9.3	33.0	27.2
Intercounty:								
0–	19.1	16.9	30.1	11.7	—	—	20.9	23.7
100–	2.6	5.1	1.3	4.9	10.5	15.0	28.2	31.2
200–	3.7	4.3	1.9	4.6	1.8	3.5	11.6	15.8
300–	3.1	2.8	.8	2.5	.7	2.1	2.7	5.9
400–	1.4	1.4	.8	2.4	—	—	2.1	5.3
500–	1.6	1.2	.5	1.5	.3	.6	.6	1.6
600–	—	—	—	—	—	—	.4	.4
700–	.4	.2	.1	.2	.1	.2	.2	.2
800–	—	—	—	—	—	—	.4	.3
900–	—	—	—	—	.1	.2	—	—
1000–	—	—	—	—	—	—	—	—
1100–	—	—	—	—	—	—	—	—
1200–	—	—	—	—	—	—	—	—
Total	31.9	31.9	60.3	60.3	50.1	50.1	169.5	169.5

Southern Sweden

	Gothenburg & Bohus Co.		Malmöhus Co.		9 remaining counties	
	Observed	Expected	Observed	Expected	Observed	Expected
Intracounty:						
Intradistrict	6.7	13.7	28.1	29.2	108.2	76.6
Interdistrict	21.3	9.5	32.3	15.7	40.6	36.5
Intercounty:						
0–	4.4	3.8	6.9	5.4	21.2	24.3
100–	2.4	4.6	2.7	5.3	30.9	43.4
200–	2.6	6.3	2.3	8.5	13.4	26.3
300–	3.3	1.9	.8	4.0	7.7	10.0
400–	.7	1.2	.6	3.7	2.8	4.7
500–	—	—	3.6	4.2	.4	1.3
600–	.2	.4	.2	.6	.4	1.2
700–	—	—	—	—	.2	.6
800–	.1	.1	.2	.9	.2	.7
900–	—	—	—	—	.2	.3
1000–	.1	.1	.1	.3	.2	.4
1100–	—	—	—	—	.1	.2
1200–	—	—	.1	.3	.1	.1
Total	41.8	41.8	77.9	77.9	226.7	226.7

The fact that most of the counties and the nation as a whole exhibit excesses of observed over expected migrants in the nearest intervals may be attributable to one of the limitations of the data, namely, the inclusion of some purely residential moves which as "opportunities" are distributed over the whole range but as observed migrants are all included in the nearest intervals. On this account the estimates of near-distance migration would always tend to be deficient compared with the observed numbers. This assumption could be tested, of course, by eliminating the majority of such moves from consideration by excluding all migrants whose last move was intra-county from both opportunities and out-migrants in the computation of expected migrants. Calculations were consequently carried through on this basis; and the results seem to confirm our assumption. As can be seen from Figs. 1 and 2 and Table 3, the two intervals which now represent the nearest migration distances do not consistently show excesses of observed over expected migrants; there is a striking improvement in the correspondence between the *patterns* of observed and expected inter-county migrants; and the relative differences between the actual and estimated numbers in each distance class are with few exceptions reduced considerably for the nation as a whole, for the geographic divisions, and for the counties which are sites of large cities. Application of the chi-square test to results of the two series of computations gave values of chi-square shown in the first two rows of Table 4. As Bright and Thomas found, the computed values are so enormous as hardly to justify their calculation; but they are impressively reduced when intracounty moves are omitted. While most of this improvement may perhaps fairly be ascribed to an increased similarity in opportunities due to the exclusion of residential moves, a part of the improvement may be traceable to a resulting reduction in the amount of overlapping between groups in our crude classification of moves by distance.

Although the omission of intracounty moves weakened or eliminated the characteristic excess of observed over expected migrants to nearest distances, the direction of the discrepancy in

TABLE 3. MALE INTERCOMMUNITY MIGRANTS IN SWEDEN 1921–30 BY REGION OF ORIGIN AND DISTANCE OF LAST MIGRATION, EXCLUDING MIGRANTS WHOSE LAST MOVE WAS INTRACOUNTY, COMPARED WITH NUMBERS EXPECTED ACCORDING TO STOUFFER'S THEORY

Thousands of Migrants

Distance (kilometers)	Total Sweden		Northern Sweden (5 counties)		Central Sweden (9 counties)		Southern Sweden (11 counties)	
	Observed	Expected	Observed	Expected	Observed	Expected	Observed	Expected
0–	102.6	107.4	—	—	70.1	68.6	32.5	38.9
100–	86.5	81.2	7.9	10.2	42.6	40.2	36.0	30.8
200–	49.0	48.3	11.5	9.5	19.1	19.1	18.4	19.7
300–	20.4	22.1	1.4	2.8	7.3	9.8	11.7	9.5
400–	14.0	15.9	5.6	4.3	4.3	6.1	4.1	5.5
500–	8.4	7.6	1.4	1.9	2.9	3.0	4.1	2.6
600–	2.9	2.6	1.7	1.6	.4	.2	.8	.7
700–	2.5	2.2	1.5	1.4	.8	.7	.2	.2
800–	1.7	1.3	.9	.6	.4	.2	.5	.5
900–	.6	.4	.3	.2	.1	.1	.2	.2
1000–	.9	.6	.5	.3	—	—	.4	.3
1100–	.2	.2	.1	.1	—	—	.1	.1
1200–	.4	.2	.2	.1	—	—	.2	.1
Total	290.1	290.1	33.0	33.0	147.9	147.9	109.2	109.2

TABLE 3—*cont.*

Central Sweden

	Stockholm City		Stockholm Co.		Östergötland Co.		6 remaining counties	
	Observed	Expected	Observed	Expected	Observed	Expected	Observed	Expected
0–	19.1	18.3	30.1	22.8	—	—	20.9	27.5
100–	2.6	4.0	1.3	3.2	10.5	10.6	28.2	22.3
200–	3.7	3.9	1.9	3.5	1.8	1.7	11.6	9.9
300–	3.1	3.2	.8	2.4	.7	.8	2.7	3.4
400–	1.4	1.4	.8	2.3	—	—	2.1	2.4
500–	1.6	.9	.5	1.0	.3	.2	.6	.9
600–	—	—	—	—	—	—	.4	.2
700–	.4	.2	.1	.2	.1	.1	.2	.1
800–	—	—	—	—	—	—	.4	.2
900–	—	—	—	—	.1	.1	—	—
1000–	—	—	—	—	—	—	—	—
1100–	—	—	—	—	—	—	—	—
1200–	—	—	—	—	—	—	—	—
Total	31.9	31.9	35.4	35.4	13.5	13.5	67.0	67.0

Southern Sweden

	Gothenburg & Bohus Co.		Malmöhus Co.		9 remaining counties	
	Observed	Expected	Observed	Expected	Observed	Expected
0–	4.4	5.7	6.9	6.9	21.2	26.3
100–	2.4	2.6	2.7	3.0	30.9	25.3
200–	2.6	2.9	2.3	3.2	13.4	13.6
300–	3.3	1.7	.8	.8	7.7	7.0
400–	.7	.7	.6	1.1	2.8	3.8
500–	—	—	3.6	2.1	.4	.5
600–	.2	.1	.2	.1	.4	.4
700–	—	—	—	—	.2	.2
800–	.1	.1	.2	.2	.2	.3
900–	—	—	—	—	.2	.2
1000–	.1	.1	.1	.1	.1	.2
1100–	—	—	—	—	.1	.1
1200–	—	—	.1	.1		.1
Total	13.8	13.8	17.6	17.6	77.9	77.9

TABLE 4. CHI-SQUARE VALUES[a]

Group of migrants	Total Sweden			Northern Sweden			Central Sweden					
							Stockholm City			Stockholm County		
	n	χ^2	$P=.05$	n	χ^2	$P=.05$	n	χ^2	$P=.05$	n	χ^2	$P=.05$
All intercommunity	14	73,100	24	13	24,147	22	6	2094	13	8	38,081	16
All intercounty	12	1,648	21	11	2,632	20	6	1359	13	6	6,631	13
Intercounty north or east	12	1,314[b]	21	4	47[b]	9	5	3274	11	6	3,262	13
Intercounty south or west	12	1,489[b]	21	11	2,188	20	5	1613	11	5	789	11
Intercounty north or east excluding migrants to St. City	12	1,470[b]	21	—	—	—	—	—	—	6	124	13
Intercounty south or west excluding migrants to St. City	12	1,103[b]	21	11	809	20	—	—	—	—	—	—

[a] Slide-rule computations. n = number of degrees of freedom.

[b] In chi-square computations, counties for which observed and expected totals were the same, because only one county was classified in a particular "direction", were omitted.

Central Sweden—*Continued*

	Östergötland Co.			6 remaining counties			Total (excl. St. City & Co.)		
	n	χ^2	$P = .05$	n	χ^2	$P = .05$	n	χ^2	$P = .05$
All intercommunity	7	9186	14	10	9577	18	11	15,423	20
All intercounty	5	57	11	8	4037	16	9	3,415	17
Intercounty north or east	5	72	11	8	1322	16	9	1,073	17
Intercounty south or west	2	20	6	5	474	11	5	417	11
Intercounty north or east excluding migrants to St. City	5	77	11	8	1044	16	9	844	17
Intercounty south or west excluding migrants to St. City	—	—	—	5	324	11	5	339	11

Southern Sweden

	Gothenburg & Bohus Co.			Malmöhus Co.			9 remaining counties			Total (11 counties)		
	n	χ^2	$P = .05$	n	χ^2	$P = .05$	n	χ^2	$P = .05$	n	χ^2	$P = .05$
All intercommunity	9	22,652	17	11	29,992	20	14	27,053	24	(not computed)		
All intercounty	7	1,846	14	9	1,590	17	12	2,622	21	12	3716	21
Intercounty north or east	7	785	14	9	1,590	17	12	1,790	21	12	2620	21
Intercounty south or west	2	228	6	—	—	—	3	1,087[b]	8	4	488[b]	9
Intercounty north or east excluding migrants to St. City	7	544	14	9	485	17	12	1,029	21	12	983	21

the first two intervals was not consistently reversed so as to agree with the pattern found by Bright and Thomas. There was, however, a fairly strong tendency toward reversal in the first interval in which two-thirds of the counties and the nation as a whole now showed excesses of expected over observed migrants. For the nation this excess would have been more pronounced were it not for the weight of the discrepancy in the opposite direction in Stockholm County and Stockholm City, where the influence of residential moves was not much diminished by the exclusion of intracounty moves.

With the elimination of intracounty migrants the factor of direction can be held relatively constant. An earlier analysis of direction of intercounty migration based on birth-residence indexes revealed that the main "routes" of net intercounty migration up to 1930 had led to Stockholm City and its environs, one route coming from the counties to the south and west, another from the counties to the north.[12] These two routes form a sort of migration axis along which, for our purposes, the counties can be so ranked that migration from any county to all counties preceding it is chiefly southerly or southwesterly in direction, and migration from any county to those following it is northerly or northeasterly.[13] No new computations were necessary, of course, for the most southerly county nor for the most northerly, but for all others estimated distributions of out-migrants were recalculated for two universes—migration northward or eastward, and migration southward or westward—determined by the position of the county-of-origin in this array. The results appear in Table 5 and Fig. 3, and the respective chi-square values in the third and fourth rows of Table 4. Almost without exception the corre-

[12] Stockholm University, Institute for Social Sciences, *op. cit.*, pp. 51—60.

[13] The ranking of counties is as follows: 1 Malmöhus, 2 Kristianstad, 3 Blekinge, 4 Kronoberg, 5 Halland, 6 Jönköping, 7 Kalmar, 8 Gotland, 9 Gothenburg and Bohus, 10 Älvsborg, 11 Skaraborg, 12 Östergötland, 13 Värmland, 14 Örebro, 15 Södermanland, 16 Stockholm, 17 Stockholm City, 18 Uppsala, 19 Västmanland, 20 Kopparberg, 21 Gävleborg, 22 Jämtland, 23 Västernorrland, 24 Västerbotten, 25 Norrbotten. The first eleven counties constitute southern Sweden in our delineation of geographic regions; the next nine, central Sweden; and the last five, northern Sweden.

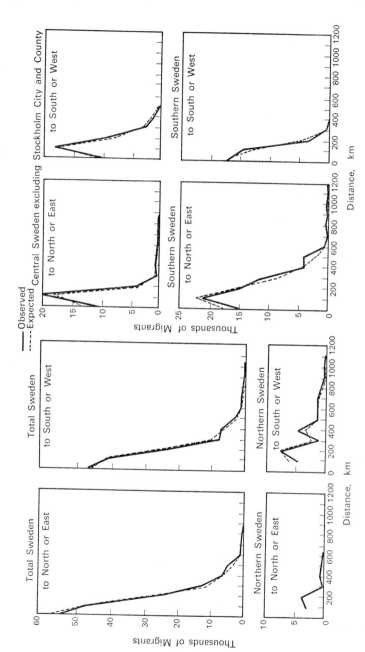

Fig. 3. Observed and expected male intercounty migrants, 1921–30, by region of origin, direction, and distance of last migration.

TABLE 5. MALE INTERCOUNTY MIGRANTS[a] IN SWEDEN, 1921–30, BY ORIGIN, DIRECTION, AND DISTANCE OF LAST MIGRATION, COMPARED WITH NUMBERS EXPECTED ACCORDING TO STOUFFER'S THEORY

Thousands of Migrants

Distance (kilometers)	Total Sweden		Northern Sweden (5 counties)		Central Sweden						Southern Sweden (11 counties)	
					Stockholm City		Stockholm County		7 remaining counties			
	Obs.	Exp.	Obs.	Exp.	Obs.	Exp.	Obs.	Exp.	Obs.	Exp.	Obs.	Exp.
To north or east:												
0–	55.1	58.0	—	—	.9	2.6	28.4	24.5	10.8	13.3	15.0	17.6
100–	46.3	46.4	3.1	3.3	.8	.9	.5	1.3	20.4	18.3	21.4	22.6
200–	25.2	25.8	3.9	3.7	1.6	.9	.9	2.3	4.2	3.6	14.6	15.3
300–	12.5	11.2	.2	.3	—	—	.3	1.0	.6	1.0	11.3	8.9
400–	6.8	6.6	.8	.7	1.0	.4	.1	.4	.9	.8	4.1	4.3
500–	4.9	3.6	—	—	.3	.1	.1	.5	.5	.5	4.1	2.5
600–	1.3	1.2	.2	.2	—	—	—	—	.4	.4	.8	.6
700–	1.0	1.1	—	—	.4	.1	.1	.5	.3	.3	.2	.2
800–	.8	.6	—	—	—	—	—	—	.4	.2	.5	.4
900–	.3	.2	—	—	—	—	—	—	.1	.1	.2	.1
1000–	.4	.2	—	—	—	—	—	—	—	—	.4	.2
1100–	.1	.1	—	—	—	—	—	—	—	—	.1	.1
1200–	.2	.1	—	—	—	—	—	—	—	—	.2	.1
Total	155.1	155.1	8.2	8.2	5.0	5.0	30.5	30.5	38.5	38.5	72.9	72.9

To south or west:

0—	47.5	46.4	—	—	18.1	15.9	1.7	2.2	10.1	10.4	17.5	17.8
100—	40.3	41.5	4.8	6.1	1.8	3.0	.8	1.1	18.3	18.1	14.6	13.2
200—	23.7	23.9	7.6	7.7	2.1	2.6	1.0	.6	9.3	8.1	3.7	4.8
300—	8.0	10.0	1.2	2.4	3.1	3.7	.6	.5	2.7	3.1	.4	.4
400—	7.2	6.6	4.8	3.5	.4	.9	.7	.4	1.3	1.7	.0	.0
500—	3.4	2.9	1.4	1.4	1.3	.8	.3	.1	.4	.6	—	—
600—	1.5	1.4	1.5	1.4	—	—	—	—	—	—	—	—
700—	1.5	1.3	1.5	1.3	—	—	—	—	—	—	—	—
800—	.9	.5	.9	.5	—	—	—	—	—	—	—	—
900—	.3	.1	.3	.1	—	—	—	—	—	—	—	—
1000—	.5	.3	.5	.3	—	—	—	—	—	—	—	—
1100—	.1	.1	.1	.1	—	—	—	—	—	—	—	—
1200—	.2	.1	.2	.1	—	—	—	—	—	—	—	—
Total	135.0	135.0	24.8	24.8	26.9	26.9	4.9	4.9	42.1	42.1	36.3	36.3

ᵃExcluding migrants who made subsequent moves within the county.

TABLE 6. MALE INTERCOUNTY MIGRANTS[a] IN SWEDEN, 1921–30, EXCLUDING THOSE WHOSE LAST MOVE WAS TO STOCKHOLM CITY, BY ORIGIN, DIRECTION, AND DISTANCE OF LAST MIGRATION, COMPARED WITH NUMBERS EXPECTED ACCORDING TO STOUFFER'S THEORY

Thousands of Migrants

| Distance (kilometers) | Total Sweden[b] | | Northern Sweden (5 counties) | | Central Sweden | | | | Southern Sweden (11 counties) | |
| | | | | | Stockholm County | | 7 remaining counties | | | |
	Obs.	Exp.	Obs.	Exp.	Obs.	Exp.	Obs.	Exp.	Obs.	Exp.
To north or east:										
0–	24.9	27.8			2.6	2.4	6.4	7.9	15.0	14.9
100–	40.9	37.5			.5	.8	15.0	13.3	21.4	19.2
200–	20.3	20.2			.9	.8	2.9	3.0	11.0	11.8
300–	5.2	6.8			.3	.3	.6	1.0	4.0	5.2
400–	5.6	5.4	See Table 5		.1	.1	.9	.8	2.9	3.4
500–	2.0	2.1	(no change)		.1	.1	.5	.5	1.1	1.4
600–	1.3	1.3			—	—	.4	.4	.8	.8
700–	1.0	.7			.1	.1	.3	.3	.2	.2
800–	.8	.6			—	—	.4	.2	.5	.5
900–	.3	.2			—	—	.1	.1	.2	.1
1000–	.4	.3			—	—	—	—	.4	.3
1100–	.1	.1			—	—	—	—	.1	.1
1200–	.2	.1			—	—	—	—	.2	.1
Total	103.1[b]	103.1[b]			4.6	4.6	27.4	27.4	57.9	57.9

To south or west:

							See Table 5 (no change)
0–	44.4	42.1	—	—	7.1	6.1	
100–	37.3	36.9	4.8	4.5	15.3	15.1	
200–	18.6	20.4	5.5	5.6	6.3	6.7	
300–	8.0	9.6	1.2	2.0	2.7	3.1	
400–	4.8	5.2	2.4	2.3	1.3	1.6	
500–	2.8	2.5	.8	1.0	.4	.5	
600–	1.5	1.4	1.5	1.4	—	—	
700–	.7	.8	.7	.9	—	—	
800–	.9	.6	.9	.6	—	—	
900–	.3	.2	.5	.2	—	—	
1000–	.5	.3	.1	.3	—	—	
1100–	.1	.1	.2	.1	—	—	
1200–	.2	.1		.1	—	—	
Total	102.0[b]	120.0[b]	18.9	18.9	33.1	33.1	

[a] Excluding migrants who made subsequent moves within the county.
[b] Includes migrants *from* Stockholm City as shown in Table 5.

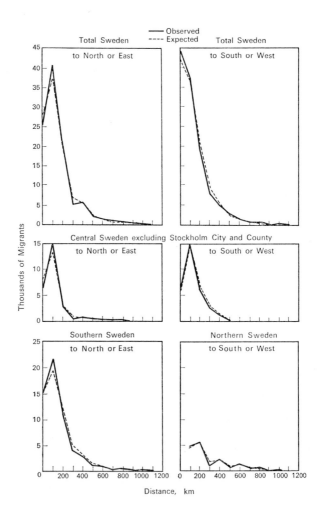

Fig. 4. Observed and expected male intercounty migrants, 1921–30, excluding those to Stockholm City, by region of origin, direction and distance of last migration.

spondence between the observed and expected distributions is again considerably improved. The outstanding exception is Stockholm City, where classification of all movement to Stockholm County as southward grossly violates the facts.

Inspection of this series of curves suggested that the major discrepancies now consisted of excesses of observed over expected migrants to the distance intervals containing large cities, principally Stockholm. Expected migrants were therefore recalculated omitting moves to Stockholm City from both opportunities and out-migrants, and the results were the most satisfactory yet obtained (see Table 6 and Fig. 4). The chi-square values (fifth and sixth rows of Table 4) show that the fit of the respective pairs of curves has again improved in nearly every case. That the opportunities in the capital have a distinctive character, attracting migrants regardless of the number of intervening opportunities cannot be doubted.

Something of the kind is presumably true also of the other large cities but inspection of the distributions of migrants from the separate counties does not suggest that excluding migrants to these cities from the calculations would remove the discrepancies in our final results. There are quite consistent excesses of observed over expected migrants in the second distance interval and frequently similar excesses in the first interval, where the opposite might be expected from the nature of the formula. It is possible that these excesses of observed migrants to nearer distances may be explained by Thomas' findings in a study as yet unpublished. With thoroughly adequate Swedish data she has shown that migrants to near destinations have tended to comprise disproportionate numbers of family members; migrants to far destinations, disproportionate numbers of "lone" persons. In our calculations, family members, like residential moves discussed above, are distributed as opportunities over the whole range of distance, but as observed migrants they may tend to be concentrated in the nearer intervals and consequently underestimated there. A desirable next step, if possible, would be to apply Stouffer's formula separately to "lone" migrants and to those who are heads of families, omitting other family members entirely. The hypothesis might account for the distributions of the separate groups of migrants better than for their combined distributions; but if distance *per se* appeared to influence one class more than the other, Stouffer's assumption of no necessary relationship between mobility and distance might need qualification.

The results of this study emphasize the need for testing Stouffer's theory with more homogeneous data than were available, if a conclusive demonstration is to be had. As in Bright and Thomas's study, increasing the similarity of opportunities and of the group of migrants under consideration repeatedly strengthened the evidence supporting the theory, but that evidence is still inconclusive. It is suggested that more convincing tests of the theory will depend upon refinement of definitions of opportunities.

Japan

Family, Migration, and Industrialization in Japan*

I. B. TAEUBER

DIVISION of labor is characteristic of all human societies, the essential distinction between cultures lying in the extent of the segregation of specialized economic activities from the cohesive functioning of the primary group. Analysis of the relationships between society and economy in transition thus becomes complex. If the world is viewed in static focus, the gamut of adjustments extends from the integrated functioning of the numerically small non-literate cultures to the diversified functioning of the great industrial societies. A dynamic focus indicates a directional drift in change. Movement is proceeding from the subsistence to the monetary economy, from the integrated to the differentiated functioning. In this transition there is a diversity of pattern that is at once economic and the product of compulsions deeper than the structures of imported and imposed economies.

Resources, people, technologies, social structure, economic organization, and political order are intermeshed in the processes of change in manpower utilization that permit and are created by economic development. The episodic utilization of the African in commercial agriculture, mining, and government activities led to a fragmented interpenetration of subsistence and monetary economies that created cultural detribalization and thwarted economic development. In Southeast Asia commercial and industrial economies producing primarily for the export market

* Paper read at the annual meeting of the American Sociological Society held in Denver, Sept. 7–9, 1950.

coexisted with native agrarian economies whose redundant people furnished the reservoir for the labor force of the commercial economy. In Taiwan and Korea export crops were produced by native peasants, but living remained integrated as long as residence continued in the villages, labor was familial, and subsistence was locally produced. In the complex industrial economies of the West, advanced technologies and increased capital utilization tended to break the direct relationship between labor and subsistence. The technological revolution made agriculture itself a capitalized enterprise.

The changing patterns of manpower utilization in most of the areas for which even rudimentary data are available indicate both the generality and the diversity of the agrarian-industrial transition. The analytical difficulties to other than a theoretical approach to the problem of the social aspects of this transition are formidable, however, for the industrial economies of the differentiated society are European in origin, whereas the economies in early transition are non-European. Moreover, the crucial aspect of the transition, whether viewed demographically or culturally, is the utilization of manpower during the long period when the rapidly increasing numbers of an already densely settled people impose the dual requirements of increasing rates of economic expansion and precipitant geographic and occupational redistribution on any society that is to complete the movement from integrated localism to mature industrialism. Modern Japan thus achieves pre-eminent relevance as a case study. Her culture and her earlier people–technology–resources relationships were Eastern, whereas her industrial transformation was patterned after the West. In three-quarters of a century she moved from the rice economy of Monsoon Asia to middle industrialization by Western economic criteria. The statistical record of changing people and economy is voluminous and increasingly accurate over time, and it is available for analysis. Thus in Japan there can be analysis of the actual relationships between social institutions, population movements, and economic transformations rather than speculative structuring of hypothetical relationships that may occur in remote areas of economic development at some future time.

Decades of Transition: 1920–40[1]

In Japan the commercial revolution, the organization of handicraft manufacturing and the widespread diffusion of the monetary economy began within the presumably stable society of the Tokugawa shogunate in the late eighteenth and early nineteenth centuries. With the opening to the West, the alteration in the balance of power, and the Meiji Restoration there was a planned industrial transformation that involved a widespread but generally selective imitation of the West. Looking backward from the middle of the twentieth century, it appears that the Japanese movements were oriented toward the achievement of power through science and technology without such alterations in social structure as would forfeit the specifically Japanese aspects of Japanese culture.

INDUSTRIALIZATION

Industrialization occurred gradually, with occupational and residential shifts, broadly comparable to those that occurred earlier in the West.[2] At the time of the Meiji Restoration in 1868 some 85% of the families were dependent on agriculture. In 1920, when the first enumerative census was taken, 46% of all gainfully

[1] Detailed citations of the sources of the basic data that underlie the numerical and verbal generalizations of the following pages would be unnecessarily verbose. The official demographic publications of the Imperial Government of Japan for the period prior to the Surrender are cited in: Irene B. Taeuber and Edwin G. Beal, Jr., *Guide to the Official Demographic Statistics of Japan. Part I. Japan Proper, 1868–1945*, Supplement, *Population Index*, **12** (4) (Oct. 1946). Reports and studies of the period after 1945 are cited currently in *Population Index.*

[2] There is a voluminous literature on the economic development of Japan from the Meiji Restoration to 1940. See particularly Elizabeth B. Schumpeter *et al.*, *The Industrialization of Japan and Manchoukuo, 1930–1940*, New York, Macmillan, 1940; Teijiro Uyeda, *The Small Industries of Japan, their Growth and Development*, London, Oxford University Press, 1938; John E. Orchard, *Japan's Economic Position: The Progress of Industrialization*, New York, McGraw-Hill, 1930; International Labour Office, *Industrial Labour in Japan*,

occupied males reported agriculture as their major occupation. Between 1920 and 1940 agriculture declined consistently in relative importance, whereas industry and construction increased. In 1920 some 49% of Japan's gainfully occupied men were in agriculture, forestry and fishing, 42% in industry, trade and transportation. In 1940, two decades later, 36% of the gainfully occupied men were in agriculture and fishing, 52% in industry and distribution. Occupational differentiation had occurred among women, too, as increasing proportions entered gainful employment outside family agriculture. And, as in the West, increasing school attendance and lessened labor force participation in old age had shortened the period of life in which gainful employment was customary.

URBANIZATION

Rapid urbanization accompanied the economic transformation. The men and women who moved to the cities for industrial employment provided the nucleus of purchasing power for concentrations of people engaged in the preparation of food, the making of the traditional household products, and the distributive trades. And so, in 1920, only half a century after the legal termination of feudalism, Japan had 16% of her total population in cities of 50,000 or more, 12% in cities of 100,000 and over, 8% in the six great cities of Tokyo, Yokohama, Nagoya, Osaka, Kyoto, and Kobe. Twenty years later, in 1940, 34% of the people were in cities of 50,000 or more, 29% in cities of 100,000 or more, and 20% in the six great cities alone.

Industrialization and urbanization occurred in Japan as they had earlier in the West, and the demographic correlates were similar. Age at marriage was higher in the cities, and the limitation

Studies and Reports, Series A, No. 37, Geneva, 1933; Ryoichi Ishii, *Population Pressure and Economic Life in Japan*, Chicago, University of Chicago Press, 1937; Warren S. Thompson, *Population and Peace in the Pacific*, Chicago, University of Chicago Press, 1946; Ernest F. Penrose, *Population Theories and their Application, with Special Reference to Japan*, Stanford University, California, 1934.

of procreation within marriage was more widespread. The traditional urban–rural fertility differentials existed within a general matrix of decline that extended to the most remote parts of the country. Mortality likewise followed its earlier course in the West, public health and sanitation permitting the cities that had once been consumers of men to become more healthful than the rural areas. Internal migration was an essential aspect of the economic-demographic transformation. In the most highly industrial provinces from three-fifths to two-thirds of all persons in the productive ages of 20–50 were in-migrants from other provinces of Japan Proper; in the most agrarian provinces, on the other hand, in-migrants constituted only 7–10% of the population in the major productive ages. In Japan, as in the West, this cityward trek of the peasant was viewed alternately as wrenching apart the traditional structure of an ancient and integrated society, or as creating a new economic order that utilized what would have otherwise been the excess population of the rural areas under conditions that were conducive to cultural modernization, the transition from high to low fertility, and the eventual cessation of the population increase generated by modernization.

THE ECONOMIC TRANSITION

Japan's industrialization appeared on superficial observation to represent a direct transition from a subsistence agrarian economy to an industrial urban economy. The actuality was not so simple as broad census statistics would indicate. The process of economic readjustment mirrored in these statistics was achieved primarily through the reallocation of youth, and that reallocation occurred through the family system. The movements for employment and for marriage that created one of the most rapid urbanizations in the modern world were controlled through a household system whose ancient roots and modern formation were alike components of a feudal social structure. Integral and differentiated functioning co-existed. Industry and commerce became added functions of a family whose cohesiveness in the metropolis became in some ways even greater than it had been in the village, and monetary values permeated a culture sizable portions of whose people worked without wages.

To understand Japan's movement toward an industrial economy with its consequent changes in the occupational composition and the rural–urban distribution of the population, it is necessary to move backward in history and assess the social transformations that were at once basis, cause and consequence of industrial development. Japan's industrialization occurred under unique conditions, as indeed does all social change if the distinctions are fine enough. The Period of Seclusion initiated by the Tokugawa in the early seventeenth century failed to achieve its goal of the unchanging society, but two and one-half centuries of isolation, relative stability and peace resulted in the fusion of once disparate cultural elements, the solidification of the social order, and the inculcation of habits of discipline and obedience. Feudalism was ended by the Restoration, but social transformation and economic development proceeded in intimate relationship to each other under the guidance of an oligarchic group speaking in the name of a paternalistic emperor. Early developments were halting, sometimes even contradictory. The historic patterns of the early twentieth century evolved primarily because the decisions made in specific situations reflected, however crudely, the basic economic and demographic factors that circumscribed the areas of potential choice. Whatever the relative roles of central decision and unplanned evolution, the consequences of the transition that occurred are indisputable. The integrated culture of the rural areas was gradually intermeshed with the monetary economy of the cities through the modification of both in ways conducive to political stability and economic development.

Japan had a population of some 30 million at the time of the opening to the West, 35 million at the time of the first attempted count in 1872. The possibilities for the expansion of the cultivable area were severely limited by the mountainous terrain within Japan itself and the comparatively dense settlement of adjacent

Asian areas. The raw materials for industrial development were generally deficient. Levels of technology within Japan were those of the sixteenth century; levels that must be acquired were those of the late nineteenth century. Industrial capital was almost non-existent, and borrowed capital even if available might have involved the colonial status that had been the fate of the remainder of Asia. The population was over-dense on the land, and the entrance of Western imports ruined many of the small industries that had existed during the feudal period. The situation was one of all-pervading poverty. And, given the continuation of the population increase that began during the Period of Seclusion itself, rapid economic expansion would be required to maintain even a stationary economic position.

The transition from feudal regime to national state was peaceful. Japan avoided the catastrophic human costs of revolution, famine or mass liquidation. The living of the people was maintained by agricultural expansion to new areas such as Hokkaido, some increase in acreage in the previously cultivated areas, improved yields and, later, imports. The mass requirements other than food were met primarily by the extension of household industries. In the broad segments of the economy in and through which the majority of the people lived there was little mechanization in the Western sense, but instead a more intense use of human labor. Capital accumulation was critical, as were directive and managerial problems. These also were soluble, for heavy taxes on the rural areas yielded revenues that the state could use to stimulate the Western-type industries that were later transferred to private ownership. The funding of the rice stipends of the *daimyo* and the *samurai* gave capital to a group long acquainted with the techniques of social status if not of business management. Development of the *zaibatsu* organizations facilitated capital accumulation and economic expansion in fields involving risk. The labor supply was plentiful and rapidly increasing, so that remuneration was low. It was a precarious equilibrium, maintained by virtue of the fact that the traditional culture with its reciprocal responsibilities and obligations of social classes and family members survived

within what was overtly a Western type of economic transformation.

THE AGRARIAN-INDUSTRIAL INTERPENETRATION

The predominant number of industrial plants remained small,
with a relatively minute apex of great industrial plants such as we
of the West envision when we think of manufacturing industry.
In 1930, at the culmination of the traditional textile-type industrialization, over 50% of all persons engaged in manufacturing
industry were in plants having fewer than five workers; over
seventy per cent were in plants employing less than 50 persons.[3]
With an industrialization of this type the lines between agricultural
and non-agricultural, rural and urban, became blurred. Agricultural families had to have income outside agriculture to survive,
and so members would work in nearby factories or on a piece-
work basis within the home. Some members might go elsewhere
during the slack season in agriculture, or the sons and daughters
might leave permanently for the cities or non-agricultural employment. In practice these differing adjustments to the severe pressures
of people on the land co-existed in varying degrees. In 1946, only
55% of the farms reported that all their working members were
engaged in agriculture, whereas 45% had one or more members
engaged in another occupation. Of these latter families, 64%
reported agriculture as the major family occupation, while 36%
reported it as secondary.

The redundant population of the rural areas facilitated the
location of small factories and piece-work distribution outside
the cities. As late as 1930, cities of 50,000 or more population
included less than half of those engaged in manufacturing industry,
the precise proportions amounting to 45% for men and 28% for
women. In fact, 21% of the men and 36% of the women who were
classified as gainfully occupied in manufacturing industry were
enumerated in *mura* with populations of less than 5000; 36% of

[3] Teijiro Uyeda, *The Small Industries of Japan, Their Growth and Development*, London and New York, Oxford University Press, 1938, p. 9.

the men and 49% of the women were enumerated in communes, generally *mura*, where the total population was less than 10,000.

Employment and working conditions within the cities partook of the characteristics of those in the rural areas. The proportion of farmers in the incorporated cities was low, but household industries flourished, and the processing and distribution of the commodities of daily living occupied rather large proportions of the total urban population. A geographic stability almost comparable to that of the rural areas existed for many of the nominally urban people. Movement from place of origin, whether rural or urban, proceeded directly to the industrial area without intermediate moves. Peasant and familistic relationships of work, leisure and living continued in the metropolis. In Tokyo in 1930, place of work and place of residence were identical for 60% of the gainfully occupied males, 80% of the gainfully occupied females. Comparable percentages for Osaka were 46% for men and 61% for women. In general, the coincidence of place of work and place of residence was greater in the rural areas than in the cities, but everywhere the cultivation of the soil, the household industries and the distributive trades knit gainful occupation and household functioning together.

Implicit in the preceding discussion of Japan's industrial development is the compulsive functioning of the integrated family. Whether the hard necessities of the industrial transformation created the familistic organization which made that transition economically feasible and humanly bearable or whether the family system channeled the industrialization into the only course feasible under the totality of the circumstances is perhaps irrelevant. The low rates of remuneration made it essential that all persons who could do so work, for the head of the household working alone could not maintain even the low levels of living that characterized the Japanese family. Family members who could not secure remunerative jobs outside the family labored as unpaid workers in the family enterprise. In general, additional family workers were most numerous in the subsistence occupations, least numerous in the more industrialized segments of the economy. As late as 1940, almost one-third of the total gainfully occupied persons, including three-fifths of the gainfully occupied women, were employed in family enterprises where they worked in most instances without specific monetary remuneration.

The magnitude of the use of unpaid family labor complicates the distinction between the subsistence and the commercial segments of the Japanese economy, for income and distribution were in major part familial rather than individual. Even in the more pecuniary industries wages were related only indirectly to individual productivity. Special allowances, family benefits and seniority increments resulted in a rough relationship between income and number of dependents, while paternalistic practices in maintenance during periods of depression created a stability of tenure that minimized insecurities for the individual at the same time that it made even more remote the relationship between industrial employment and individualism that is so often assumed to be a necessary correlate of industrialization.

The Role of the Family

The preservation of the reciprocal obligations of labor and maintenance that existed between household head and household members was a reflection of the intensity of the struggle of the people to maintain themselves at the levels which had come to constitute standards of living. The family was Japan's social security system. For most Japanese there were neither unemployment allowances, sickness benefits, old age pensions nor public welfare grants. The family substituted for all these luxuries of rich and advanced economies, for the individual who lost a position in the commercial economy could rejoin his family of origin, secure subsistence, and become an additional worker attached to the family enterprise, be it farm or small shop. Alternatively, he could start a shop or sales enterprise or seek piecework, thus becoming a "small operator" while his family became "unpaid family labor". Unemployment was an ill-defined concept.

The pre-eminence of the family in the economic structure is reflected with great clarity in the patterns for the utilization of women. In all cultures women have a dual role, the economic and the demographic. In Japan the pressure to maximize both roles was severe, for poverty necessitated universal labor, while the imperatives of the ancient culture, the adjurations of the emperor, and economic self-interest emphasized abundant reproduction. Here, as elsewhere in Japanese culture, there was no selection between apparently conflicting developments, but rather adjustments and compromises were made that integrated them. There was little conflict during youth, for compulsory school attendance ended at age 12 or 13, whereas marriage occurred during the early twenties. In 1930, the percentage of girls gainfully occupied increased sharply from 20% at ages 12 and 13 to 44% at age 14 and 62% at ages 15–19. As marriage approached, labor force participation rates declined. In the age group 20–24 the percentage of women employed had dropped to 54; at ages 25–29 it was 47. But proportions increased again after age 30. Forty-seven per cent of all married women were reported as gainfully occupied.

This seeming inconsistency between economic activity and socially sanctioned modes of behavior is illusory, for married women entered the labor market in ways consistent with their family role, i.e. they labored within the home or in the family enterprise, not outside it. In 1930 over three-fourths of all gainfully occupied married women were in agriculture, and a further 12% were in distribution. Agriculture, household manufacturing and the family shops account for perhaps 95% of the total utilization of married women within the Japanese economy. It is significant that even the Japanese war effort of 1944 did not alter this picture; 83% of the girls 18 and 19 years of age and 70% of those aged 20–24 had been drawn into the labor market, but the proportion of gainfully occupied women at ages 25–29 was the same as it had been 14 years before when the census of 1930 was taken.

Migration

Occupational reallocation and geographical redistribution were achieved predominantly through the cityward movement of the surplus youth of the countryside. Here also, in a process generally regarded as highly individualistic, the role of the family was paramount. The codified household law prohibited a change of residence without the consent of the head of the household; the individual decision might be paramount in the actual move, but it need not be so. The assumption that this familial control would minimize migration is again to over-simplify processes by assuming that relationships observed at particular time periods in specific cultures are necessary and therefore universal. The Japanese did move, and they did so in sufficient numbers to maintain the agricultural population virtually unchanging from the Meiji Restoration to 1930 and to reduce it thereafter. The decisions and the adjustments tended to be familial rather than individual, but this was a social mechanism that facilitated the initial movement, minimized the adjustments in the new environment, and maintained acceptable patterns of living among individuals and the continuity of the social structure through the arranged marriage.

The role of the family in structuring migration is revealed in fascinating detail in the data of the 1930 census, where statistics on place of birth were tabulated by age. The interprovincial migrations under age 10 were proportionately similar for boys and girls, for children were dependent migrants. With adolescence the proportions of boys and girls involved in the provincial exodus and influx diverged. Decisions were still familial, but the opportunities for sons and daughters differed sharply. Over 300,000 girls were in factory dormitories located in the rural areas, while many had gone directly to the cities. Specific migration patterns were related to local factors of pressure and of attraction, but whether the broad currents or the local eddies are considered, the complex of pressures and opportunities were specifically female. The migration of boys had only a rough relationship to that of girls. By the time youth reached the middle twenties, however, proportions migrant were converging for men and women, and by the early thirties the relationship between the migrant status of men and women was very close. The explanation lies primarily in the prevalence of the arranged marriage. For women in their twenties there was a movement to the cities and the industrial areas to marry the men who had migrated earlier and a return from the cities to the villages to marry the men who had remained there.

The role of the family in migration, great as it was, was probably surpassed by the role of migration in transforming the family. The rice agriculture of Japan had not been a mode of living that produced local or regional flux within an agrarian matrix. In fact, the heritage of Tokugawa and more remote periods to modern Japan was stability in both geographic residence and social structure. These people with their venerable traditions of stability moved to the great cities, and in most instances they moved directly rather than through intermediate steps that would ease the adjustments. The difficulties were lightened by the small shops, the household industries, the family labor and the relative residential stability within the cities, but they remained great.

Migrants of all ages and both sexes were present in greatest numbers in those areas for which their social background and economic training least fitted them. The economic and cultural assimilation involved in migration to the metropolitan provinces was of such magnitude as to make assimilation itself an erroneous designation. In the agrarian provinces and those with proportionately small industrialization the migrant was a minority, and assimilation in the ordinary sense could operate. But in the industrial provinces the migrant was a majority, and so assimilation occurred with those to be assimilated more numerous than those who were to assimilate them. In the most developed provinces, Tokyo and Osaka, in-migrants out-numbered the provincial natives almost two to one in the economically productive ages from 25 to 40.

The inundation of the native in the industrial centers occurred for girls and women as it did for boys and men. The positions available to the single women in these areas were filled and there was created a reserve labor force for any and all positions consistent with women's historic role as wife and mother. The wife who maintained the household and bore the children in the metropolis had as a pattern the values and the behavior of her mother and the neighbors a generation earlier in a small town or village. In that life girls married, babies arrived, and the status was enhanced. Children assisted in the care of succeeding children—and if babies died, that, too, was one of the burdens that life imposed. Adherence to the reproductive patterns of the village in the city would have produced economic and psychological maladjustments. Each additional baby meant eventually a roughly proportionate increase in expenditures. Limited space and city streets compounded the physical problems of child care, while economic return for child labor was long postponed. The ambition of the husband, the comparison of levels of living that induced striving and discontent, and the other components of urbanization of an industrial type also entered. These adjustment problems, more serious for women than for men because of women's traditional domestic immobilization, were not "social problems" of a minority of the population of the industrial areas but rather the day to day compulsions that transformed the behavior of the once peasant girls of the rural provinces who became the majority of the young married women of the industrial provinces.

The adjustments required by migration were severe, but they were predominantly the shared adjustments of family groups rather than the disruptive wrench of single men in the industrial areas, single women in the agrarian areas, or of married men in the industrial areas with wives and children at home. Furthermore, they were transitory, for migrants came as individuals but contributed their children as the indigenous population of the areas to which they went. Social problems and adjustment difficulties were involved, but they were less acute for the children of the migrant than for the migrant himself. With the continuation of the utilization of migrants the native-born supply of labor to which the migrant had contributed so abundantly would become increasingly adequate to meet the needs both of labor maintenance and of labor expansion.

The Postwar Period

The integration of subsistence and monetary economy as we have described it here is predominantly that of the Imperial period, and particularly the interwar decades. The preparations for war and war itself introduced rapid industrial developments, while the absence of men and the heightened levels of economic activity during the years from 1937 to 1945 resulted in a somewhat increased participation of women. The traditional techniques of labor utilization continued without intrinsic modification, however. War ended with the destruction of major portions of the industrial plant and mass flights from the cities. In the four years between October 1, 1945 and October 1, 1949, the net repatriation movements added five million people to the population of Japan Proper, while natural increase added 5.5 million more. The 72.4 million people of 1945 had reached 82.6 million by the fourth quarter of 1949.

The post-war censuses of 1946 and 1947, together with the current data of the Monthly Report of the Labor Force, reveal the ancient structure of the labor force in great clarity, in part because the intensity of the economic difficulties had thrust people backward toward the traditional familial ways of insuring survival. The population on the land and the people gainfully occupied in agriculture had increased, a reversal of a long-time trend that had kept virtually unchanged the absolute number of people on Japan's overcrowded farms. High proportions of the total population and of the various age and sex groups reported themselves in the labor force with a definition that made one-half hour or more of gainful activity constitute employment, but the majority of the numerous laboring Japanese worked long hours and desired further hours. The predominance of family workers continued; in November, 1949, 21% of all men in the labor force and 64% of all women were classified as family workers. In agriculture and forestry the proportions reached 40% for men and 84% for women. In commerce and finance, proprietors and family workers constituted 66% of the total for men, 76% for women. Unemployment was negligible, being only 300,000–400,000 in all Japan, for people in the rural areas became family workers while people in the urban areas became small scale manufacturers or shop-keepers.[4]

The impetus of the Occupation and the democratic reforms of the post-surrender period tend toward the abolition of those distinctive characteristics of the labor force structure that reflected its roots in the authoritarian family system. The responsibilities and the obligations of the household head are legally abolished; women have an independence of action theoretically comparable to that of men, and the arranged marriage survives only through the voluntary subservience of children to parents. Individualism is to replace familism, equality to replace feudalism. The social services and the welfare provisions of the state are to supplant those of the family. The extent to which these essentially Western modifications will alter the structure of the Japanese labor force will depend in major part on the achievement of general solutions to very difficult economic problems, for the basic characteristics of the Japanese land-resources-people relationship remain. Rapid and continuing increase in the population in labor-force ages is inevitable for at least another generation unless death rates increase sharply.

Conclusion

In Japan the unbroken pattern of an oligarchic group with traditions of leadership, and a people disciplined to obey, permitted controlled and selective modernization. The shogun of Tokugawa had wished a world without change; the elder statesmen of Meiji wished economic development within a stable

[4] Japan, Ministry of Labor, Labor Statistics and Research Division, *Analysis of Labor Economy in 1949*, Tokyo, 1950, p. 3.

social order. Thus the law of the state, the indoctrination of Shinto, and the propaganda of the educational system operated to stay the social consequences of economic transformation. The transition from an integrated to a diversified economy proceeded fundamentally as interpenetration, with a gradual shift in balance from the one to the other. During the period from the Restoration to the present, however, feudalism and industrialization, subsistence and monetary economy, familism and urbanization have coexisted.

Japanese experience is clearly insufficient for generalization concerning the future of other Asian regions. It is sufficient to suggest, however, that the changing patterns of manpower utilization that accompany population increase within a matrix of industrialization and urbanization may differ in various cultures and at various periods of time. Resources and technologies impose limitations within which adjustments must occur, but within the fairly wide range of the economically feasible social structure may be a major factor in determining both the extent and the characteristics of labor utilization.

San Salvador

The Migrant Population of a Metropolitan Area in a Developing Country

A Preliminary Report on a Case Study of Salvador*

L. J. DUCOFF†

UNDER the auspices of the United Nations and in cooperation with the government of El Salvador, a sample survey was made in early 1960 of the population of the metropolitan area of San Salvador.[1] A random sample of approximately 900 households containing 4560 persons was interviewed and various demographic and socio-economic data were obtained. This sample constituted somewhat under 2% of the total population of the metropolitan area. The survey was designed to serve substantive and methodological objectives. A dominant substantive theme was the securing of information that would be helpful in studying the impact and the process of urbanization within the context of a country undergoing economic development. Central to this theme is the problem of internal migration, particularly from rural to urban areas. Both the Population Commission and the Social and Economic Council of the United Nations have placed a high

* Paper to be presented at the International Population Conference of the International Union for the Scientific Study of Population, New York City, Sept. 1961.

† Economic Research Service, US Department of Agriculture, Washington DC.

[1] For a fuller report on this survey see *A Demographic and Socio-Economic Survey of the Metropolitan Area of San Salvador*, *El Salvador*, Economic Commission for Latin America, Mexico, DF (Doc. No. E/CN.12/CCE/233/ TAO/LAT), Jan. 1961.

priority on studies of internal migration, and especially rural–urban migration, in underdeveloped countries in relation to problems of urbanization and industrialization.

In the design of the schedule for use in the San Salvador survey, emphasis was placed on data that would shed light on the following aspects: (1) the number and relative importance of migrants in the current population of the capital metropolitan area; (2) the rural, urban, and the geographic origin of the migrants; (3) the differential flow of migrants over time; (4) the demographic and socio-economic characteristics of the migrants and the differentials between migrants and non-migrants; (5) the degree of acculturation or social integration of the migrants as exhibited in their levels of living, educational and cultural characteristics, fertility patterns, and other aspects compared with non-migrants.

Only partial and preliminary results are as yet available from the survey as circumstances have not permitted the completion of all of the tabulations and their analysis. In this paper we shall summarize and elaborate on some of these findings.

San Salvador is the largest urban center in the country, with a population, at the end of 1959, of 235,334; for the entire metropolitan area of San Salvador the population at that time was officially estimated at 275,535, which represented a gain of 45% over the 1950 level of 190,224. The preliminary results of the survey, made in February 1960, indicated that the largest absolute and percentage increase since 1950 occurred among children under 10 years of age. This age group increased by 82% compared with much smaller percentage increases in all other age groups. Children under 15 accounted for nearly 53% of the total population increase of the metropolitan area during the 1950-60 decade. Persons of this age group among families who in-migrated into San Salvador accounted for only one-seventh of this increase. Hence higher birth rates and lower mortality among children are the factors principally responsible for the large gains among children under 15 years of age. The ratio of children under 5 to women 15–49 years of age for the metropolitan area was 26% higher in 1960 than in 1950, and again indicates the considerable gain in the effective fertility of women that occurred during the 1950–60 decade. One consequence of this large increase in the number of children and youth in the area's population has been a considerable increase during the decade in the "dependency load"; i.e. the ratio of persons too young to work to persons of working age. The proportion of the old population (65 years of age and over) did not change significantly during the decade.

Role of Migration in Population Growth

If we define non-migrants as those persons who have lived all of their lives in the San Salvador metropolitan area (except for temporary visits, vacations, etc., elsewhere), and migrants as those who have maintained a permanent residence at some time of their lives elsewhere than in the San Salvador metropolitan area, and if we make some further sub-classification among the migrants, some interesting results of a type previously not available emerge from the survey. Forty-two per cent of the entire population of the metropolitan area in February 1960 were migrants; 36% were Salvadoreans who came to the metropolitan area from other parts of the country; 3.4% were foreign-born; and 2.8% were migrants who were originally born in the metropolitan area, but had lived elsewhere for some period of their lives and returned to the metropolitan area. The proportion of migrants among the female population of the metropolitan area is higher than the male population; 46% of the female population are migrants compared with 37% of the males.

Of the native-born migrants (i.e. born in El Salvador) living in the metropolitan area early in 1960, two-thirds came here in the past 15 years, and 40% of them came during the past decade. Nearly half of the foreign-born population came to the metropolitan area only in the past 5 years. For the native-born migrants the periods 1945–9 and 1955–9 seemed to be especially heavy periods of migration to the capital area. Since we are dealing only with the population currently living, the proportion of the presently living migrant population that came to the metropolitan area many years ago represent, of course, only the survivors of the original migrants. The figures for earlier periods particularly prior to 1940 cannot, of course, be interpreted as measures of the total volume of in-migration to the capital in the earlier years, as many of the persons who came have since died. Also some of the migrants who came left the area later to live elsewhere.

By restricting ourselves to a very recent, short period, we can, however, obtain a fairly good idea of the relative importance of migration to the growth of the population of the metropolitan area. Of the migrants living in the area early in 1960, nearly 30,000 arrived during 1955–9, with 84% of them being Salvadoreans and the remainder foreign-born. The official estimates of the total population of the metropolitan area show an increase of approximately 52,000 between the end of 1954 and the end of 1959. However, it is quite probable that the official estimates understate the growth of the population as they are based on the estimates of births and deaths and do not specifically take account of net migration to the metropolitan area.

Characteristics of the Migrant Population

Salvadoreans have migrated to the capital area from every *departamento* (major civil division) of the country. Women comprise a considerably larger proportion of the migrant population of the metropolitan area than among the non-migrants—61% of the migrants are women compared to 52% for the non-migrants. This is not an uncommon migration phenomenon as many young women come to the large urban areas to seek employment as domestic servants or in other occupations or to improve their marital opportunities. Other women who have separated from their husbands or have been widowed also frequently migrate to urban areas to seek employment.

The migrant population has a heavy concentration of persons in the young adult ages, as for most of them migration does not begin until they have reached their late teens or early twenties.

Forty-six percent are in the age groups 20–39, and 57% are between 15–39 years of age. This is their age distribution at the time of the survey. Among female migrants there is a fairly substantial proportion in the group 15–19 years of age in addition to the 20–29 and 30–39 age groups.

An important difference in age composition between the migrant and non-migrant population is the much lower proportion of children under 15 among those who have migrated. Over half of the non-migrant population consists of children under 15 years of age compared with only 10% for the migrants. Of course, some of the children in the non-migrant population belong to families where the head of the household or his wife are migrants. These are children who were born after their parents' arrival to San Salvador and have continued to live there since then. However, this does not alter the fact that each incoming stream of migrants brings a group that is preponderantly in the most vigorous and productive ages. Thus, for example, the migrant population that arrived to the metropolitan area during the 5 years 1955–9 were currently in the following age groups: 66% in the age groups 15–44, 25% under 15, and only 9% 45 years of age and over.

Information on marital status was obtained in the survey for every male 16 years of age and over and for every female 14 years and over. For the migrant population in the age limits stated above, the survey showed that 43% were single, 27% married through a civil or religious procedure, 19% were living in a *union libre* (referred to in El Salvador as "unidos"), 8% were separated or divorced, and 3% were widowed. Although the population in the age groups 25 and over legally married exceeded the free or consensual unions, the latter still accounted for a large proportion of all matrimonies. From a fourth to over a third of all male migrants 25 years or older reported their marital status as that of free or consensual unions. For women migrants 25–49 years of age, this proportion was from a fifth to a fourth. Substantial proportions—from a fifth to a fourth—of the women 25 years of age and over reported themselves as single (i.e. never married). Some of this is undoubtedly true, as the excess of females over

males in the marriageable ages in the population of the metropolitan area makes it more difficult to contract a marriage. In
part, however, it may reflect the tendency on the part of many of
these women to report themselves as *solteras* when in reality their
marital status is more akin to either *unida* or *separada*.

Literacy and Education—Trends and Differentials

During the past decade there has taken place a considerable
reduction in illiteracy despite the large increase in the population
of the metropolitan area of San Salvador. Whereas 19 % of the population 10 years old and over were illiterate in 1950, only 12 % were
illiterate in 1960. Among males illiteracy had been reduced from
11 % in 1950 to a mere 5 % in 1960. For females the reduction has
not been as dramatic—18 % still continued to be illiterate in
1960, compared with nearly 26 % in 1950. The result is that five
out of every six illiterate persons in the San Salvador metropolitan
area are females.[2]

Illiteracy has delined since 1950 for each age group and among
females as well as males. Within the metropolitan area population
there is a much higher frequency of illiteracy among the migrant
than among the non-migrant population. The proportion of
illiterates among the migrant population in February 1960 was
double that of the non-migrant population—16 % compared with
8 %. The higher proportion of illiteracy among the migrants
shows up in the various age groups for males as well as for females.

For nearly 60 % of the adult population (25 years of age and
over) some primary school education is the most they have gotten;
another 16 % completed the 6 years of primary school but did
not go any further. A little over a fifth of the population had one
or more years of secondary education, with only approximately
5 % of the population having graduated from a secondary school

[2] In rounded numbers there were in the metropolitan area at the time of the
1950 census 28,100 *analfabetos*—7400 males and 20,700 females. The preliminary estimates from the Feb. 1960 survey are 24,300 *analfabetos* consisting
of 4300 males and 20,000 females.

but not continuing on with university training. The remaining 4% of the population was divided about equally between those who had university degrees and those who had some university education but had not as yet graduated or had discontinued their university education.

As between the migrant and non-migrant adult population of the metropolitan area, no marked differences in educational status show up except among the groups with the barest minimum of education—those who have had one year or less of primary school. Approximately 23% of the migrant adults are in this category, compared with 13% for the non-migrants. At the other extreme, the migrants show larger percentages with some university education or degrees reflecting the gravitation of professional people to the capital metropolitan area.

Contrary to what might be expected, the migrants who arrived in the last decade show, in some respects, higher educational attainment than those who came to the San Salvador area in years before 1950. Relatively fewer of the recent migrants have failed to complete less than 3 years of primary school. Also relatively more of the recent migrants than of those who came before 1950 have managed to graduate from a secondary school. This is partly a function of the improvement in educational facilities in the more recent years as well as the growth of appreciation of the importance of more education.

Economic Differentials

INCOME DISTRIBUTION

Approximately half of the families in the sample of the metropolitan area reported their total 1959 income from all sources as less than 2500 colones.[3] For 12% of the families the income was under 1000 colones. The income distribution shows a bimodal pattern, with the modal group of 26% of the families being in the 1500–2499 colones income group. A secondary concentration

[3] The exchange rate is 2.5 colones per US dollar.

families is in the highest income group of 10,000 and over colones which was reported by 10% of the families in the sample.

The income distribution shows no significant differences among families classified by the migration status of the head of the household. Three categories are used: (1) the head of the family lived all his life in the metropolitan area; (2) the head migrated to San Salvador during the 1950–9 period, and (3) the migration of the head of the family occurred before 1950. The proportion of families with incomes in 1959 of less than 2500 colones is practically the same among the three categories, and the differences among them at the various income levels are not marked. Families belonging to migrants of the 1950–9 decade showed the largest percentage in the income group of 10,000 or more colones in 1959. However, the number of cases underlying this percentage is small and it should, therefore, be interpreted with caution.

RENT EXPENDITURES

Of the 904 families in the sample, 726 (or 80%) were living in rented dwellings, the remaining 20% owned their own homes. Among families where the head of the household was a migrant who came to San Salvador during the past decade, 90% of these families lived in rented units and only 10% owned their homes. For migrants who came before 1950 as well as for the heads of households who have lived all their lives in the San Salvador metropolitan area, the proportions of renters and owners were the same as in the general population—approximately 80% renters and 20% owners.

Rent expenditures were reported by five-sixths of the renter families. For the remaining one-sixth the preliminary tabulation does not show the monthly rental. Of those reporting on rent nearly half of the families were living in very low-rent, generally inadequate, housing of the *meson* type with a rental of less than 25 colones per month. Another 28% were living in housing with a monthly rental of 25–50 colones, and 14% were in the rental groups of 50–150 colones per month. The remaining 11 % were in the high-rent groups of 150 or more colones per month.

As between families of migrants and non-migrants the differences in quality of housing they have are not marked, as judged by the rentals paid. If anything, the families headed up by migrants who came to San Salvador in the last 10 years have a *lower* concentration in the poorest rental groups of under 50 colones per month. Two-thirds of these families were in the under-50 colones rental groups, compared with four fifths of the families of migrants who came before 1950, and three-fourths of the families headed up by persons who lived all their lives in San Salvador.

OTHER INDICANTS OF LEVEL OF LIVING

Each of the families in the sample were asked as to whether or not they owned various specified items considered indicative of the level of living. The list included 10 items, such as sewing machine, refrigerator, radio, television, record-player, automobile, etc. Three-fourths of the families in the sample did not have a mechanical refrigerator, and 97 % did not have an icebox. Hence only approximately a fourth of the families have some type of refrigeration. There follows a summary of the percentage of families who reported having the specified items:

	%
Sewing machine	43
Water heater	4
Refrigerator (electricity or gas)	24
Icebox	3
Record player	20
Radio	64
Television	11
Automobile	13
Motorcycle (or scooter)	1
Bicycle	4

When the families are classified according to the migration status of the head of the household, no significant differences appear in the percentages who have or do not have these items between the migrant and non-migrant families. Only in the case of the automobile do the recent migrants (those who came to San Salvador in the past decade) show a higher proportion who have automobiles than either the non-migrant families or the migrants who arrived before 1950. Nearly 20% of the 1950–9 migrant families have automobiles compared with 10% and 12% for all other migrants and for the non-migrants respectively. This is consistent with the findings previously noted that the 1950–9 migrants contain a larger proportion of families in the high-income group of 10,000 colones or more per year, and a larger proportion of individuals with a university education or degree. The capital metropolitan area, as the seat of the government and the economic and cultural center of the nation, serves as a focal point for many professionally trained people who have migrated to the capital for governmental, university and other professional services. A substantial proportion of these people are among the migrants of the past decade, and they are concentrated at the relatively higher income levels.

Although the above data suggest no marked economic differentials between the broad categories of migrant and non-migrant population groups, it should be noted that there are marked contrasts *within* each of the three broad categories which far exceed any differences *between* these categories. Each of these groups (i.e. the non-migrant, the migrants of the 1950–9 decade, and the migrants who came before 1950) is characterized by a large concentration at the very low income levels. Another general conclusion suggested by the preliminary findings is the existence of age selectivity among migrants and of a differential level of educational attainment among them. The education differential, however, exists at both ends of the scale; namely, a higher concentration among migrants of persons with very little schooling as well as of persons with high educational attainment. The presence or absence of other significant differentials of a demographic or socio-economic nature between the migrant and the non-migrant population groups will need to be explored after more detailed tabulations and analyses are made of the data secured in this study.

Summary

This paper presents preliminary findings from a demographic and socio-economic sample survey made in early 1960 of the population of the metropolitan area of San Salvador, El Salvador. This survey was part of a United Nations Technical Assistance project carried on in cooperation with the Economic Commission for Latin America and the government of El Salvador.

The survey revealed that 42% of the entire population of the metropolitan area are migrants—i.e. persons who have not lived there all their lives. Less than 4% were foreign-born. Among the female population of the area 46% were migrants compared with 37% of the males. Two-fifths of the migrant population came in the 1950–60 decade. The migrant population has a heavy concentration of persons in the young adult ages as for most of them migration does not begin until the late teens or early twenties. Only a small proportion migrate after reaching 45 or 50 years of age. Thus, each incoming stream of migrants brings a group that is predominantly in the more vigorous and productive ages and helps to redress the city's imbalance between the working and the dependent age population.

During the past decade there has taken place a reduction in illiteracy despite the 45% increase in the population of the metropolitan area of San Salvador. Whereas 19% of the population 10 years old and over were illiterate in 1950, only 12% were illiterate in 1960. The decline in illiteracy was noted for each age group and for females as well as males. Within the metropolitan area population there is a much higher frequency of illiteracy among the migrant than among the non-migrant population—16% compared with 8%. The migrants who arrived in the last decade had, in general, a higher educational attainment than those who came to the San Salvador area in the years before 1950.

When families are classified into the three groups, (1) non-migrant, (2) migrants of the 1950–9 decade, and (3) migrants who came before 1950 (with the classification being based on the migration status of the head of the household), no marked differences show up in terms of income distribution, distribution by level of rent paid, or in terms of the possession of the specified level of living items. There are marked contrasts *within* each of these broad categories, which far exceed any differences *between* these categories. Each of these groups is characterized by large concentration at very low income levels. In addition to age selectivity among migrants the data also suggest educational selectivity. The educational differential, however, exists at both ends of the scale; namely, a higher concentration among migrants of persons with very little schooling as well as of persons with high educational attainment.

Biographical Notes

BASTIDE, H. Research Worker with Institut National d'Etudes Demographiques.

Major publications include: (jointly with Professor A. Girard), "Niveau de vie, mode d'emploi et croissance de la population: une enquête auprès du public" *Population*, 1962, 4; "La stratification sociale et la democratisation de l'enseignement", (*ibid*, 1963, 3); Two surveys dealing with the primary-secondary education transfer, (*ibid*, 1963, 1); "Enquête nationale sur l'entrée en 6ᵉ et la démocratisation de l'enseignement" and "Orientation et sélection scolaires. Cinq années d'une promotion: de la fin du cycle elementaire à l'entrée dans le 2ᵉ cycle du 2ᵉ degré", *ibid.*, 1969, 1 and 2.

BROWN, JAMES S. Professor of Rural Sociology, University of Kentucky and a previous Fulbright Research grantee. Has been a principal investigator of *The Beech Creek Study: The Social Adjustment and Personal Stability of Eastern Kentucky Migrants in Ohio and Neighbouring States*, a study sponsored by the National Institute of Mental Health and the Kentucky Agricultural Experiment Station. A number of papers, including the one reproduced in this volume, have been written, and two monographs on the study are to be published soon.

Major publications include: Dr. Brown has contributed to *Kentucky Agricultural Experiment Station Bulletin*, University of Kentucky; *The American Journal of Sociology; The American Sociological Review; Rural Sociology*; and has presented papers to the Conference on Rural Appalachia in Transition, the Commission on Religion in Appalachia, and the Symposium on Migration and Behavioural Deviance. Author, with G. A. Hillery, Jnr., of a chapter in *The Southern Appalachian Region, A Survey* (ed. T. R. Ford).

DUCOFF, LOUIS. Chief of the Social Affairs Section of the Economic Commission for Latin America of the United Nations at the Regional Office in Mexico.

FINLAYSON, MRS. ANGELA. Research Officer, working on the epidemiology of mesothelioma in the Department of Social Medicine, University of Dundee.

Major publications include: "Familial Aspects of Pre-eclampsia and Hypertension in Pregnancy" (with E. Adams), *Lancet*. Married Women who Work in Early Motherhood (with B. Thompson), *British Journal of Sociology*.

FOFI, GOFFREDO. Literary editor of a Milan publishing house, co-director of *Quaderni Piacentini*, official organ of the Italian student movement.

Major publications include: (jointly with Danilo Dolci, with whom he worked for three years), "Inchiesta a Palermo"; "Una politica per la piena occupazione"; "Processo a l'articolo 7"; subsequently, contributions to *Il Ponte Nord e Sud*, and the volume *Immigrazione e industria*. *L'immigrazione meridionale a Torino* appeared in 1963 (Feltzinelli). Active in several cinema revues, he is at present making a full-length film and writing a book on concerned European intellectuals in the 1930's. He claims that he is "not a sociologist".

GEORGE, PIERRE. Professor of Human Geography and Urban Studies, Faculté des Lettres et Sciences Humaines, Sorbonne.

Major publications include: *Sociologie et Géographie* (Collection SUP, Presses Universitaires de France); Précis de Géographie urbaine; Précis de Géographie rurale; Précis de Géographie économique; Introduction a l'étude géographique de la population; Questions de géographie de la population; Géographie de la consommation; Géographie sociale du monde. He is a frequent contributor to *Cahiers Internationaux de Sociologie*, *Population*, and *Tiers Monde*. He aims to promote contact between the field of human geography and sociology.

GIRARD, ALAIN. Professor at the Sorbonne, Technical Consultant for the Institut National d'Etudes Demographiques.

Major publications include: *Français et Immigrés* (with Jean Stoetzel); *Developpement economique et mobilite des travailleurs*; *La Péussite sociale en France*; *Le choix du conjoint*.

ILLSLEY, RAYMOND. Professor of Sociology and Head of the Department of Sociology, Kings College, University of Aberdeen. Honorary Director, Medical Sociology Research Unit (Aberdeen), Medical Research Council. World Health Organization Consultant. Member of the British Sociological Association, International Sociological Association and Society for the Study of Human Biology. Fellow of the Eugenics Society.

Major publications include: *Family Growth and its Effects on the Relationship Between Obstetric Factors and Child Functioning*; *Social and Genetic Influences on Life and Death*; *The Sociological Study of Reproduction and its Outcome*. Many articles on obstetrics, childbearing, etc., in the *British Journal of Preventive Medicine*, *British Medical Journal*, *Nursing Mirror*, and *Sociological Review*, etc.

ISBELL, ELEANOR C. Executive Associate of the Social Science Research Council and editor of its publications.

Major publications include: *Population Movements and Industrialization in Swedish Counties, 1895–1930*; Contributions to Research Memorandum on Migration Differentials and to Observational Studies of Social Behaviour.

MANGALAM, DR. J. J. Associate Professor, University of Guelph, Ontario.

Major publications include: *Human Migration, Lexington, Kentucky*, University of Kentucky Press, 1968. Has published in *Year Book of Education, Rural Sociology, International Migration Review*, etc. Dr Mangalam has been a co-investigator with J. S. Brown and H. K. Schwarzweller in the Beech Creek Study described in Dr. Brown's biographical notes.

MANNUCCI, CESARE. Executive Editor of *Comunità*, a bi-monthly cultural magazine founded by Adriano Olivetti. Doctorate, Rome University; graduate research Harvard.

Major publications include: *Lo spettatore senza libertà*; *Radio-televisione e communicazione di massa, Laterza, Bari*; *Societa di massa*; *Analisi di moderne teorie sociopolitiche*. Essays in other volumes including *Alla ricerca de tempo libero* and *Annuario politico italiano*.

MOINDROT, CLAUDE. Lecturer, Faculté des Lettres et Sciences Humaines, Université de Caen.

Major publications include: *L'Amenagement de territoire en Grande Bretagne; Villes et campagnes britanniques*.

PETERSEN, WILLIAM. Robert Lazarus Professor of Social Demography at Ohio State University.

Major publications include: *Planned Migration: The Social Determinants of the Dutch-Canadian Movement*; *Population*; *The Politics of Population*; *Migration*; Social Aspects in *International Encyclopedia of Social Sciences*.

POURCHER, GUY. A prominent research worker with Institut National d'Études Démographiques from 1960 until his death in 1965 at the age of 34.

Major publication include: A major work, *Le Peuplement de Paris, origines régionales, composition sociale, attitudes et motivations* (Paris, PUF, 1964). He was a contributor to *Population, Cahiers de sociologie et démographie médicales* and *le Concours médical*, writing on psycho-sociological aspects of migration and urbanization, especially with reference to Paris.

ROSE, ARNOLD M. (deceased). The late Professor Rose died on 2 January 1968. He had previously been Professor of Sociology at the University of Minnesota and was, until his death, President Elect of the American Sociological Association.

Major publications include: *The Power Structure*; *Libel and Academic Freedom*. Professor Rose had written or edited many books on social psychology, methodology, and race relations.

SCHWARZWELLER, HARRY K. Professor of Sociology at West Virginia University. Was previously a Fulbright Research Fellow in New Zealand and a Fulbright Scholar in Germany where he researched on social change and migration from a rural village and the problem of career choosing among German rural young people.

Major publications include: He has contributed articles to *Rural Sociology, Social Forces, Journal of Marriage and the Family* and *Comparative Education*. He is at present completing the work on *The Beech Creek Study* with J. S. Brown and J. J. Mangalam and is completing research for a comparative study of career planning in the United States, Germany, and Norway.

TAEUBER, IRENE B. Senior Research Demographer, Office of Population Research, Princeton University. Member of the American Sociological Association, the American Statistical Association and the American Association for the Advancement of Science.

Major publications include: *Public Health and Demography in the Far East*; *The Changing Population of the United States*; *The Population of Japan*; *The American People in the 20th Century*; *The Population of the Chinese Cultural Area*.

THOMPSON, BARBARA. Sociologist, Medical Research Council, Medical Sociology Research Unit, Foresterhill, Aberdeen. Has been a temporary Advisor, World Health Organization, Geneva.

Major publications include: Has published many articles in *Lancet* and other journals as a result of studies of childbirth and infant care in rural West Africa. Other articles include Social Study of Illegitimate Maternities; Women from Broken Homes; Follow-up of 186 Sterilized Women.

ZIMMER, BASIL G. Professor of Sociology and Acting Chairman, Department of Sociology, Brown University, Providence, Rhode Island.

Major publications include: *Rebuilding Cities*; *Effects of Displacement and Relocation on Small Businesses*; *Metropolitan Area Schools: Resistance to District Reorganization*. Has contributed to *Cities and Society, Studies in Human Ecology, Community Political Systems, American Journal of Sociology, American Sociological Review*, etc.

It is regretted that it has not been possible to obtain biographical notes for F. Alberoni and R. Duocastella.

LIBRARY

Tel: 01244 375444   Ext: 3301

This book is to be returned on or before the last date stamped below. Overdue charges will be incurred by the late return of books.

Chester

A College of the
University of Liverpool

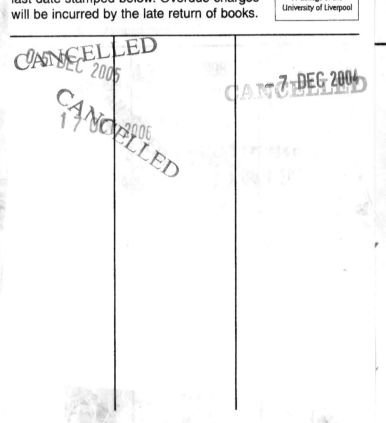